From Ship's-Boy to Skipper

From Ship's-Boy to Skipper

With Variations

BY

H. Y. MOFFAT

PAISLEY: ALEXANDER GARDNER
Publisher by Appointment to the late Queen Victoria
1910

LONDON :
SIMPKIN, MARSHALL, HAMILTON, KENT & CO., LMD.

PREFACE

FIVE years ago I retired from active service after half a century of strenuous work, in constant action, on sea and land. The sport of Fortune in my earlier years, and with a nomadic strain in the blood, few can have experienced a greater variety of life and incident or endured greater hardships and changes. The transition from such a life to the easy leisure of retirement was not altogether plain sailing. It was here my good friend and late colleague, Mr. Spencer E. Colchester, of London, came to my aid with the suggestion that I should write my memoirs. Knowing somewhat of my eventful career, he wisely thought that in fighting my battles over again—on paper—I would gradually get into the stride of my new life.

To me the suggested task seemed perhaps the hardest of a hard life. The hand that has grasped the capstan bar and the wheel, the stock-whip and the gold-digger's spade, the harpoon and the gun, may well falter when it takes up at last the mightiest instrument of all. But I was " ever one who never turned his back, but marched straight forward," and so to the last task I set myself.

1

Who shall wonder if I found the pen but a feeble weapon in my unpractised hand? Literary style and grace, polished phrases, illuminated descriptions and dramatic treatment of exciting episodes were not for me. All I could compass was a sailor's yarn, told in plain, unvarnished, but, let me add, truthful language. Now that my work is done, no one can be more conscious of its defects than myself. But yet the writing of my life story has not failed of its primary purpose in that it has lightened and brightened many of my leisure hours, and if it does a similar service to my indulgent readers I shall be well repaid.

In addition to the kind assistance of Mr. Colchester, I have to gratefully acknowledge the interest and help of my valued friend, Captain Francis Brown (the retired marine superintendent of the City Line in Glasgow), and of Mr. J. A. MacKeggie, Glasgow, without whose encouragement this work might not have seen the light.

H. Y. M.

HERNE BAY,
September, 1909.

CONTENTS

CONTENTS

PAGE

CONTENTS

PAGE

FROM SHIP'S-BOY TO SKIPPER

CHAPTER I

EARLY DAYS

IN the fair city of Edinburgh, on the 24th November, 1844, I was launched upon the sea of life ; but my memory will only carry me back as far as my fifth year. At about that time I first went to school, being placed in the first class to begin with, and everything went smoothly until I was promoted to the second class, when my troubles began.

It was a rule at this school that when four members of one family were attending at the same time the fourth member was not charged for, and as I had three elder brothers at the school, I became the unfortunate fourth. The proprietor of the school taught one of the higher classes, while two of the lower grades were under the charge of his two sons —Mr. Peter and Mr. John—who received as salary so much per head for the pupils in their classes. This was the only possible reason for the brutal treatment to which I was subjected from the day I entered the second class—taught by Mr. John—

until I left school. Day after day—most frequently without the faintest shadow of an excuse—I received a severe caning, or a sounding blow on the side of the head if the cane was not at hand at the moment. I used to go home with long, red-coloured streaks across my neck and cheeks, but all the consolation I received from my parents was: " You must have deserved it, or Mr. John would not have done it! " Although I have had over half a century in which to smooth over my resentment, I can still honestly say that I was treated with great cruelty, which was wholly undeserved.

Before proceeding · further with my unhappy schooldays, I must describe our Sundays, as my religious training will be called in question in another chapter. All hands were called at 8 A.M.; breakfast at 9; Bible Class at 10 o'clock in a room behind the church, which class was broken up at the first sound of the church bells at 11 A.M. We then took our seats in the church, where we had to sit as quiet as mice, for our mother's eye was on us if ever we budged. My brother, who was two years my senior, and I, had to write down the heads and as much of the sermon as we could grasp; this was to keep our attention fixed and prevent our thoughts from wandering.

At the close of the service at one o'clock we walked to the Dean Cemetery (weather permitting), and finding a seat in a quiet corner, we were allowed a few minutes' grace to refresh ourselves with a slice of bread and butter or a biscuit, after which we had to read our notes to our mother and hear her opinion, and also a lecture on the heads of the sermon.

This was all very brief, for we had to be back at the church at 2 P.M. for the afternoon service, which lasted two hours, at the close of which the elder members went home, and we young ones formed into our respective Sunday School classes, which were dismissed at 5 o'clock. We returned home for tea about 5.30, as hungry as hunters, having had only a small snack since breakfast, for in very few houses was dinner thought of on a Sunday.

When tea was over, the dishes were piled up on the kitchen dresser to be washed on Monday, and then the order was issued, " Get your books." We all produced our Bibles and took our seats in the best room, which was only used on Sundays. There we formed a half circle, with our mother in the centre; round the window in summer, and round the fire in winter.

My mother wished us to read through the whole Bible in the course of each year, so we read verse and verse about for a few chapters, when we would close our books, and our mother would give us an exposition on the sermons we had heard that day, pointing out various illustrations the minister had used. Then one of my elder brothers would be called upon to read aloud from some such book as Bunyan's *Pilgrim's Progress*, Milton's *Paradise Lost*, James' *Sermons Amongst the Tombs*, or sometimes *Gleanings Among the Mountains*—Scotch Covenanter stories being allowed on Sundays.

At nine o'clock, before going to bed, we had each

a slice of bread and butter, and a cup of milk, for porridge was never made in our house on the **Day of Rest**, though we had it twice a day during the **week**, and perhaps brose for dinner on washing day.   I will conclude my description of Sunday in our family by saying that I had the best of characters at the Sunday School and Bible Class, I could always repeat the lesson which had been set for me to learn, and I gained more prizes than any of my brothers.

Now I will return to the account of the relentless treatment I endured at the day school.   I cannot speak for my qualifications as a scholar, though no doubt I was the same in that respect as the average boy of my age, but I am sure that, when I joined the Second Class, I was as quiet and orderly a boy as ever entered it.

A change came over the scene; I became very dull and hated school, and I tried shamming illness to get clear of it, but my mother was not to be caught that way.   One of my elder brothers, who was in the highest class, spoke to her over and over again about my learning nothing, for which he blamed Mr. John, but, although she consulted him in many things, she would not hear a word against my teacher, of whom she held a very high opinion. This went on for some time, until at last I began to play truant, which I did successfully for a considerable time.   I think Mr. John was rather pleased than otherwise at my absence, and he never reported it to his father, as he should have done, for the father would have communicated with my mother if he had known.

One morning when I left the house as though going to school, I met a boy chum (not a school-mate) named Bruce, who had received such a thrashing from his father that he had made up his mind to run away to Glasgow, and he asked me to join him. Money was necessary for our expedition, and as I had ten shillings in the Savings Bank, I ran home for my bank-book and lifted the money; we then had about fifteen shillings between us.

We took train to Glasgow after buying our tickets, which were five shillings each, no seats being provided, and arrived there, three hours after leaving Edinburgh, as black as sweeps. We walked about the city for some time, but people seemed to know we were runaways, for we were asked a dozen times where we had come from and where we were going, until at last we were stopped by a policeman.

"Whaur dae you boys belong to?" he asked.

We told him we were from Edinburgh.

"Are you here by yoursels?" was his next query.

"Yes," we answered, trying to look innocent. "Our uncle was to have met us at the train, but we didn't see him, and we don't know where he lives."

"Whaur are you gaun to sleep the nicht?" the policeman then demanded. "Hae ye ony siller?"

"Yes, a little," we replied.

"Well, come wi' me," he said, "and I'll show you a guid place."

He took us to the George Hotel in George Square, where we got a bed for the two of us for half a crown. We were out early next morning and got as far as the Broomielaw Bridge where we found a passenger steamer about to sail for somewhere, and as we did not care where it was, we went on board, and to this day I am not sure where that steamer called. All I can remember of our day's outing is that, when she got round the Cloch, it was very rough and we were both very sick, and that we arrived the same evening at the Broomielaw with empty stomachs and empty pockets.

The sea-sickness had left us, but home-sickness had set in, so we started there and then on our homeward journey. I cannot say how we steered our course to begin with, but I remember we came to some large iron-works on the outskirts of the town, and the big blazing fires looked very comforting to the two small, cold, and hungry bits of humanity.

The gate stood open, so we ventured in, and as it was, doubtless, very unusual to see two little boys there at midnight, some of the workmen asked us what we were doing out at that time of night. We told them we were going to walk to Edinburgh, and seeing the big fire, thought we would like to warm ourselves by it before proceeding further on our way. They took us to a little wooden shanty where they kept their coats and cans of tea, the latter standing at the side of a nice, bright fire, and there they shared their tea and contents of their parcels with us. That disposed of, they told us to lie down on the seats with their coats for pillows, and they would call us at six A.M. and show us the road we should take to Edinburgh. We gladly availed ourselves of this kind offer and slept soundly till we were called at six o'clock, when the men supplied us with more tea and all the eatables they could scrape together. They then showed us the way to the Canal, which was not far off, and advised us to keep beside it so that we should not lose our way. We parted with these kind, hard-working men, and set forth on our journey like giants refreshed.

Late in the evening of that day we reached Falkirk, where Bruce had an uncle to whom he had decided to go, but I, being very home-sick, was determined to keep on, so we parted company. As I was walking towards the town, a young fellow and his sweetheart overtook me. He asked me where I was bound for, and on hearing that my destination was Edinburgh, he advised me to go no further that night, but to go and sleep at the neighbouring lime-kilns and start fresh in the morning. However, the girl took another view of the matter and rounded on him smartly.

"I think shame of ye," she cried, "tae tell a wee laddie like that tae gang tae the lime-kilns! He'd be deid gin the morn's morning. I'll tak' him hame tae my mither and see what she says."

Which the compassionate lassie did. The cottage was a thatched one, the inside neat and clean; but there was only "a but and a ben," and there were a man and his wife, with eight or ten children.

They treated me very kindly, and as it was bed-time and the porridge all consumed, they made me a bowl of brose, while the little ones gathered round and stared at me as if I had descended from the moon. They then made me up a little bed on the

lid of a chest, with a big chair at the end to lengthen
it, the family being stowed away as follows. The
guidman and his wife, with the youngest child, had
a concealed bed, from underneath which a truckle-
bed (called in Scotland a "hurly") was pulled out,
and it accommodated four boys; the girls all slept
"ben the house," and, I have no doubt, were disposed of in the same compact manner.

I can still remember some of the good woman's
remarks to her man anent my appearance.

" He's rale weel cled," she said, as she took stock
of me. "They're a nice pair o' buits he has on, and
his claes are a' o' the best. Aye, he must be somebody's bairn : we'll hear some day maybe."

Next morning I was sent on my way again, with
twopence in cash, and a piece of bread in my pocket.
The road ran no longer beside the Canal, but
towards Queensferry and Cramond, and farther on
Comely Bank.

Soon after passing Craig Leith, my attention was
attracted by a bill stuck on a tree, offering a reward
of £10 for a lost boy, who, I found on reading the
bill, was my valuable self! I was too young to
think of dodging home to save the £10, but anyway
I managed to get into the house without being seen.
I was at once taken to my mother's bedroom, where
I found her in bed, surrounded by a dozen or so of
friends who had come to comfort her. They left
on my arrival, and I was soon dispatched to bed,
which I was glad to reach, for I was footsore and
weary, and there I remained till well on next day,
when my mother put me through a severe question-

ing as to my travels, my reasons for setting out, etc. After a long, sharp lecture that scene closed.

The next day I was packed off to school, where I took my place as if nothing had happened, but Mr. John announced that in the afternoon he would settle with me for having run away from school. I informed my eldest brother of this during the mid-day interval, and he told it to the other boys in the highest class, who were very indignant. After thinking it over, it was arranged that, if Mr. John started to punish me in the cruel manner I had so often experienced, I was to give a great shout and all the senior boys would leave their room and come to my rescue.

At the opening of the class that afternoon I was told to go upstairs, which meant I was to receive my punishment on a tender part. Up I went, followed by Mr. John with his map pointer, which was nothing more nor less than a billiard cue. Without saying a word he lifted the pointer and brought it down on my shoulders with such force that it broke in two, and the heavy end fell on the floor. My blood was up, and this was an opportunity not to be missed. I caught hold of the broken cue and, with the heavy end, gave him a blow on the forehead with all my might. Before he had recovered from the effects of the blow I was downstairs and out in the street. The worm had turned !

That *striking* episode concluded my school-days. A court-martial was held that night in our house before my mother and Mr. John's father. I had asked that my brothers might be allowed in, for I knew they would speak the truth and clear me to a great extent, but they were not admitted. I do not know what passed between my judges, but I do know I never went to school again. I was about ten years of age at that time, and very big and strong for my years, for on my eleventh birthday I weighed eleven stones two pounds.

For a time I continued my lessons at home under the supervision of my eldest brother, learning them during the day and being examined by him at night, but he found it a thankless job, for my studious proclivities had been thoroughly beaten out of me. He had now left school, and was with a firm of publishers in Edinburgh. Through his interest I was eventually installed as an errand-boy with another publishing house, but soon afterwards, again by his intercession, I was sent for by a large printing firm, with whom he did business, to see if I could pass an examination in reading, writing, etc., but I failed, with the result that, instead of becoming a compositor, I became a printer's devil, which was quite to my liking. The following Monday morning at six o'clock I appeared on the scene, arrayed in all the splendour of a new white jacket, white apron, and paper cap, and was first instructed to watch how the other boys laid on and removed the sheets of paper.

It was a large printing office with about eighteen hand-presses and six steam-driven machines. During the forenoon one of the boys came to me and told me I was to go to B——, the blacksmith, and ask him for the black file. I went off at once to the smithy, and found Mr. B—— was out, but his son, a young fellow of about twenty, was at work at the bellows, so I went up to him and said I had been sent for the black file.

"All right," he said, "just stand there and I'll give it to you directly."

He proceeded to pour some oil over the palm of his hand, which he then rubbed over the sooty smoke-plate, and immediately applied it to my face and spotless white jacket, which so enraged me that I closed in on young B——, got hold of him round the waist, and swinging him off the ground, sat him down on the fire.

I will say nothing of the result, except that it necessitated a visit to the hospital as well as to the tailor. The story spread like wild-fire, and effectually put a stop to any more tricks being played on me.

The men in charge of the machine-room were very kind in showing me my work, so I got on well and rose over the heads of boys who had been there a year before me, and my wages were raised from half a crown to three shillings a week after the first month. I had also plenty of overtime, as we were paid half a crown for a night's work, when the machines had to be kept going all the time, and we relieved each other for meals as well as we could.

After three months I was laying on at the cylinder printing machine, and that was as high as I could get as a "devil". I have no doubt that my brother's influence had a great deal to do with my rapid promotion; he made a point of calling from time to time to see the manager, whose reports of me were always very favourable.

To encourage me in my business my brother presented me with a small wooden printing press, worked by a wooden screw, and with it I printed the addresses of all letters written at home, an ordinary-sized envelope being the largest-sized paper the press would take.

Then I tried cutting out pictures in wood as frontispieces for books, and printed them on every book I could lay hands on, and in so doing brought fresh trouble on my devoted head. One of my wood-cuts represented a big, dirty laddie in flowing robes with a big bundle on his back. To my youthful intelligence this seemed a singularly appropriate frontispiece for the *Pilgrim's Progress*, but, unfortunately for me, my mother thought otherwise!

I made another wood-cut of a rabbit which everybody agreed was my masterpiece, and even my foreman said it was very good. This rabbit flourished on the pages of every book in the house, from *Robinson Crusoe* to the Bibles, and for the latter offence the original " bunny " was taken from me and cast into the fire.

While I was amusing myself thus during the evenings at home, everything was going smoothly at my work, though I cannot say how long it was before a storm arose. My employers were great Bible printers, and I had a stereotyped one on my machine, large print and easy paper for me to lay on. We were printing between five and six hundred sheets per hour one day, and everything was going nicely when, unknown to me, a pin went through with the paper, with the result that it broke the type on two plates, which had to be taken out and sent to the foundry for the broken parts to be taken out and new let in. That gave us an hour's leisure, which was much appreciated by us youngsters; it had not occurred to me that I might be suspected of putting the pin through in order to get a rest.

We started again, and had gone on steadily for over an hour when another pin went through. The machine-man looked very hard at me, though he said nothing, but when the manager heard of the second pin he sent for me at once. I went up to his office without fear, thinking he was going to send me with a message to his home, as he had frequently done before, but to my dismay he gave me my wages up to date and ordered me to clear out there and then.

It was a great blow to me, for I liked the work and my foreman was pushing me on well. I can remember still that I cried all the way home, and when I reached the house I fairly howled. I explained it all to my mother, and this time I could see she believed my version and would take my part against my accusers.

In less than two hours a boy arrived from the office to fetch me back; he told us that when the type came back from the foundry and my machine had started again, another pin went through, and then there was an enquiry, as there should have been at first. They examined the paper and found several more pins, not lying loosely between the sheets, but stuck through and back again, as a woman puts a pin into a shawl, and they were rusted into the paper, so that they might have been there for months or even years. It occurred to them to look at the sheet which had got me the sack, and they found that that pin was also rusted into the paper. The manager then sent for me to go back, but my mother said I should not go till my brother had been consulted. When he came home we found he knew all about it, for the manager had called on him and begged him to allow me to return, but my brother was so annoyed at the summary treatment which had been meted out to me, that he stood upon his dignity, and I believe those two never spoke to one another again.

Thus, through no fault of my own, my printing career came to an end.

Shortly afterwards a very decent working man, who lived near us and was known to my people, though not intimately, was about to open a shop on his own account, and, wanting a boy, asked for me. The matter was arranged, and a few mornings later beheld me taking down the shutters of the new shop in St. Andrew's Street.

My new master was no other than Alexander Henry, the inventor of the Henry rifle, and, at that time, the best shot in Scotland. I need scarcely say how Henry's business increased ; he soon had seven men working in the flat above the shop, and a year later, finding the premises too small, he bought a larger building a few doors farther down the street.

Great alterations had to be made, and while they were being carried out, Mr. Henry's son and I frequently had a look over the new premises. On one of these occasions we were in the backyard when young Henry picked up a stone and threw it at a pane of glass in a window on the second floor. I remonstrated with him, but he said the old glass was all to be taken out and new put in. Whether he really believed it himself or not, I cannot now say, but I accepted his statement in good faith, picked up another stone and threw it at another pane of glass. Mr. Henry happened to be inside at the time, so we were caught in the act; the other boy received a thrashing there and then, and my misdeed was reported at home by letter, which resulted in my leaving Mr. Henry's service.

Home tuition was again planned for me as I was so very far behind the other members of my family as regards education, but I did not take kindly to it, and sighed for other worlds to conquer.

At that time H.M.S. *Pembroke*, one of the old 72-gun line-of-battleships, was lying in Leith Roads, and I made up my mind to try to join her, for I had decided that the sea was the career for me. However, it required much thought and manœuvring, for I was only twelve and a half years old, and the age limit for the Navy is fourteen, and also, I knew my mother would never give her written consent, which was a *sine quâ non*.

At last one evening, as we all sat by the fireside, I learning my lessons, and my mother darning stockings, I put a neat little plan of my own invention into operation. I managed to abstract a sheet of notepaper from the stationery drawer, and under cover of my lesson-book, folded it into a narrow strip, about an inch in width. That done, I remarked :—

"Mother, you very seldom write now, and, do you know, I have no idea what your signature is like. Just write your name there."

So saying, I laid before her the narrow strip of paper and a pen, all ready inked, and she at once complied with my request. Thus I overcame the first difficulty. After studying the signature for some time, and passing a few remarks, I slipped it into my pocket, and the following morning I proceeded to make use of it. I had a chum whose father was a coal merchant, and the two of us repaired to a little office in the coal-yard to fill up my sheet of paper. After a few experiments on another sheet of paper, our combined efforts produced something like this :—

"*To the Captain of H.M.S. 'Pembroke.'*

"Sir,

"Having a great desire to go to sea, and hearing that you are taking boys, I beg to offer myself. I was fourteen years old on my last birthday. I am strong and healthy, and I have my mother's consent.

"I am, Sir,

"Your obedient servant,

"HENRY YOUNG MOFFAT.

"My mother's signature—MARGRET MOFFAT."

CHAPTER II

THE NAVY OF FIFTY YEARS AGO

IT was on a Saturday in the month of May, 1857, that I made my way to Leith Pier, where the *Pembroke's* first cutter was lying, having come ashore for the mail, and as I stood there trying to keep a tight hold of my courage, the coxswain suddenly appeared on the scene, and called out :—

"Hallo, white-headed Bob! what do you want?"

I said I wanted to go on board to join the ship if they would take me, and he answered :—

"All right, my boy, get into the boat and I'll take you off."

I afterwards found the coxswain's name was Leach (nicknamed "Stickey" Leach); he was a good old sailor with a very jolly face, as brown as a berry, and slightly bandy legged which gave him a rolling gait: also, like most sailors, he was a fine hand at spinning yarns.

He took me off to the *Pembroke*, and, on arriving at the top of the gangway ladder, he said to the master-at-arms :—

"A boy come to join."

The master-at-arms took out his note-book in which he jotted down my answers to various questions he put to me, such as: what was my name and age, where did I live, and had I my parents' consent. In answer to my last question, I handed him my letter, with my heart beating like a sledge-hammer, and he said: "Stand there till I come back," which he did in a very short time, followed by the First Lieutenant, who asked me if I wanted to enter the Navy, and I said: "Yes, sir."

The master-at-arms then read out my former answers from his note-book, and the Lieutenant said: "All right, take him down to the doctor."

I stripped, was examined and passed in a few minutes, the master-at-arms then taking me to the office where a young clerk asked me the same questions as before. I was then enrolled as a second-class boy in the British Navy.

When I came out of the office, I was taken under the wing of a ship's corporal, who carried a cane in his hand—a most unwelcome sight, for I thought I had left all that on shore. He took me to the purser's steward to be entered in his books, so that on Monday I would be able to draw my cloth, serge, flannel, duck, drill, knife, etc.

I was appointed to a mess on the lower deck. All the sailors were divided into messes of twenty to twenty-four men with one or two boys, and the mess-tables hung between each gun on the lower deck, the pigeon-holes formed by the timbers of the ship-side being stowed with pannikins, plates, and similar utensils.

The next day was Sunday and a very strange Sunday it seemed to me, with the Bos'n's pipe whistling away like a lark, and everybody hard at work, washing decks, flemish-coiling ropes, and cleaning wood and brasswork.

At 9.30, the drummer beat to divisions, when all hands mustered, dressed in their best, and arranged themselves in a single line right round the upper, main, and lower decks. When the junior officers found that all the men of their several divisions were present, they went on the quarter-deck and reported to the First Lieutenant, who reported "All present" to the Captain, and a small procession was then formed, consisting of the Captain, First Lieutenant, and the officer of the division, with the master-at-arms in their wake, carrying the book of good and evil under his arm, and a pencil in his hand, ready for action.

The second-class boys, of whom there were eighteen, were stationed by the port fore-rigging in charge of the schoolmaster with a cane in his hand —oh, that cane!

As my uniform was still to be made I appeared in mufti, the only one so clad out of a crew of about six hundred. I might say here that it was unusual for a strict Captain to go the rounds without finding fault with something or somebody, and I never saw divisions pass without the master-at-arms being called upon to enter something in his book.

Divisions over, we were dismissed by the sound of the drum; then the bos'n's mate piped: " Aft all mess-stools on the main deck," and a few minutes afterwards the church bell began to ring, when all hands assembled on the main deck, except Roman Catholics, who were excused from the church service

—a strange service it appeared to me, who had been brought up in a strictly religious family, according to the customs prevailing fifty years ago in the United Presbyterian Church of Scotland.

The second-class boys sat on the first two forms in front, the next two being occupied by a brass band, which accompanied the hymns and anthems. As the trombone player was seated immediately behind me, I got the blare of that instrument (called a stomach-pump by the sailors) full in my ears, and it seemed to me a very irreverent demonstration for the Sabbath.

Out of the eighteen second-class boys, fourteen were Scotch lads who had joined previously at various periods ranging from a week to six months, but none of them had been in the service long enough to have been converted to the Anglican form of worship.

I had been in the *Pembroke* six months when a new chaplain joined the ship, who was very strict in all matters connected with the church service, and he soon complained that the boys, in repeating the Creed, did not bow their heads at the words " Jesus Christ." He reported this to the schoolmaster, who cautioned us.

After school was over, we fourteen Scotch boys held a meeting in the cable tier (a place in the orlop deck for coiling down the stand-by hemp cable), and for the first time in my life I was called to the chair. We all agreed that bowing and scraping belonged to the Roman Church, and we gave our word that, happen what might, we would never bow. We then closed the meeting by shaking hands all round.

When the critical moment arrived the following Sunday we held our heads erect, and the schoolmaster, who was usually as white as chalk, turned as red as a turkey with anger. After service we were called to muster on the after-part of the main deck, where the schoolmaster demanded from each of us an explanation of our conduct.

I remember the first boy's answer was: " The musical instruments knock me fair stupid, and I didn't notice we had got to the place for bowing till it was too late." Ingenious youth! When it came to my turn I replied: " Well, sir, I have been brought up in the Scotch Presbyterian Church by religious parents, and we would not be allowed to bow in our church."

The thirteen other boys then spoke up to the same effect, and the dominie seemed amazed at our effrontery. We were entered in the master-at-arms' little book, which meant we were to appear with the defaulters next day on the half-deck at seven bells (11.30 A.M.). That night we held another meeting in a snug corner of the upper deck, and pledged ourselves to stand firm and true to one another in our trials. The whole affair had become known on the lower deck, and the men were ragging us in a joking way, with such remarks as: " I say, white-headed Bob, if you don't bow your head when you're told you'll have to kiss the gunner's daughter when you go before No. 1 " (First Lieutenant).

We duly appeared before No. 1 at seven bells,

and when he heard the charge against us, he flared up in a mighty passion. " What ! " he cried. " Because you have been dragged up in an irreligious manner, you think you are going to dictate to us what is right and what is wrong in the church service ! I will give you each one week's first watch, and we shall see if that won't make you bow next Sunday."

A week's first watch meant that every evening at eight o'clock we had to march on to the quarter-deck and stand, seven of us on each side by the mizzen rigging, toeing a line for four long hours without speaking or moving, and as we did not get to bed till 12.30 and were called, with all hands, at five o'clock, we only got four and a half hours' sleep. A first watch punishment nowadays is from eight to ten only.

The next Sunday found us in our usual places, with the " stomach-pump " at the side of my head as before, and every eye in the ship turned towards the fourteen " heretics." When the Creed started, the men who usually sat as far back as possible pressed forward to see us bow, but they were disappointed, for we stood as straight as hand-spikes.

When the service was over we were put in leg irons in the after cock-pit with a marine sentry over us, which meant we were in the Captain's report for Monday. When the Captain came on board we were mustered on the quarter-deck, and he sentenced us to three dozen strokes with a cane.

They were administered in this way :—a small

field-piece was run out to a convenient part of the quarter-deck, and each of us in turn stood with a foot at each axle, with a leather strap to secure them there and another strap round each wrist. Then one of the ship's corporals, who was standing ready with his cane, pulled the prisoner's blue frock and flannel out of his trousers, leaving only the thin No. 1 blue cloth between the cane and his flesh. Each prisoner had to bend over the gun, and a corporal bound his wrists tightly to it to prevent him squirming during the infliction. Then, all being ready, the corporals turned to with their canes, each giving a dozen strokes, which were counted by the master-at-arms.

I consider this punishment quite as bad as the cat, for I have seen blood coming at the second or third stroke, whereas with the cat I do not remember it appearing before the first dozen were over.

I think we all tried our best to keep back any sound of pain, but it was no use, we all had to yell. At the sound of the shouts three boys gave way and promised to bow, so they were dismissed, leaving eleven of us to be treated as above, and after the punishment was over we were taken right aft abaft the mizzen-mast and placed under a marine sentry till sunset, which was to prevent us from doing anything rash while in such pain. We were allowed to sit down on the signalman's grating if we liked— a permission which might safely be granted, for we were not likely to avail ourselves of it, a standing position being more comfortable than sitting just then.

During that week we sailed from Leith Roads for a cruise, calling at Cromarty, and were then ordered south to Sheerness. Thus we were at sea on the Sunday after the flogging, and they tried a new way of making the unregenerate Scotch boys bow the head. Six of us were placed on the first seat with a ship's corporal at each end, and five on the next seat, guarded in the same way, with the band well back to give the corporals room to swing their canes. When we stood up to repeat the Creed the corporals raised their canes, and when we came to the words "And in Jesus Christ" they brought the canes down on our bare necks with a force that made us bow with a vengeance, and the sky-pilot left the deck with a smile on his face. We used to think he was the cause of all the trouble, and I still think so.

The Captain went on the quarter-deck after church and called the First Lieutenant to him, and they both laughed heartily. I often heard the men say afterwards that was the only time they saw the Captain laugh; he was known in the Navy as "Black Jack," or, more frequently, "Chin-stay Jack," because he always wore his chin-strap down on his chin. Nicknames were very prolific among us, and they always showed in what estimation a man was held. Flogging was very frequent in "Chin-stay Jack's" ship, but mostly among the men.

I will conclude this chapter by giving a short account of the daily routine of the second-class boys' work in those days.

All hands were called at five o'clock, and while

the men washed decks the boys scrubbed out the wardroom or the gun-room. Breakfast was at 6.30, and an hour later the boys mustered on the quarter-deck, with trousers turned up to the knee, sleeves up to the elbow, and neck exposed to show they were properly washed and had left no " high-water marks." If they all passed the First Lieutenant's inspection without a fault the order was given to go aloft, when they made a rush for the main-rigging, ran up to topmast head, over the cross-trees, and down the other side. If anyone was observed easing down, even passing over the futtock-shrouds, he would be received on the deck with a cut of the cane and sent to do it over again.

On the other hand, if a boy was found to be untidy, or with a " high-water mark," two of the biggest boys would be told off to take him to the head pump and scrub him with canvas wads, and also with sand if it was a second offence.

We had a boy on board at one time whose name was Willie, but as he hailed from St. Andrews he received the nickname of " East Neuk." He was a long, lanky boy with a very dark skin that made him look dirty when he was actually as clean as any of us, so he had frequently to submit to the scrubbing operation. I remember one cold winter's morning, when it fell to my lot to assist in scrubbing him with sand and canvas, he tried to get out of our hands and jump overboard.

Our little climbing exercise over, we had to attend on our masters at the wardroom breakfast at eight o'clock, and after that to tidy up their rooms.

At nine o'clock we were mustered at our guns, and about half an hour afterwards the bos'n would call the watches to their respective duties for the day. For the boys that might mean sail drill, knotting and splicing, palm and needle, gun drill, rifle and cutlass, boat drill, down and up top-gallant mast and royal yards, etc.

I think knotting and splicing was our favourite work, as we were then sure to be under a sailor, while in the other branches we might be under a corporal of marines, and that we did not like. Fancy work in plaits and sennits we usually learned in our mess from any of the men who happened to be working at some fancy article, such as a knife lanyard or yoke-lines, and I always found them very willing to teach us.

We learned tailoring in the same way, for all the men could cut out and make their own clothes; though there was a ship's tailor on board no one went to him, except for his first suit.

Dinner was from twelve to one o'clock, and during this hour we had also to wait at lunch in the ward-room. Afterwards we resumed our duties till 4.30, when decks were cleared up, and the boys again tidied up their master's room before tea, which was at five o'clock.

The bugle would sound at 5.45 to dress for dinner, and we had to smarten ourselves up before appearing in the wardroom at six o'clock to attend at dinner. At 6.30 the order was given to sling hammocks, and we enjoyed ourselves in various ways till nine o'clock, when we all had to turn in.

CHAPTER III

REMINISCENCES OF THE NAVY

WHEN the *Pembroke* arrived in Sheerness we were paid off and put in barracks, but we soon received orders to join our new ship, the *Edinburgh*, a ship of the same class as the *Pembroke*, but, I should say, much shorter. I have heard that she was called the "Grog Tub" in the Baltic during the Russian war, not that they had any more grog than the rest of the fleet, but on account of her relative length and breadth.

We sailed for the north again, and this time made Queensferry our headquarters. There were many changes in the crew, both among men and officers, and they had also got rid of several of the noted eleven, but I had been spared.

The boy called Willie, or "East Neuk," whom I mentioned in the last chapter, joined the ship about this time, and we boys all liked him though he was not very bright in the intellect. He used to speak very broad Scotch, especially when he was rebuked by an officer for mistakes in his work, till the officer was nonplussed.

Willie was gunroom boy, and the officers there used to play terrible tricks on him, one of which was as follows :—We were cruising in the Channel one day, and the dinner for the gunroom was a poor one as the potatoes were finished, so it consisted principally of soup and Norfolk dumplings, or "dough-boys" as we called them, of which there were seven. Just before dinner the Admiral had signalled to us to shape our course for Tor Bay, and the officers were so pleased at the prospect of getting into port that, when they went down to dinner, they were very independent and found fault with the fare. To add to their displeasure a half-burnt match was found in the middle of a dough-boy, and poor Willie had to bear the brunt of it all.

They got up a mock court-martial and sentenced him to sup all the soup and eat all the dough-boys, there and then, while they stood over him. I think he managed to struggle through the menu, but the groans that issued from the cockpit during the afternoon made me think that was the worst punishment the poor unfortunate ever received.

Another misadventure befell Willie not long afterwards. We returned from our cruise towards Christmas, and the master's mate had a turkey sent to him from friends on shore. It was delivered on board alive and in a hamper, which was handed over to the tender care of Willie, who stood it down by the gunroom door. A live turkey being a very unusual sight on board, everyone who passed that way lifted the lid of the basket to have a look at the curiosity, until at last someone forgot to close it again, with the result that the bird took French leave.

When the master's mate went down to tea Willie

announced in fear and trembling, "Sir, the bubbly Jock's awa'!"

"What on earth are you talking about? Why don't you speak English? Moffat, come here!" he called to me.

"Yes, sir."

"What is this fool of ours trying to say?"

"What's wrong with you, Willie?" I inquired, as if I knew nothing of the matter.

"The bubbly Jock's awa'," he repeated.

I turned to the master's mate, and by way of breaking it gently, innocently inquired: "Had you a turkey, sir?"

"Yes, d—— him! has he lost it?" he exclaimed, jumping up and discovering the empty hamper.

Willie was tried by mock court-martial, and that evening was stretched across the gunroom table while the officers gave him blow and blow about with the scabbards of their swords on his bare skin.

Each second-class boy had a master whose cabin he had to attend to, besides waiting on him at table, and my master was the Second Lieutenant, a jolly little Irishman who sported five medals and was very lame, having been wounded during the Crimean War.

He was not very prominent when the First Lieutenant was on board, but he made things hum when he was in charge. One morning after breakfast he stepped into his cabin when I had just started to tidy up—an unusual thing for him to do at that hour of the morning. He had left his razor lying on the table just as he had finished with it, and I had picked it up to wipe it and put it away, but before doing so I was trying its edge by cutting up an empty match-box, when he stepped in and caught me in the act. He told the schoolmaster to bring me up with the defaulters at seven bells, and on my appearance, sentenced me to a week's first watch, and to call out my offence every half hour as the bell struck. I stood half-way up the main rigging (that position having been appointed at my sentence) and when the bell struck, every half hour from eight o'clock to midnight, the sentry on the bridge called " All's well," and the sentry on the head gratings replied " All's well." Then a voice from the main rigging announced, " Here am I for chopping sticks with my master's razor ! "

I could hear the men below laughing at me, but it was no joke to stand on a ratline for four hours at a stretch. Then when the Second Lieutenant came on deck after his dinner, in a slightly elevated condition, he looked up at me and exclaimed : " Chop sticks with my razor, eh ? I'll teach you to chop sticks with my razor ! You would chop sticks with my razor, would you ? I'll teach you to chop sticks with my razor ! "

He "looked upon the wine when it was red" every night, but " Paddy," as we called him, was a fine officer for all that. One Saturday had been a very wet day with a strong wind, and the ship's cook had not sent his mate (who was a nigger) to coal-tar the galley funnel as usual. " Paddy," on going the rounds next day, noticed the galley funnel, and the ship's cook was put in the report. On Monday he and his mate were sentenced to a week's first watch, one in the port and one in the starboard main rigging, so every half hour, after the usual "All's well," came the nigger's voice, "Here am I for not black de ship's galley funnel!" Then from the other side came in a deep baritone voice, "Here am I for not see him do it!" followed by loud laughter from below.

Ship's cooks had very few friends on board in those days, for the men were kept on short commons, the food being of very bad quality, and they were apt to blame the cook for it, so that he was anything but popular.

I think it was about the end of the year 1859 that our First Lieutenant, having written a book which he wanted to publish, was advised by a friend to consult my brother John, which he did, and after a few meetings John asked how his young brother was getting on in the *Edinburgh*.

"What!" said No. 1, "is the boy Moffat your brother? Why did you allow him to go into the Navy?"

"We didn't allow him," replied John, "he ran away from home!"

"But the Navy would not accept the boy without his father's or mother's consent," said the lieutenant.

My brother assured him I had not had that, so he promised to inquire into the matter. When he came on board next morning he called to the sentry: "Pass the word for the boy Moffat," and although I was two decks below him at the time I could hear his stern voice, and it was enough to make any boy shake in his shoes.

I heard the words "Boy Moffat!" shouted from sentry to sentry until it reached the one on the orlop deck who came to me and said: "Here, white-headed Bob, No. 1 wants you." Nearly all hands had heard the call on its way to me, and I received much sympathy from friends as I went up to the First Lieutenant's room. The schoolmaster evidently thought I should not be allowed to enter the presence of such a great personage without a guard, for he followed me up but came to a stand a few yards from the cabin door.

When I reached the door the sentry knocked and said, "Here is the boy Moffat, sir," and the answer came sharply, "Come in!" If the ship had foundered, or gone on fire, or some other great calamity happened at that moment, I would have hailed it with joy! However, nothing happened, so I stepped in and found No. 1 sitting with his back towards me, looking at some papers on his desk, but he turned round in a few minutes and looked me in the face.

"How did you manage to enter the Navy without your parents' consent?" he demanded. "Come, speak out!" I nearly collapsed, but I saw there was nothing for it but to make full confession, and I managed to get through my story with a struggle. Then I saw him as I had never seen him before, for he was quite kind and gave me words of advice. He said my brother had told him of it, and that my mother, through John, would probably apply for my discharge, but I had laid myself open to three dozen with the cat.

At that I showed signs of excitement, and to calm me he said, " But I will try to get you off the flogging. I am very pleased to say that both the wardroom steward and the schoolmaster have reported to me that you behave very well. Now you may go."

When I got outside of the door I felt as though all the eyes on the ship were on me. The schoolmaster was standing where I had left him, but he had been joined by the master-at-arms, bos'n, gunner, and a few of the lesser lights. The bos'n was a very loquacious man, who would surely have been in danger of exploding had he been compelled to hold his tongue for an hour, so he was the first to speak on my appearance.

" What little hanky-panky trick have you been up to now?" he asked. " I've told you before you will never be drowned. Hanging will be your lot some day; see if it isn't!"

Then he walked away, and I told my tale to the schoolmaster but to no one else, though, somehow, it soon spread over the ship, and for the remainder of my time in the service everyone seemed extraordinarily civil to me—even " Paddy." He gave me many little punishments, but, on the other hand, he gave me many presents. We were often allowed on shore on Sunday afternoons from one to five o'clock, when " Paddy" always gave me half-a-crown, and when it came to my turn for twenty-four hours' leave he gave me five shillings.

About three months after my interview with the First Lieutenant I was sent for and told to pack up and go. I did not pack much, for I distributed most of my belongings among my friends, whom I was very sorry to leave, and then went home, where I was again set to my lessons, but with a very bad grace— for who could meekly sit down to study the Rule of Three after having roamed the wild ocean from the North of Scotland to the South of England?

CHAPTER IV

EXPERIENCES IN A COLLIER BRIG

ONE of the boys in H.M.S. *Edinburgh*, who had been my particular chum, deserted soon after I left, and went to Shields, where he joined a ship in the coal trade. He wrote to tell me how comfortable he was, and gave me an address to go to in South Shields if I would like to join him. Soon afterwards I again cleared out from home, with a few articles of clothing, and went to Leith, where I took my passage by the Newcastle steamer, and eventually reached South Shields. I found the people my chum had told me about, and they took me in and were very kind to me.

I intended waiting there till my friend returned from a voyage to London, but there was some delay, as his brig had only got as far as Yarmouth Roads when she, and a number of others, were caught by strong northerly winds and detained there ten or twelve days. Then the captain of the brig *Premium* called one day at the house where I was staying, as he had heard there was a very likely lad there, wanting a ship, and he wanted an apprentice.

I was close at hand and was called in, the bargain being fixed for three years, at £8 the first year, £10 the second, and £12 the third. We went off at once to a lawyer, who drew up the agreement, and when all was settled I went on board my new home, then lying in the Howdon Dock.

I had not mentioned my previous experiences, and they thought they had the usual "green" boy to deal with, so the only job I was entrusted with the first evening was to sweep down the deck.

In the coal trade the men were engaged by the voyage, but they would do certain work while the ship was in Shields, such as putting her under the shoots to load, without pay; they all lived on shore and were mostly married men. The mate came on board every day, and frequently brought his wife with him for the day. While I was sweeping the deck that first evening, just before the mate went away, he brought a small coil of hemp-rope out of the cabin and laid it in the galley, saying to the other boy, "Leave that there till morning; I am going to reeve a new lanyard in the fore rigging in place of that stranded one." After that he called the other boy to scull him ashore—the brigs in the coal trade had two boys as a rule.

When my new friend came back we made our tea in the galley and then adjourned to the forecastle for a good tuck-in, which I much enjoyed, for no one had asked me if I had a mouth all day.

The forecastle seemed both small and dirty to me, but nevertheless we made ourselves very snug. Being strangers to each other we had much to talk over and it was late before we got into our hammocks.

Next morning I was up first and lit the galley fire, then the other boy appeared on the scene and started to cook our breakfast, while, to amuse myself, I unrove the broken lanyard, rove the new one, and worked the knot on the end, but I did not know about the tackle to set it up, so let it stand at that. When my shipmate saw what I had done he looked small, for he was quite ignorant of the way to manage it, and he was the oldest apprentice. Only by six weeks, it is true; but still he had that much seniority, and every sea-faring man will remember how he felt when he became the oldest apprentice— almost a third mate!

When the mate arrived during the forenoon, he noticed the lanyard was all ready for setting up, and remarked, " I say, boy, I didn't know you had been at sea before? "

I said nothing, for I did not want anyone to think I knew anything about a ship, knowing that the time would soon come when I would be found very green, say, in reefing a top-sail, I did not know what to do with the points, for I had been used to strop and toggle reefing.

However, I think they were very pleased to get me, and we sailed in two or three days for Hamburg.

In the middle watch of our first night at sea, the mate gave us a hurried call out in this way :— " Below there ! Jump out, boys—shorten sail ! Hurry up now—every other button ! "

We soon appeared on deck and found there was a very strong wind, with heavy rain and vivid lightning. In a few minutes I was on the fore-topsail-yard, tying a reef with the help of the flashes of lightning. I managed it somehow, but I think I learned more next day when I went up to shake out the reef, for I saw the points I had tied were too slack, and the spare canvas was not snug. I also noticed that there were no cleats at the yard-arm for each reef as there are in the Navy. Of course I had tied many a reef before, though always as a part of sail drill in fine weather, but I soon learned how to do it properly by watching the others.

At Hamburg we had to discharge our own cargo, so I had to learn how to handle the shovel and bell-ropes, for the "Geordies" never discharged with winches, but by jumping. It was very hard work for a crew of eight to discharge coal at the rate of about a hundred tons per day, especially for a beginner, but I soon got used to it.

The ballast was always put in by shore men, though we had to trim it, but that was not very hard work as the brig took only sixty tons of ballast.

In the summer months we traded steadily to Hamburg, with the exception of two trips to Rotterdam, and in the winter months to London, where gangs from the shore discharged our cargoes.

Now I shall recount a few of the remarkable events that happened in the old brig *Premium*.

On our second voyage from Hamburg we sailed at daybreak, about half ebb, but had only got a few miles down when the brig took the ground, and in taking soundings all round we found she was hung by the heel, under which there appeared to be a stone.

We soon noticed, as the tide fell, that she was pushing the rudder up, and all the spars we could muster were used to shore it down, which kept it all right, as we thought, but when we got into clear water lower down, we found that the rudder was broken and we had only nine inches of it under water. However, we went on, for it takes more than that to stop a crew who are paid by the voyage.

If the weather had kept fine we should have got on all right, but we had a fresh beam-wind and a little swell, and to steer her anything like straight was out of the question. She, like the greater number of the colliers of those days, was steered with a tiller, and we might be trying to push the tiller to windward when all at once she would lift her rudder out of the water, and flat on the deck we would go. All things have an end, and so had that passage, but it gave us plenty of trouble.

On another voyage from Hamburg we had unusually bad weather for summer-time and our position was not very well known. Our captain was not a navigator, so I do not remember whether the sun was obscured or not, it being no other use to us than to supply us with light and warmth, but there was a consultation at noon between the captain and the mate.

I was at the helm till eight bells, and, on walking past the skipper, I heard him say to the mate: " I've a good mind to take the fore-sail in now, for we must be drawing well in towards the Bar. Well, let them have dinner first."

The mate came forward and said: " Be handy, my lads, get your dinner, and then we'll shorten sail. We must be close in."

"So I was thinking," said one of the men, and the others answered: "Aye, aye, Charles, we won't be long—it's pea soup for dinner."

We went below, and in less than fifteen minutes I, as ship's-boy, was first up with the soup-kid to return it to the galley, but first I went towards the lee bow to throw the remaining soup overboard, and to my great surprise found I had thrown it on to a red-painted buoy. I roared out at the top of my voice and all hands came running to see what was the matter with me, but they saw the buoy and recognised it as the Bar buoy at Shields. They did not wait for orders, for every man knew what to do, and at once set about it.

Before we had gone very far the fore-sail was up, and the top-sails lowered, and it fell a dead calm as we got under the lee of the Tynemouth land. The tide was half ebb, the anchor down, a tug alongside —all within a few minutes from the time I threw the pea soup on the Bar buoy.

I used to think Hamburg a much nicer place than London, for the weather was always bright there, but in London it was always blowing or raining, if it was not foggy. Of course that is accounted for by the time of the year, for we sailed to Hamburg in summer, and to London in winter, when we had long, dark evenings, sitting round the bogie-fire.

The men usually went on shore, leaving us two boys in charge, and that was what we liked best, for then we got the full benefit of the fire. If the men stayed on board there was no room for us, and we had to retire to the galley. We were better off if it was Saturday night, for then we had to read Reynold's newspaper, which was the favourite with Shields men. Very few of them could read at all, and none was sufficiently proficient to read aloud, so it fell to the lot of the two boys to read in turn while the men got into their hammocks out of the way to listen, and passed remarks to one another after the finish of each article. We were always pleased when the remarks developed into a hot argument over our heads, for then we got a rest from the reading.

There was a little peculiarity in our reading which may have a very amusing effect if tried nowadays. Every time we came to a big word which we could not pronounce we simply said "Liverpool" in place of it, and went straight on. It was just as intelligible to the men as if we had managed to struggle through the right word.

There was one very bad thing we had to face in the London trade; the captain went on shore every evening after tea, leaving orders for the boat to be sent for him at nine or ten o'clock, which meant that, just as the men turned in for the night, we boys were sent on a job that would, in all probability, keep us out of bed till midnight, and sometimes long past it. I do not remember the captain ever making his appearance till several hours after the appointed time, and there we had to sit in the boat, perishing with cold and hunger, for there was not even a quay for us to walk about on to keep our blood in circulation, as there were only steps leading down to the river at the end of some alley. Nearly all the steps we were sent to led up to Ratcliff Highway, and one favourite landing-place was called Stone Stairs; I looked for them a few years ago but a wharf seems to have been built in their place.

When sent on those expeditions we thought ourselves lucky if we could get hold of two potato sacks, for then we would get right inside them, which made a welcome addition to our scanty clothing, as we seldom had either jackets or boots with wages of £8 or £10 a year.

Being kept up so late did not excuse us from being on duty again by six o'clock next morning, but we had plenty of companions in misfortune—so much so, that, soon after my boy-days, the police stepped in and summoned any captain who kept his boat waiting for him after nine o'clock.

Another Act, of which I missed the benefit, was that compelling the ships to take fresh water from water-boats; we always filled our water casks from the river at half ebb, and we did the same at Hamburg, but there the river was clearer water than the Thames.

On one of our winter voyages we had orders to discharge coal for the Government at Woolwich Dockyard, and we arrived alongside the dockyard wall one night at ten o'clock. Next morning we were rather alarmed to find our ship was not floating, though it was within an hour of high water, and the water was washing over the deck. We sounded the pumps and found just the usual water, but we soon discovered that she had stuck in the mud, so all hands set about doing something to get her out of it, for she would soon have filled by the hatches and other ways.

We started the pumps first, for that is a good way to shake a vessel, then one man and I went aloft to jump and swing about the topmast rigging, while another man got into the boat alongside with a long pole which he stuck into the mud near the bilge to make a blow-hole. In the meantime a party of about two hundred and fifty men was dispatched from the guardship *Fisgard* to our assistance, and a number of them ran our best six-inch rope along to the capstan on the quay, while others went aloft to shake her, which they did right heartily.

When the water had reached about half way up the coamings the rope was hove taut and they intended to let go sharp, but just as the pipes sounded " 'vast heaving," the rope broke, and that did the trick ! She jumped up like a porpoise and our trouble was over.

The captain was pleased to see her all safe, but he was very down-hearted about the good six-inch hemp rope being broken, and I ventured to make a suggestion to him. One of the sailors having pointed out to me the Superintendent of the dockyard, I advised the captain to ask him for a new rope, telling him it was the only one we had to depend on, and freights were so low he could not afford to buy another. He was doubtful of success, but he tried it, and next morning a six-inch hemp was delivered alongside, with a letter which the captain was to hold as long as the rope lasted, for it had the

Woolwich Government mark in it.   That was a fine rope, and was there doing its work well when I left the brig.

That reminds me of another occasion when I got the captain out of trouble by telling him how to work the oracle with Navy people.   We were tacking up Woolwich Reach, and when nearly abreast of the frigate *Fisgard* we were reaching on the starboard tack so that we would just fetch about the stem of the frigate.   At the same time there was a barque running down, which should have passed across our bows, but did not like to venture for fear we did not put our helm down.   He starboarded to go under our stern, and to assist him and save ourselves, our captain stood on rather too long, so that, when we did put our helm down, our mast carried away the flying jib-boom of the *Fisgard*.   When we were clear and standing over to the north'ard, I approached the captain and said that if he went on board the frigate and told them he was very sorry, but he had been placed in such a position that the mishap was unavoidable, it would probably smooth matters over; otherwise, he would have to pay for the damage.

He said to the mate: "Keep her going, but with a good allowance of watermen's nips," then got into the boat and I sculled him alongside the *Fisgard*, and we were back again, with the matter amicably settled, before the brig got far away.

For the benefit of the uninitiated I will explain the meaning of a "waterman's nip."   In the days of which I write, a waterman was always employed to assist in the navigation of small coasters, of which he took charge anywhere between Woolwich and Greenwich. They were usually Greenwich men, and a hardy lot, but very fond of grog. When they were beating up with the flood, in company with from fifty to a hundred brigs, it very often happened that one could not allow the vessel to head-reach for vessels ahead of him, so the watermen would put the helm down, and let her come up in the wind and shake the sails well, but he would not allow all the way to get off the vessel. With great care the waterman at the helm could take as long to reach from one side of the river to the other as would allow the crew time to take their dinner, and each time he brought her up in the wind was what we used to call a " waterman's nip."

All our berthing in those days was done without the help of steam tugs. If we were ordered to such-and-such a buoy at Gallion's Reach or Bugsby's, we had to get there under sail, and, more often than not, we managed by sailing as close to the buoy as we could steer and working the sails and braces in such a manner that the vessel's way would be checked just as we reached the buoy. Then the youngest man on board would jump on to the buoy with a handy rope, catch a turn, and make fast another rope at once, and then we would furl the sails. If we made a mess of it we had to drop the anchor and furl the sails, and then run a rope to the buoy.

We had also a good deal of kedge-anchor work, for many of the mooring buoys were well off in the fair-way, so to keep well in out of the traffic, we ran the kedge inshore and hove it taut. We shifted it to the outer bow at the change of the tide, and if another vessel was ordered to the same buoy we passed the rope to her; if four or five moored at the same buoy the inside vessel looked after the kedge and the outside ship kept the anchor watch, the middle ships being all "farmers" or "sleepers."

The anchor watch, anywhere above Gravesend, was not all beer and skittles, for the place was infested with river thieves, who prowled about, looking for a vessel with the look-out asleep in the galley; then they would set to work, and nothing was too big for them to carry off. They used to have an eye to the cabin funnel, which was always made of copper, as it, of course, stood beside the compass, but my captain always made sure of our funnel when we anchored in the river, by taking it under his arm when he retired to rest.

The thieves also looked for captains' or mates' watches, as they were frequently hung up in the cabin to keep the ship's time by, which plan works very well at sea but is decidedly risky in the river.

Although we had no clock on board we had plenty of sand-glasses—half-hour, one hour, and two hours —but they were very unsatisfactory time-keepers, though that was not the fault of the glass. Take a case of anchoring in a roadstead, wind-bound, with the watch from 8 P.M. to 5 A.M. when the "doctor" (cook) would be called. By the time he had got his fire going and the coffee ready, he might perhaps hear some clock on the shore strike five, and then "the band began to play." None of the men would admit having turned the glass before the sand had all run out, so, as usual, the boy would have to bear the blame of it. I think it was always done quite innocently. A man would look at the glass and, finding it nearly run out, would turn it, thinking such a little sand would make no difference, when it might have run several minutes longer, and that shortage would be doubled in the turning.

There was one branch of seamanship that was well drilled into the youngsters on the brigs—casting the lead. If we had a head wind anywhere between Yarmouth and London we had to keep the lead going, for we were in very narrow water all the way. There were no gas buoys then, but still we kept under way, blow high, blow low, and even fog, if not too dense, would not stop us.

As a rule, the helm was put down by the soundings we called out, and not by the bearing of the light-vessels. If it was daylight, or a very clear night, we would only heave when the captain called, " keep the lead going," but in the course of time we learned from experience when to heave.

I had not been long in the Hamburg trade before I started smuggling in a small way, and with good intentions at the outset, but, like other things, smuggling grows on one till it has a good hold. I started by bringing a pound of tobacco to an old sailor and a pound of tea to his wife, but I soon had plenty of customers for as much as I liked to bring, and the old sailor, being a boatman on the river, helped me to get my booty safely on shore.

On one occasion I had a big order for tobacco, it

being our last voyage for the year to Hamburg, and I went on shore one evening to buy my stock. The plugs of tobacco were all sticking together, so I slung the big square block over my shoulders and set out for the ship, but I stopped to rest on a low wall overlooking the shipping. While I was sitting there a gentleman came along and sat down beside me on the wall.

"Good evening," said he; "that's a fine lump of tobacco you have there."

I made some suitable response, and he immediately said, "I can hear from your tongue you are a Scotch boy. What part of Scotland do you come from?"

I told him Stockbridge, Edinburgh.

"Do you really?" he exclaimed. "I know Edinburgh very well, and the Stockbridge district too. What is your name?"

I said my name was Moffat, and he went on, "You know, I am Scotch myself, and it is nice to fall in with a countryman when you are abroad. What ship do you belong to?"

"The *Premium*, of Shields," I replied.

"Is that tobacco for the ship's stores, or is it your own?" he inquired.

"It's my own," I explained. "I can make a few shillings each voyage by buying it here at 1s. 2d. a pound of eighteen ounces, and selling it at Shields for 2s. 6d. a pound of sixteen ounces."

"Oh, that is very nice," said the interested gentleman, and soon after that we parted.

We had a good run across, and arrived in fine weather at nearly low water, so we could not cross the Bar, but let go the anchor and hove out our ballast. That was a usual practice when tide and weather permitted, and for which the men were allowed a shilling a ton, which in our case came to twelve shillings each, the mate drawing the same as the men, out of which each man gave a shilling to the boys, making five shillings between us, and it was understood that the boys should do the lion's share of the heaving. My old sailor saw us at this work, and knowing we would be in about half flood, he came well below the Low Light to meet us.

I had my tobacco in a bag at the bow of the long-boat, and I also had a gasket made ready for lowering it over the side after crossing the Bar. I could see my boat, for she was painted blue, but I also noticed the Customs boat further seaward than usual, and just abreast of my man, who was pulling seaward, supposed to be looking for a job to moor strangers. Then I realised that there was danger afloat.

It was customary for the tug to stop towing as we drew close to the boat and that suited my man also, for both boats came alongside at the same time, my boat on the port side and the Customs on the starboard. I did not give my man a rope, but lowered the bag close down, and as he came under it, I let go, and at once ran round to the other side to see the Customs come on board. There were two officers on that duty, one we called the little Englishman, who was a very pleasant officer to deal with, the other we called the big Scotchman, and he was a terror. As luck would have it, it was the Scotchman, whom no one liked, who boarded us that day and set his rummagers to work as usual while we went on with ours. In a very short time the ship was moored in her tier and ropes coiled down.

The Customs' boatmen were the rummagers, and by the time we were fast they had all been aft to report to the Scotchman. The other boy and I had started to sweep down the deck when the big officer came up, and in my hearing, said to the captain, " Well, sir, I know that there is a large quantity of tobacco in your ship and we have failed to find it." Taking a letter out of his pocket, he continued, " You have a lad of the name of Moffat on board ?"

The captain was smoking his usual yard of clay and the only notice he took of the officer was to remove the clay from his mouth and point it at me. The Scotchman turned to me and said, " Your name is Moffat, is it ?" I replied, " Yes, sir," and then he opened out on me.

" You have a quantity of tobacco on board which you have not declared, and if you tell me where it is at once it will be better for you, for I must and will have it, if I should pull the ship to pieces." He went on at such a rate that I could not get in a word edgeways, and he finished by saying, " Now I will ask you for the last time—have you any tobacco in the ship that you have not declared ?"

Loudly and firmly I answered " No !" and then the fun started, for they turned over everything, loosed the sails, turned the cable over, and emptied the bread locker, but of course, as I had no tobacco in the ship it was impossible for them to find it, and so far, my mind was easy.

They tried every way they could think of to coax me to confess, but it was of no avail, so they left two men on board and relieved them night and morning. I think one of them was intended to shadow me if I should go on shore, but I knew the tobacco was in good hands so I did not trouble about it, and the big Scotchman was nonplussed.

We sailed again in two or three days for Rotterdam, with a general cargo of fire-bricks, fire-clay, and coke, and on leaving Rotterdam on our return, to save time and expense, we came out by the Hook of Holland Channel, and not by the Maas and Helvoet Sluys that we entered by. All went well till we were nearly out; we were then with square yards and all sail set, and the tide had just started to ebb, when all at once we were caught flat aback with a fresh N.W. breeze, and before we could box the fore-yard and get her head off, she was ashore and bumped heavily until the tide left her hard and fast.

When she was high and dry at low water we carried away our big kedge and a small one, led one to the windlass end, and the other along the deck with a luff upon luff, and hove both right taut, then waited for high water. The sea was very rough and she bumped so much that we were all very sick, while the pilot had been crying like a child all the time, and was past taking any part in the re-floating.

At high water we hove away on the kedge rope, and could have hove more, but the anchors were coming home, and the brig herself was complaining very much. The butts were all started, and when we lifted off a hatch to see how the hold and ballast looked, we found every stanchion unshipped and lying on the ballast, and we were afraid that, if the wind did not take off, we would find the beams beside the stanchions.

Next low water we took away a bower anchor with the help of tackles and skids, then took the cable along and shackled it on, and went aboard again, where we hove right taut. We then decided to go on shore during the bumping hours as we stood much in need of a rest.

We had no boat in the water, so we slid down ropes and set out for terra firma; the water was only knee-deep at the ship, but the beach was so flat we had a long way to walk before we reached dry land, nor did we get the expected rest when we reached it, for we found the place was full of rabbits, and we bagged fifty or sixty between us. There were no houses there in those days, but the place is greatly changed now, the Great Eastern Railway Company having two mail steamers and one cargo boat arriving there daily, and the same number sailing. When we went on board again we found the wind had shifted to N.N.W. and had done so before high water, the brig having shifted into a much better position, and we thought she would come away next time. We therefore remained on board and took in the two kedges. We set the main-topsail and braced it flat aback, and after that was done we had some spare time, so I looked for something to eat, but just as it was ready the ship floated. In a minute all was excitement, and "all hands on deck," "shiver the main-topsail," "drop the bunt of the fore-topsail," "heave away the windlass," and numerous other orders were rapped out in quick succession.

We soon got through them all and shaped our course for Shields, where we arrived leaking badly, and she was at once placed on the Gridiron to be examined and caulked.

CHAPTER V

SAILORS OF THE OLD SCHOOL

SOME time ago I read a book called *Windjammers and Sea Tramps*, by Walter Runciman, which, on the whole, I liked very much, but I take exception to his remarks on the sailors of his time, which was also my time. He speaks of the sailors of the present day being very superior to those of forty or fifty years ago, but I must say I cannot agree with him there; his experience must be a strange one if it has led him to that conclusion.

Men of the present day are better educated, for they have all grown up under the Compulsory Education Act, but truly a little learning is a dangerous thing—they know how to calculate the freight on a cargo, but they do not understand, or they ignore, the value of the ship and the great expense of sailing her, and look upon it as all clear profit. For instance, they may read in the newspaper that freights are twenty shillings a ton, and their ship has 3000 tons on board. "That's £3,000," says Jack. "There's ten of us with £3 a month—that's £30—and the officers and petty officers get another £30 between them, and we'll say the old man has £15 a month—that's £75—we'll be three months on the passage—that's £225—and if we bring it up to £500 for grub and other expenses, that gives the owner £2,500 for this trip, and we only get £9 each for doing all the work."

This discontented spirit was unknown to the sailors of my young days, most of whom could neither read nor write, but I maintain they were steadier, better-disposed, and better-conducted men than the seamen of the present day, but under the protection and dry-nursing of the Board of Trade they have gone so very far down the hill that they have nearly all disappeared out of sight.

If a ship were to sign on twenty A.B.'s at the present day, how many of the twenty could pass a very ordinary examination in seamanship so as to fully entitle them to that rating?

Not very long ago I told two sailors to get into the boat and take another rope to the buoy, but when one of them had got on to the buoy the other managed to get adrift with the boat. When I observed that, I called to him to scull up to the buoy for his mate, but alas! he knew no more about sculling than he did about flying!

Three or four years ago I went on board a ship that I was superintending; she was at Northfleet and the crew had joined the previous day. They had been sent to bend the main-sail, and they had got it along, laid it athwart just before the main-mast, opened it out, and were in the act of bending on the gear when I arrived. I came over the side just abaft the fore-rigging, so that I had a good view of all that was going on, and I saw at once that she had a crew of " know-nothings," but it was a most amusing sight. Nobody had noticed my arrival, so I asked the second mate to tell the captain I was on board, and when he—a good old salt—came forward, we both enjoyed the joke for a little, but I could not stand it long, so the captain went on the starboard side and I on the port, and I can truly state there was not a man on the port side who could clinch on a buntline.

I wonder where Sir Walter Runciman finds the sailors who are better than they were fifty years ago; where are the boys of the old brigade? I ask—echo answers, " Where ? "

Many of them may be found in the Australian bush, in the backwoods of America, farming in Canada—in short, everywhere and anywhere but the forecastle, for the grandmotherly protection of the Board of Trade has disgusted them and they have all left. I see there are a number in Herne Bay, where I now swing my cot, and I can tell them by the cut of their jib, although I have not spoken to many of them.

One day last summer I was on the beach watching a boat race, and I had my glasses with me, the case of which I had made from a piece of No. 5 canvas, and coated it with Japanese black. This took the eye of a man (who, I have since noticed, is a pick-and-shovel man about the town), and after gazing at the case for some time he remarked, "It was a sailor made that."

I wonder how many sailors of the present day carry the ditty bag which, in my time, was hung up at the head clew of every sailor's hammock, and which contained marline-spike, pricker, palm, rubber, sail-hook, a case with needles, usually hitched all round with twine, the tip of a horn full of grease, and a fancy little serving-board.

A mate or a bos'n had very little trouble in sending a full crew to their jobs here and there about the ship, and every man liked to work with his own tools, but to turn to the same number of men at the present day a mate would require the contents of a chandler's shop. The "Geordies" had one tool more than I have mentioned above; if the brig they were going in had no patent windlass they went on board with a well-scrubbed handspike tied to the outside of their bag of clothes.

These old north country sailors were very guilty of blaming the boy for everything that went wrong, and I have noticed the same thing on shore, as the following story shows. A keelman was hauling his keel up alongside H.M.S. *Castor*, then a drill ship at Shields, and on this occasion the crew were at big gun drill as if in a rough sea, which means that every time they fired the guns and she recoiled, they let go the port-tackle-fall, and down went the port with a slam, to be traced up again when the gun was loaded. Now, when Geordie had his hand on the port sill down came the port on his hand, so he immediately hauled to the gangway, which he ascended, but was stopped by the sentry who asked him what he wanted.

"Where's that boy?" Geordie demanded. "He's lowered the clapper down and jammed my hand!"

I have mentioned the pay the boys got in the brigs, and I need hardly say it was impossible to keep ourselves provided with many clothes on that princely sum, so we had to do without oilskins and many other articles. I was always on the look-out to make a little whenever possible, and I frequently got a shilling for sculling people on board of their ship while I was waiting for my captain, and I saved these odd shillings till I had enough to buy something of which I stood in need. The sleeved waistcoat of bye-gone days was a friend in need, for it fitted closely, and kept out wind, rain, and cold better than a " monkey-jacket," but, if fairly good, it cost from twelve to fifteen shillings.

On one occasion I had five shillings saved and fifteen shillings wages due, so one Sunday morning in London I asked the captain to settle, which he did after a growl, and I asked the mate for permission to go ashore, as I wanted to go to Petticoat Lane for two pairs of moleskin trousers. He granted the permission, adding: " Mind you don't get taken in."

" Oh, no fear," said I ; " I'm Scotch ! "

" Well, we'll see when you come back," he responded.

When I reached the great clothes market I decided to walk through first and view the land before buying, and I had not gone far when I overheard a Jew at his stall say to a young man : " I vill give you sixteen shillings ; I have no more monish."

I took no notice of the remark, but went on, and

further down the market I bought two pairs of moleskin trousers for eight shillings, the shop price being seven shillings and sixpence a pair. With my parcel under my arm I was leaving Petticoat Lane when a man touched me on the shoulder and whispered, " Will you buy a gold ring ? "

" No, I have no money," I answered.

" I'll let you have it cheap," he persisted, " I must get rid of it. Just step up this passage and I'll show it to you."

We stepped aside from the crowd, and he cautiously produced the ring, saying casually as he did so, " An old Jew in the market offered me sixteen shillings—all he was worth—for it, but I would rather let you have it than a blooming old Jew."

I offered him eight shillings, which he accepted, and I went on my way rejoicing, looking about me all the way down the Minories for a quiet corner that I might stop and gaze on the noble ring that was to be the means of lifting me from poverty to riches.

When I reached the brig the mate was performing his ablutions on the main-hatch, and he called out, " Well, Harry, come and show me how you got on."

I produced the trousers and said I gave four shillings a pair for them.

" Did you ? " said he. " Fools and their money are soon parted."

" Why, look at them ! " I protested, " did you ever see anything better for the money ? Thick moleskin trousers like that would cost seven and sixpence at the Milldam-bank, Shields."

By way of answer he put one of the trouser legs in the bucket and gave it a slight rub, as if washing it, and to my great dismay, he washed all the thickness out and left something no thicker than a cambric handkerchief! I could see I had been taken in on that deal, but I had another shot in the locker, so I produced the ring.

"Ah, look at that!" I said exultingly. "You wont wash the starch out of *that!*"

"Well, well! what have you been doing now?" exclaimed the mate. "What did you pay for that—twopence?"

I told him I had expended eight shillings on it, and he was very angry with me, for he said it was only brass. However, I was convinced that he was wrong, and next day I went to a jeweller and asked him to tell me what the ring was made of, but he said he charged sixpence for his opinion. I felt so sure of the result that I ventured a sprat to catch a whale, but, after a minute's examination, he informed me that the ring was brass and only worth a penny. So there was nearly all my money gone and very little to show for it, but it taught me a lesson which I have never forgotten, and I am sure it saved me many a pound in after years.

The north countryman's idea of the four quarters of the globe is well-known—"Roosha, Proosha, Memel and Shields"—but it is not so generally known that they used to say there were only three inspired books—the Bible, the *Pilgrim's Progress*, and the *Farmer of Inglewood Forest*. They would lie in their bunks while the boy read aloud from one of these works as mentioned previously.

These old salts had little or no book-learning, and they were very far behind in things spiritual. I remember one day when we had finished our dinner, consisting of pea-soup and pork, one of the men, in the act of wiping his spoon and sticking it up on the beams in a little sennit becket, remarked, as he got up, "Thank God for that!" A "blue-nose," who heard it, jumped to his feet and cried, "I don't see what you have to thank God for, we've only had our Act of Parliament!" This was said in all sincerity, and he evidently thought the Lord should only be thanked for extras.

One day on the Bank-tops in South Shields, where pilots most do congregate, a missionary appeared, but he did not get on with them very well for they all claimed to belong to some particular sect. Presently another pilot, very well known in those days, arrived on the scene, and the missionary said to him, "Well, Mr. Larboard, of what persuasion are you?"

"What per-sway-shun am I?" he replied. "I've been a licensed pilot for twenty-five years, and I've never put a ship on the Herd Sands yet!"

The old pilots of Shields were a hardy set of men, though not over-burdened with education. One of them boarded a man-of-war off the Bar on one occasion, and as soon as they reached the Bar, he shouted in the usual North country tongue, "Clew the fore-top-gallan'-sail up!" But the captain said,

"That is not how we do it here, pilot, we take in all sails together. You just let me know and I'll call the bos'n, then he will call the men and we will take them all in together."

"Ah reet, hinny," returned the pilot, "I'll tell ye and ye'll tell another, ah reet."

When the ship was close to her appointed moorings, and all hands standing by for orders, the pilot drew a long breath and rattled out without a pause, "Clew the fore main and mizzen top-gallan'-sails up haul the foresails up lower the topsails down brail the spanker up haul the jib down fower hands in the boat and run a warp ashore to the post!!!"

Another man-of-war, cruising in the North Sea, came close in to the Bar one day, and a pilot, thinking he might get a job, went alongside, but the captain told him he was not going in.

"But if you like," he added, "I will engage you to take some letters to the post and to buy us £2 worth of vegetables."

So Geordie went on shore with the mail, and on his way along the street he met another pilot whom he asked for the meaning of vegetables.

"Wegetables? Oh, they're just wegetables. Green peas are wegetables, and scallions,* and er——"

"Oh, green peas are wegetables, are they? Ah reet, hinny."

Off he went to the market-place, where he expended £2 on green peas, which pretty well filled his cobble, and then returned to the ship with his

---

* Scallions—onions.

purchase.   He mounted the ladder, and on reaching the deck, called out, " Pass down the buckets."

The captain advanced and said, " Oh, never mind the buckets, pilot, we have plenty of men, so we will pass them up one at a time."

Geordie exclaimed, " Wan at a time, sir ! It would take ye ah day the day, and ah day the morn, and then ye wouldn't have them up ! "

With which the captain agreed when he had had a look at the cobble.

I must leave this digression about pilots and return to the sailors. The old Geordies were very prejudiced against whistling, and I had not been long at sea when they recited to me :—

" All you young sailors take warning from me,
   Never whistle when you are at sea ;
   For if you do you are sure to rue,
   For the wind will howl and whistle too."

Another verse they taught me was the following :—

" He that doth a rope belay
   Coils it up and walks away,
   Excepting 'tis the Mr. Boiler (cook),
   Who belays a rope and calls another coiler."

They had another bit of advice for the benefit of raw boys. " Never throw anything over the weather side of the ship except hot water or ashes—the one will blow back and scald you, and the other will blind you."

One man in particular stands out clearly in my recollections of the collier brigs. He was cook with us for over a year, and was a very tall, well-made man, about sixty years of age, with a striking-looking nose. It was long, straight and thin, and resembled a flying jib in a dead calm with the sheet hauled right taut, so although we had to call him "Doctor" to his face, he got no other name but "Flying Jib" behind his back. We did not dare to address him as cook, but though he was for ever growling at us boys, he never lifted his hand to us.

One of his peculiarities was his solemn belief that it was the object in life of every steamboat to run down all the sailing ships they fell in with. If a steamboat was seen ahead, the cooking had to stand till she was past, for "Flying Jib" would not take his eyes off her, and if he heard at night that there was a "Doctor's Shop" ahead (the Geordies' name for a steamboat's three lights in sight ahead), he would run on deck and stand there till she had passed, though it gave him many a sleepless night. The poor man was very sensitive about his nose, and was always on the look-out for insults on account of it. By a mere chance I met him one night in Poplar, close to a music hall, and he kindly invited me to go in with him. As we entered we met a man and his wife going out, who seemed to look very hard at the "Doctor," and he, as usual, took it as an affront. He put his hand up to his face, pressed his nose over against his cheek, and said to them, "Can you manage to get past?"

"Flying Jib" always went on shore with his moleskin trousers, sleeved waistcoat, and long hat—silk hat was hardly a suitable name for it because it was always brushed the wrong way. He thought so much of the long hat that he would start to wear it from Gravesend, or Woolwich at the latest. He was a typical old Geordie with regard to his shore-going rig and many other characteristics, but he had a number of fads peculiar to himself. If a steamboat came alongside while we were at the moorings, and threw us a line with the usual " take a turn of our rope—thank you," " Flying Jib " would pay no attention, even if he were the only one on deck.

I do not know why he left our brig, but I remember he was out of employment for a very long time, and his wife was beginning to feel the pinch of hunger, so one day she ventured to say, " Robert, I hear you could easily get into the steamers; they are wanting men, and the pay is thirty-six shillings a week, and find yourself."

" Flying Jib " was so wild at his wife's suggestion that he should go into a man-killing steamboat that he walked straight out of the house, and it took the combined efforts of all their friends to bring them together again.

CHAPTER VI

MEDITERRANEAN VOYAGES

WHEN I had served my three years in the brig *Premium*, the owner, who was a pilot, thought he would be doing me a good turn by taking me in his cobble, and bringing me out as a pilot, so I accepted his offer, as I understood the work perfectly. He had a brother who was also a pilot and they usually went out seeking together, the direction and strength of the wind being an unfailing guide to them to go out.

We would sail or pull out, according to circumstances, and when we got into position a little south of the Bar, we would heave to, or drop the hook, or just let her drift right in the track of vessels coming from the southward. When both my bosses were on board vessels, I sailed home, if possible, but if not, I towed in with the last one to board, and when in harbour I had full charge of the cobble, to keep her clean and the gear in order.

This went on for some time, until all the youngsters became very uneasy at the news that the Tyne Commissioners were going to have a large dredger built which, rumour said, would be so powerful she would walk away with the Bar in one season.

We lived in the hope that nothing would come of it, but in a very short time the contract was given out, and a number of young fellows then left Shields for pastures new. I have since fallen in with only one of them; he became one of the best pilots of Calcutta, and was well liked by all who had the good fortune to obtain his services.

At the general exodus I shipped as A.B. in a Welsh schooner bound on a voyage to Malaga, then to Pomeron, and back to Liverpool. We had seven of a crew, all told, of which the captain, mate, second mate, and one A.B. were Welsh; then there were myself, an ordinary seaman who was a fisherman, about thirty-five years of age, and the cook—a little Dundee boy on his first voyage.

When I was having my first chat with the captain he said, with quite a fatherly air, " You know we all mess together in the cabin, and you get the same food as myself."

I thought I had got " a home from home " this time, but I was soon to be disappointed. The captain, being a part owner and very " near," had taken care to buy cheap food, but as all the Welshmen belonged to the same village and the captain was a pillar of their church, there never was the slightest murmur from them. The pork did not contain the slightest particle of lean, and it was packed in dry salt in two boxes—one box for the outward passage and one for the homeward. It was the very same article that was sent in some ships for greasing masts until the cook had collected some slush.

We each had a hearty appetite and we did not let the fat pork annoy us much, but we did object to a little incident which occurred daily at dinner. The captain would take a mustard pot out of a little cupboard beside him, help himself and pass it to the mate, and if the latter at any time omitted to return the mustard pot to the captain to be put back in the cupboard, he would reach over for it. The fisherman and I did not like that, so we agreed that the next time the mustard pot was left on the table, whoever was nearest to it should help himself and pass it on to the next.

We put our little plan into action next day. The fisherman took the mustard pot, then passed it on to me, and I helped myself and passed it to the Welsh A.B., but there it stopped, for he was afraid to touch it. The captain reached over and snatched it away, saying sharply as he did so, " Remember this is a privilege pot ! " " Privilege pot " was the name I gave to a mustard pot for years afterwards.

There was one good point in the catering on that schooner : we each had a basin of tea and a biscuit at midnight, and I think this was only right. We had then been existing for seven hours on—at best— a biscuit and pork tea, with another seven hours still to run, and when work is the same, night and day, food should be the same also.

Old Captain Welshman was a fine helmsman, and if the ship was steering badly, or going along with the wind well aft, he never left the wheel, but ate his food there, and never asked to be relieved until he altered the course or the wind shifted. In port he used to work with us, discharging cargo, and if he had to go on shore to the agents he would hurry back, change into his working garments, and take his place at the winch, thus allowing another man to go down the hold.

The Welshmen never spoke in Welsh to one another if the fisherman or I was about, which I thought was very good of them, for they did not feel at home with English, and sometimes would make amusing blunders. Of course we knew very well that none of the three of us would have been there if Welshmen had been obtainable.

After discharging at Malaga and taking in forty tons of ballast, we sailed for Pomeron, an ore port up the river Guadiana, which at that time was only visited by schooners and small brigs. We loaded at a shoot about three or four miles below Pomeron, which we had to ourselves; but the loading was a very slow process, for the cargo was brought in small baskets on donkeys' backs, a donkey's load being about four good shovelfuls. The river was, at that time, very narrow and very shallow, and there were no tugs, so we had plenty of work on the way up. Square sail was out of the question, the high land causing calms and variable winds, and we had to make our way up with stay-sails, and with the boat under the bow with a small kedge ready. If the wind drew ahead, or a dead calm fell, we could run the kedge away with only a two-and-a-half-inch rope bent on, which is heavy enough when it has to be sculled away. A small vessel cannot spare two men in the boat, and I was appointed to the boat, for I was always a powerful sculler.

At that time, when steamers were unknown there, the banks of the river at low water were covered with tortoise, and every time I went under the bow to get the kedge I passed up the little reptiles till the decks were nearly full.

One Saturday night, after the work was done and we had had our tea, one of the Welshmen and myself were told off to get the boat ready to take the captain to Pomeron. We had the flood-tide with us, so we soon reached our destination, where we found several Welsh vessels. In fact, they were all Welsh except one schooner hailing from Dublin, who had broken her back trying to carry a cargo of manganese ore: she was only three parts loaded when she began to buckle up.

We boarded one of the schooners, hailing from the same port as ourselves, and on our arrival the other captains, three or four in number, all met in the cabin, while we betook ourselves to the forecastle. The night wore on, and I tried to get to sleep across the chest lids, but the sound of twelve or fourteen men, all speaking Welsh around me, did not prove a soothing lullaby. When I could stand it no longer I made an excuse of going on deck to pass the boat aft, though I knew it was lying alongside all right.

I was the only one on deck, so I had a peep down the cabin skylight, and what a sight I saw! All the captains drunk, and very drunk too! All speaking and singing, and none listening.

I saw we were in for a night of it, so I returned to the forecastle and looked for a soft plank to lay me down to sleep, but I was awakened by a voice calling,—"Come up here, Harry," followed by a stream of Welsh.

I drew my wits together and ran up—to be greeted by my captain, mad drunk, with a long knife in his hand!

It was clear that it was I on whom he wanted to operate, and in an instant I had him by the throat. I stuck my thumbs hard in on each side of his throat, and had the upper hand of him in so short a time that he was quite unable to use the knife, but I would not let go till my mate arrived on the scene and took the knife away. As soon as the knife was overboard I let go, and he dropped at my feet like a dead man, though I am sure I had hold of him only thirty seconds.

I might mention in passing that I have found this the best way to subdue a man in similar emergencies.

The captain and I had always been the best of friends, but I have heard it said that men suffering from delirium tremens always attack their friends. I, for one, could do without the friendship: when they come armed, at any rate.

In an hour's time we were able to lift him into the boat and return to the ship, which we reached before anyone was out of bed, so my boat-mate helped the captain to his bed and the matter was never spoken of afterwards. He treated me just as usual up to the time I left.

We made a fair passage to Liverpool, where we stopped by the ship for two days at the captain's request—I think to allow him to go home for money to pay off the three of us.

As we left the ship we passed a grocer's shop, and I said to the fisherman, "Let us go in here and send them down two pounds of butter for auld acquaintance sake." This we did, and saw the grocer's boy off with it. No one in the ship had tasted butter during the whole voyage, and the pork fat was finished a week before we arrived. I knew, therefore, that the butter would be welcome, and it would repay the captain for our solitary raid on the "privilege pot."

I went straight to Glasgow from Liverpool by the steamer *Blenheim*; it was calm all the way and she took twenty-four hours to reach Greenock. I arrived in Glasgow with a few pounds, but no friends, for I had not been there since my youthful escapade, recounted in the first chapter.

I asked a pointing porter, who offered to take my baggage, if there was a Sailors' Home at hand.

"Yes," he answered, "but take my advice and don't go there—it's only niggers that go there. You come with me, and I'll take you to a house that will be like home itself."

I acted on his suggestion, and that was my first experience of sailors' boarding houses. It was close to James Watt Street and the Shipping Office, and the old lady who owned it had many good qualities, and perhaps a few doubtful ones, but, as sailors' boarding houses go, it was not the worst by a long way.

I had been in Glasgow two weeks when I joined a Glasgow-owned, but American-built, brig, then loading in Ardrossan for a voyage to Havre, where she was to get a cargo of machinery for Port Said, consisting of the first dredger and engine stores for the Suez Canal.

The captain, whom I will call Pannikin, was a native of Glasgow and well known on the Clydeside, and the mate, Mr. Abel, was English, but also well known on the Clyde. There were ten of a crew, and they lived in a house on deck. The cabin was also in a deck-house, fitted with bath, pantry and store-room, none of which I had ever been shipmates with before, so I thought I was in clover this time.

We made a fine run to Havre, and were soon on the berth for loading, but the charterers discovered that our main hatch was too small to take in the boiler, and our owners would not allow the hatch to be cut.

The case went to court, and on the day of the trial Captain Pannikin, as he was going on shore, told me to accompany him on board one of the old "Black Ball" packets, which was lying close at hand, taking in passengers for New York. He had his tape-line with him, which I held while he measured her main-hatch, and it was lucky for our owners that he did so, for that measurement gained the day.

When the case was hanging in the balance the captain said that he had that morning measured the main-hatch of the largest ship in the harbour, and had found it to be two feet smaller than ours. It was, therefore, decided that we had only to take what would go down the hatchway without cutting it.

Whisky was only a penny a glass at Havre, and it caused much trouble; the mate had to be discharged, and there was some difficulty in getting another, but at last Captain Pannikin agreed to take the mate of a Shields brig that was discharging beside us. He had no sextant, nor would he have known what to do with it if he had had one, but he had plenty of good clothes (of the sleeved waistcoat type), and was clean and tidy at all times. He was a very fine fellow and a thorough sailor, so we left with him, trusting to Captain Pannikin being at all times able to do the navigation.

The cook and steward left at Havre with the same complaint as the mate, and we shipped in his place a " coloured gentleman "—as he was always careful to call himself. He was undoubtedly one of the best cooks that ever went to sea, and he never did any work without singing some appropriate song—such as " Ham fat! ham fat! smoking in the pan "—but he had such big ideas of his own importance and dignity that he would not listen to a reprimand from anyone, and he left before the voyage was over.

It was the month of July, and we made a fine passage up the Mediterranean, hugging the African coast, where we got a sea-breeze or a land-breeze, and she could lay her course with either, so we reached Port Said in thirty days. It was well for us that the weather was fine, for, as it afterwards turned out, the fine little brig was the heaviest roller that ever sailed the seas, but we did not know it just then.

We had no chart for Port Said, for there was none published then, so we anchored off Damietta, and the captain went on shore to make inquiries; but the health officer would not allow him to land, and there was no one about who could speak a word of English, so he had to return unsatisfied.

We remained at anchor all night, hove up at four A.M., and kept the lead going till we found our port. We could see a great number of tents on shore and a flag-staff with the French flag flying, and we approached with caution so that we might get as close as possible. We anchored in five fathom, and it turned out that Captain Pannikin had done well, for we were never asked to shift our anchorage.

The brig had a nice, smart boat, very light and handy, to which I and another young fellow were appointed, and we had plenty of boating when we took the captain on shore. There was a little outlet from the Lakes with about two feet of water, but there was a bar to cross with only a few inches of water. When we were taking the captain on shore and drawing close to the bar, we would give way to try and make the boat jump the bar, but we usually stuck, so the two of us would get out and lift her over into deeper water again.

Soon after our arrival the natives were set to remove the bar, for our cargo had to be landed by barges, which were only square boxes with no hold. They placed two to four tons weight on them and hauled them ashore with a small line which they had run from the shore to the ship for that purpose.

Port Said at that time was a very miserable place with no housing accommodation but tents, and the flies were unbearable.

In walking about that part which was allotted to the native labouring class, it was quite a common thing to see little boys laid on the sand with their hands tied to their sides and their right eye greased to attract the flies, with the result that they would lose the sight of that eye and so evade conscription.

The highway from Damietta into Syria was along the sea-coast, and the caravans used to cross the outlet close to where the main street is now. We always contrived to be about when the caravans arrived, for they had plenty of pomegranates, oranges, vegetables and such like articles which they willingly sold to us.

There was a butcher's shop in a small, round tent, and I shall never forget our first visit to it. We had been directed to it, and on looking in we could smell butcher-meat, but there was none to be seen, for the whole place had the appearance of being draped with black. When the proprietor observed us he started swinging an empty bag round about his head, and the flies came pouring out in such a dense cloud that the captain and I had to beat a retreat for a little. When we returned, the meat had become visible, but after that sight the captain struck a bargain to be supplied at six o'clock every morning.

Mons. De Lesseps lived in a tent a little removed

from the others, and he was of great service to Captain Pannikin, for he was the only man there who could speak English.

We had run out of oil; in fact, I think none had been sent in the stores and we had only had enough to burn the side-lights as far as Gibraltar, so we had burnt slush in the forecastle and candles in the cabin. There was no oil to be had at Port Said, but as there was a great number of porpoises playing about the mouth of the outlet, the captain suggested that we (the boat's crew) should try to harpoon one, so we took the harpoon with us one day, and after we had landed the captain we pulled out to a position just outside the breakers, where we dropped our anchor, bent the harpoon on to a line of twelve-thread manilla, saw all clear for running, and then looked for the fish. There were none in sight, so we lit our pipes and sat down for a chat, but very soon we saw a few of the fish curling round under the boat, and, without waiting to see if all was clear, I stuck the harpoon into a fine, big porpoise.

The result was unexpected; the line had got round my leg, and next moment I was dragged overboard. Away went the fish and away went the boat in tow, leaving me in the water, but my chum, not wishing to make a voyage by himself, took out his sheath knife, cut the rope, and then sculled back to me.

All the porpoises in the sea appeared to have arrived on the scene, and in one minute after I had driven the harpoon home they were all passing our ship, and the mate, who saw them coming, shouted to the others to look. They could see that the leading fish had a harpoon in him with the line streaming behind, and the mate declared he saw me fast to the line, being towed feet first with my yellow hair showing. The fact was, it was a manilla rope that we had on the harpoon, and when my chum cut it, it would naturally fray out, so, my hair being the colour of jute, it deceived the mate.

The harpoon was lost, and we had to burn slush for the remainder of the voyage.

Our next trouble was the want of fresh water, and there was none for sale in Port Said, but we were told of a spring about seven miles up the canal track, so we borrowed a square, flat punt, that would draw only six inches with a cask of water in her, and started early one morning. We found it to be a long seven miles. We poled her along in turns and so kept on the move, but we took three and a half hours on the passage, and then our punt could not reach the spring, and we had to carry the water in buckets. We noticed it had a strange taste and a milky appearance, but for want of anything better we took it and returned to the ship.

I will make a short digression here.

During the twenty years I regularly traded through the canal, I met with only one man who knew of the existence of that well. This was Mons. Stamata, pilot from Port Said to Ismailia, who, before the canal was opened, was master of a dredger. For years I had noticed that steamers became unruly as they passed the well, and when I became master I amused myself by trying the density of the water just a little to the north of the first station from Port Said, until I was able to fix the spot. Now that the canal has been deepened the little tantrums in the steering when crossing that spot will not be noticeable. In the earlier days, when a steamer had coaled down to the last inch the Canal Company would allow, and was creeping along very close to the bottom, if she crossed over a spring, or, in other words, passed through about four to five hundred feet of comparatively fresh water, her draught would be increased about four to six inches, and she would be apt to cut some capers, the blame of which would be laid on the man at the wheel.

CHAPTER VII

ADVENTURES IN THE HOLY LAND

WE were glad to get away from Port Said after a stay of several weeks, but before we sailed a barque and a schooner had arrived. The former fetched in all right, but the schooner's master, not seeing Port Said where he had expected to find it, went to another port, further along the coast, called Said, and could not work back again as he had to stand well out to sea to avoid the easterly set of the current; so it was six weeks from the time he had sighted land about Port Said before he arrived back again.

Captain Pannikin could do better than that, but, I am sorry to say, at this part of the voyage he was always a full pannikin, and he was in that state when we left Port Said. When he did not appear next day all hands went aft to see him, in the last dog watch, and though he tried to get out of seeing us, we would not go away till he came out. Then we read the Riot Act to him, and he promised not to touch any more liquor.

I think it was the following morning at daybreak that we found we were close in shore, though we had not expected land so soon, but the captain settled matters by taking in sail and coming to anchor as if he knew the place. He ordered the boat to be manned, and said he would go on shore and see if he could get fresh water, for the Port Said water was not fit to drink. We rowed him ashore, and as he left the boat, he said, " Wait till I come back, I won't be long."

After waiting for an hour I thought I had better go and look for him. I walked into the town— which was a small place several miles south of Joppa—and inquired for him at the first grog shop or café that I came to, but all I could get out of the man in charge was, " Gone—gone ! "

I would have gone too, after that answer, but, as I turned to leave, I caught sight of the ship's box, which contains all the ship's official papers, and I turned on the man and charged him with telling a lie.

Fortunately an Arab who could speak English came in then, and, after hearing the story on both sides, he explained that the captain had been there for grog and a young native had coaxed him away, but before going he had left the box in charge of the café-keeper till his return.

I asked the English-speaking Arab to go with me to trace out the captain, and promised to pay him for his services. He consented to accompany me, and we soon learned that the object of our search had taken a donkey and gone to Jerusalem. I ran down to the boat with the box and the news, and told my chum to go off and tell the mate that I would take the best donkey I could find and give chase even unto the gates of Jerusalem.

7

After some persuasion the Arab agreed to finance me, on the promise that he would be well paid if he would assist me in getting the captain back. About noon we set out with the usual donkey-boy in attendance, who sang snatches of songs by the way to break the monotony.

If I remember rightly we had to make a journey of twenty-six to twenty-eight miles, in the course of which we learned from several travellers that they had passed a man answering to the description I gave, which was as follows:—white trousers and shirt, white shoes, Turkish fez, and no vest or jacket.

At last we arrived within the walls of Jerusalem, where the first thing I saw was a café. I made straight for it and looked in, and there descried the captain, again a full Pannikin.

I suggested lashing him to a donkey and returning there and then, but no one would agree to start before the next morning, for it was then nearly dark, and I had to submit; but I was determined not to leave the captain for a minute. I could not take him to an hotel for the night in his condition, and on searching his pockets I found he had only five or six shillings. I discovered that my interpreter had a friend close at hand who had a donkey-house empty, so I had the captain put on my back and carried him there, where I deposited him on some straw with myself beside him. They had promised that all would be ready to start at five A.M., and I slept well, for I was thoroughly tired after jogging all day on a donkey's back.

It was six o'clock when we got away, and just before leaving the town I bought a newly-baked loaf of Arab bread, which was light in weight but very dark in colour. I offered a bit to the captain, but he could not touch it, so I polished it off myself.

Towards the end of our journey I saw that the interpreter was getting a bit anxious about his money, and when we reached the beach I asked him to come on board for payment; but he was afraid to do so, and suggested that I should go and he would look after the captain till I came back with the cash. But after so much trouble in getting him there half sober, I was not going to be induced to leave him till he was safe on board. It was finally arranged that we should employ a boat with four of a crew, all natives, and the Arab agreed to come with such a strong bodyguard. He asked for £5, but there were only £4 on board the ship, and he accepted that with thanks.

We got under way (but without the water) next morning at daybreak, with the captain in a fair condition and not a drop of spirits on board.

I had become the captain's right hand man and he sent for me very often, for his nerves had been much shaken and he was quite childish. Every time I visited him he would say, " If I could only get a half glass of spirits I would be all right. If you can get me that from anyone forward I'll promise not to taste a drop this voyage again."

We had learnt from experience to put no faith in his promises, so he would not have got it if there had been any on board, but every time I called on him I had to make up a mixture from three bottles in the medicine chest as a substitute. I do not remember the quantities, but the ingredients were sal volatile, peppermint and laudanum. In a few days we reached our port—Beyrout—where we had to await orders from our owners. It is a very fine bay to anchor in, for it is possible to anchor quite close to the beach, and the water is marvellously clear. We anchored in about seven fathoms with forty-five fathoms of chain, and we could see our anchor from the knight-heads, even at that distance and depth.

We found there were some fine sights to be seen within two miles of the ship, including caves of enormous size. We could sail our boat into one very large one with the mast up, and once in, there was room for a ship of any size.

The water was very deep, and so clear that, after our eyes had become used to the dim light, we could see the bottom, and the fish swimming about.

When we arrived at Beyrout there were two British corvettes and one frigate, also one French frigate and one corvette, lying on the opposite side of the bay, which gave us a little amusement twice a day, at least. At eight o'clock every morning the five warships sent up their top-gallant-masts, and crossed the top-gallant and royal yards. In the evening they sent them down again, and unlucky the ship, whether French or British, that was last. I might say, in parenthesis and without prejudice, that the British crews did the work far more smartly than the French.

Shortly after our arrival we set out in search of fresh water in the long-boat with two water-casks and all available tubs and buckets. Acting on the advice of the inhabitants, we proceeded along the Northern coast to what was called the Dog River. It was very narrow at the entrance, but it widened out considerably, and the water was beautifully clear. When we had got the boat into a position where she would float when loaded, two of us jumped into the river, but we jumped out again in double-quick time for the water was bitterly cold.

It came from Mount Lebanon where, travellers tell us, snow lies all the year round, but I saw none when I went up in November, though I saw it put its white cap on two months after our visit. We made two trips to the river for water, and the mate and carpenter came the second time so that all hands might see the place.

Our elegant cook and steward left us at Beyrout, and I was asked to take the appointment till other arrangements could be made. I consented, for I had always had a turn for cooking, but it was rather difficult to fill the post efficiently after it had been occupied by such a smart " coloured gentleman."

We had been in Beyrout three or four weeks when we received orders to proceed to Mersina for a cargo of cotton for Smyrna to be transhipped there to a steamer for Liverpool. The American War had stopped the supply of cotton to Lancashire, and the working people there were in great straits, so we had to do our part with all dispatch.

We left Beyrout with a strong southerly wind, and should have reached our port next day, but Captain Pannikin was worse than ever. On the evening of the next day we found land right ahead and well out on each bow, but the captain was useless, and the mate had no idea what land it was.

We started to take in sail, brought her down to two close-reefed topsails, and put her head off for the night. In the morning the land was still in sight, and we were nearly land-locked. The men came aft in a body to see the captain, and I went in to tell him he was wanted, but I could not find him. I told the men and they started to search for him. When I saw them trying to open the door of a certain room, I explained that the door was locked because there were stores stowed there which were sent by our ship-chandler at Beyrout to his brother, a ship-chandler at Mersina.

The men asked me if there were any spirits amongst the stores, but I could not tell them, so I opened the door and we beheld the captain— speechless! He had got in by the window, though it was a very small one. We removed him to his own room and placed a watch over him.

A shift of wind came that day which saved us from going on the beach, but it was three days before the captain was able to take a sight and work up the ship's position.

All that time we were under close reefs, so, when Captain Pannikin came on deck on the third day and found her in that rig, he shouted out, "Make all sail!" and to the man at the wheel he said, "Keep her off; steer N. W." Then he turned to the mate and said in a loud voice, "It's a strange thing the captain can't get drunk without the whole ship getting drunk too!"

He helped us to hoist topsails and so on, and we were all glad to see that, for we knew it would do him a lot of good. He soon found our position by the sun and shaped a course which brought us to Mersina, where we arrived on a very fine evening.

We could see the beach covered with hand-tied bales of cotton, and hundreds of camels arriving with more, till it seemed to me there must be enough to load the *Great Eastern*, and we threw half our ballast overboard to make as much room as possible. The captain made a good show to begin with, for he spent the greater part of his time in the hold, superintending the stowage so that the bales might be jammed in as tightly as possible, and all went well.

I knew that our biscuits were in a very bad state, being full of maggots, and I found out from the butcher one day that he had a large oven close to the beach where we could bake them, and so get rid of the maggots. He said we could have the use of the oven free, but we must do all the work ourselves. The captain, on hearing of the butcher's offer, gave his consent, and told off two men and the carpenter to do the baking, which took place on our last day in port, and was a great success so far as the biscuits were concerned, but it had other and more unfortunate results, for the men came back mad drunk. The spirits sold in that port were what sailors call " chain lightning," and the after effects were always very bad.

When the captain returned, after having been on shore all day, he was in the same state as the men, but I took care that there was no drink in the cabin, and that he brought none with him, except internally. After I had got him to bed I was about to turn in when the anchor watch called me out, as ten passengers had arrived alongside, and they had brought with them their firearms (flint-locks), four goats, two dozen fowls, and several baskets of filthy rags which they called their wardrobes. They produced a paper from the agent to the mate, stating that they were passengers bound to Smyrna by our ship, so we took them on board with all their traps. After everything was passed out of the boats the mate gave me the flint-locks to lock up in a spare room, and then I turned in.

I cannot say how long I had been asleep when I was awakened by the rolling of the ship, with the goats crying like children, casks rolling about the deck, dishes breaking, etc. I got along the deck safely and into the cabin, but just as I stepped inside I landed my heel on a broken tumbler which was sliding about on the floor, and, before I could stop myself, I had taken a step with the tumbler on my bare heel, which was very badly cut. The tumbler was as firmly fixed as if it had been nailed on, but the mate managed to pull it off. The commotion caused by the rolling did the captain and the three men a lot of good, and before long we had everything on deck secured.

It was then time to heave the anchor up, and the mate, finding the passengers, with their goats and fowls, very much in the way, gave them permission to go into the long boat, live stock and all. The ship was rolling very heavily and we were glad to get under way, for the beam swell was increasing, but as soon as we got sail on her she improved, and we were able to walk about. My foot was very sore, and everyone told me I should rest for a day or two, but I did not see my way to do so.

When the rolling had ceased and breakfast was over I went on with scrubbing out two rooms, which was all I was able to face, for I had the dinner to look after. When I started with the first room I had to pass out the flint-locks into the saloon, where the captain was walking fore and aft with a very sore head, no doubt, and I had further depressed him by telling him the laudanum was finished, though I had a little stowed away. When he saw the flint-locks he asked whose they were, and I told him they belonged to the passengers.

"What!" he cried, "have I got passengers on board? What will happen now! Tell the mate I want him!"

However, the mate was all right, for he held an order signed by Captain Pannikin :—" Please receive on board ten passengers with their traps "—so we had to do the best we could.

I found one of them who was willing to help me in the galley, and another to peel the potatoes, which I thought would relieve my heel.

When I arrived in the galley next morning I found my Arab assistant had the fire going and the copper boiling, and I was very pleased, for I thought, when I first got out of my bunk, that I should not be able to stand on my foot at all, but I think that was caused by congealed blood, because I found I could get along after I had had my foot in water for a little.

We made a fair passage to Smyrna, and the captain had a visit from the British Consul, who appeared to have an interest in the cotton, for, when we were discharging the cargo he paid the ship several visits to ask us to work longer hours, and when the last bale went out he gave the mate something and £2 to the crew to drink his health.

When we signed articles in Glasgow they stated that the voyage was not to exceed six months, and that time had now expired, but I believe the crew would have said nothing about the matter, only, having spent the £2 in drink of the "chain lightning" type, it was not long before they marched aft and demanded their discharge or ten shillings per month more wages, and, as the captain would have nothing to say to them, they got into a shore boat to go before the Consul.

I might mention here that I have been a total abstainer all my life, and so never joined in these freaks.

The captain gave chase and reached the Consulate

first, the men having stopped for a " reviver " on the way, and the ·Consul was ready for them, with five policemen in a side room.   When the men arrived to state their complaint they were in a worse condition than when they left the ship, and, as they fell out with each other about which of them was to have the honour of addressing Her Britannic Majesty's Consul, he called in the police and had them marched off to goal, so the mate and I had a very quiet ship for two days, which benefited my foot considerably.

I have already mentioned that the mate was a Shields man who knew nothing of navigation, but he was a good seaman and an honest, hard-working man whom we all liked very much.   He never read books or papers.   If he picked up a piece of paper and found there was printing on it he would lay it down again as if it were poison, but he could sign his name if he were not hurried over it.   During one of our quiet chats, while the men were locked up, he said to me in his broad Shields dialect : " On your first voyage up the Mediterranean didn't you expect to find the Straits of Gibraltar so narrow you could barely work a brig through ? "

" No," I replied, " when I was in the Navy I heard many yarns about it."

" Do you know," he went on, " I've often heard the Straits were so narrow you had to stand in close to the shore, so that sometimes you couldn't swing the mainyard for monkeys' tails getting in the brace-blocks."

I looked solemn, for he was my senior, and said :

" Yes, I have often heard it said, but generally by men who had never been off the coasting trade at home, and they, I suppose, heard it from someone who was told by another who knew a man whose son had been ship-mates with a man who had seen it." If sailors were not allowed to spin yarns they would die of melancholia.

When our men returned from durance vile they were in a better frame of mind. Our ship was now fixed to load to Glasgow, which was a bit of luck for us all, and also, which was of more importance to me, a cook and steward had been engaged. The first part of our cargo was two hundred tons of emery stone, and the remainder was a light general cargo.

About four or five days before we had finished loading, a large fire broke out in the town, and, when the captain and mate were called out and saw the blaze, the former asked for four volunteers to take him on shore. I was first in the boat, although still lame, and the captain, as usual, was half-seas-over. When we reached the fire he spied a ladder standing against a burning house, and he made straight for it, followed by a Kanaka (a South Sea Islander) and myself. When the captain reached the top of the house he jumped down through a skylight, and apparently disappeared for ever, but in a few minutes he returned and called Louie, the Kanaka, who was one of our A.B.'s, so we both went to the skylight, and he passed us up an old woman, saying as he did so : " Come back, I have another." I helped Louie to get the woman on his back at the top of the ladder and then returned to the skylight where the captain passed me up a little child, and called to me to come back quickly for he could not stand the heat and smoke much longer. We were both back in an instant and pulled him out more dead than alive.

I was glad to get down, for the soles of my feet were sorely burnt, but the Kanaka fared better because the skin of his feet was as thick as the sole of a sea-boot. Well, those were two lives saved by us, and while we were at it there were four or five hundred Turkish soldiers and about the same number of Turkish sailors standing around, supposed to be keeping order. The British Consul's house was very close to the fire and we proceeded there to help carry out the furniture for fear the fire should spread, and to watch that no one appropriated any of it. Two days after the fire we were called to the Consulate to receive thanks. Captain Pannikin had been offered a money gift for his services, but he refused it and said that neither would his men take money—although he had not consulted us on the point. On the day we sailed, the Consul sent each of us—the captain, Louie and myself—a framed card of thanks for saving life and property. My card found a home on a spare nail on the walls of the boarding house which was close to the Shipping Office in Glasgow, and it may be hanging there yet for aught I know to the contrary.

We sailed from Smyrna one bright, cold morning in January, but that night it came on to blow a heavy gale from the north, and although we would have liked to carry on sail and get clear of Khios Island, which was on our lee, the wind was too strong and she was reduced to two close-reefed topsails. With her heavy rolling, we made little or no headway, and we could see the black-looking island to leeward with the sea breaking on it. We could see the westernmost point, and we thought if we could only reach that we should be safe, but at times there seemed to be little hope. All hands remained on deck throughout the night, and about four in the morning there was a very slight lull, so we at once hoisted up the main-staysail and hauled out the foot of the main-trysail. By five o'clock she started to show a little improvement in her speed, and by six we were able to keep her off a little and shake a reef out of the main-topsail, then we were sent to coffee and a rest for two hours.

When we were called at eight o'clock to make sail it was still blowing hard, but we were then running before the wind. We therefore set the whole top-sails, foresail, and main-top-gallant-sail, and off we set—homeward bound in earnest. She could do ten knots easily, but she did not forget to take a heavy roll at times. I never had such a run of fair wind as on this passage, and as there was not a drop of grog on board all went well. Our royal yards were still across, and we could not get a chance to send them down, though we expected to do that in the Straits of Gibraltar, but we could not manage it even there, for she rolled as much as ever and it still blew hard.

It eased at Trafalgar, but we had a nice breeze to

St. Vincent, where it fell a dead calm for three or four hours, and the royal yards were got down, wet clothes and sails dried, and our beds carried out for an airing.   Altogether it was a great change from what we had had for the last twelve days.

After our short spell of calm a breeze sprang up from the south-east, so off we started again with smooth water, and before long passed a steamer—a rare sight in those days—going the same way as ourselves. To our great joy we out-distanced her so that we were soon out of sight. This fair wind followed us across the Bay of Biscay, through St. George's Channel and up to Greenock, making the passage from Smyrna to Glasgow in twenty-two days.

Just as we were finishing loading at Smyrna fifty bales of rags were sent off to us, and we stowed them around the main hatch.

When the "lumpers" took off the hatches the morning after our arrival in Glasgow, it was discovered that the bales of rags had been burning, unknown to us, for the flames came rushing out of the hatchway and forced the men to retreat until the fire brigade arrived and extinguished the flames.

That was the concluding incident of an eight months' Mediterranean voyage.

CHAPTER VIII

WRECKED ON LUNDY ISLAND, AND ANOTHER VOYAGE TO THE MEDITERRANEAN

I TOOK up my abode in the same boarding house as last voyage, for I had seen nothing much wrong with it, though I knew it was not conducted on teetotal principles; at the same time I saw very little drink about. There never was as much as a glass of beer on the dinner table, but, if a homeward - bounder wanted to get into Mrs. Boardinghouse's good graces, he had only to go to the kitchen and call for whisky. The homeward-bounders were men just off a voyage who had plenty of money and were usually very lavish with it, consequently they received much better treatment than those who had had time to spend all theirs, and who were allowed to stay on in the hope that they would pay the debt with their month's advance when they got a ship. I noticed that Mrs. Boarding-house had never to send out for the whisky, for she had a cupboard in her bedroom from which she could supply anything that was asked for, and that was very convenient for some of the boarders who had not been in Scotland before, and who found the public-houses closed all day on Sunday.

That reminds me of a tar's first trip to Scotland. He had been the worse for drink on Saturday, and on Sunday forenoon sallied forth to wet his whistle, but, to his great astonishment, found every public-house closed. He asked a passer-by for an explanation of the phenomenon, and was told of the Forbes M'Kenzie Act which was in force in Scotland. He then continued his walk along the street, casting his eyes all round, till he came to a pillar-box which he walked round and round, and, after his "great circle" round the letter-box for the third time, he came to a stand, and, addressing the people whose attention had been attracted by his circumnavigation —"Damme if Forbes M'Kenzie hasn't unshipped the handles of the pumps!" he exclaimed wrathfully.

Though Mrs. Boardinghouse had no objection to selling drink on Sunday, she would not allow anyone to whistle on that day, and I once heard her order a man out of the house for persisting in the offence, although he owed her two weeks' board. She was well up in years, of great size, and, as might be expected, was not very lively on her feet. She sat all day on a big chair at the kitchen table where she could do all the talking and other sitting jobs, such as cutting and buttering bread for the table. I was a close observer of her methods on this point, for it was very seldom I could see any trace of butter on the bread, and I managed to solve this problem :— How can you butter two quartern loaves with half a pound of butter, and, when you have finished, have three-quarters of a pound of butter left on the plate? This is the explanation of the seemingly impossible feat :—Mrs Boardinghouse spread the butter on a slice of bread, and then scraped it to remove superfluous butter, but she did it so thoroughly that she scraped crumbs off as well. The scrapings were deposited on the butter plate to do duty for the next slice, when the process was again gone through, and at each repetition more was scraped off a slice than had been applied in the first place. Thus when the two loaves had been operated on, the butter plate was in a very flourishing condition.

At this time (during the American Civil War) everybody was talking of running the blockade, for they were paying good wages out to Bermuda or Nassau, and after that the pay was better still, and if one only had the luck not to be taken prisoner, there was a good deal of money to be made in a very short time. As there were a number of men going from the Clyde, I set about finding a ship, which I did very soon. She was being built at Renfrew, and I journeyed there to see the mate, but, finding one had not been engaged, I saw the captain, who said he wanted all smart young men, and if I returned in two days, when his mate would have arrived, he would put in a word for me. I went back as arranged, but it was unnecessary to speak to the mate on my behalf, for he turned out to be Captain Pannikin.

The captain had just been telling his new mate that he wanted four leadsmen whom he could trust to give him correct soundings when he was running the blockade, so when I arrived Mr. Pannikin took me to the captain and said, " Here is the first leads-man." The captain thought I was too young for the position, but, after a few minutes' conversation, he saw I understood the work thoroughly, and that was settled.

A few days afterwards we signed on, and the following day went down to join her on the stocks, and had the pleasure of a slide down the ways—the first, and last, time that I have seen a steamer proceed on her way to adjust compasses straight from the launching. By the time we got to Greenock the steam was up. We went to the Gareloch to adjust compasses, and while that was going on Mr. Pannikin managed to fall down the main hold. We returned to the Tail of the Bank and sent a boat to Greenock with the mate, who had been unconscious since he fell. I went on shore with him, left him in the hospital, and returned to the ship; but on my way back I noticed a great stir and a crowd of people, and asked a man the cause of it. He told me there had been an explosion, the boiler of a steam scow had blown up, and two men were missing. When I arrived on board I learned that the scow had had coals for our steamer. It appeared that she had a look round the Tail of the Bank, and, not being able to find us, was making for the harbour when the catastrophe happened.

We had a little coal on board, which had been supplied by the builder for the trial trip, but we dispensed with the trial trip and proceeded to Cardiff at easy steaming. We filled up at Cardiff with coal, but, before it went in, we shipped a large number of big cases—in fact, a whole train-load, pulled alongside by two locomotives. I never knew for certain what they contained, but I do not think I should be far out if I called it rifles and ammunition. The work of loading was carried out with great dispatch, and, although news of a very unsatisfactory nature to blockade runners appeared in the papers the day before we sailed, it did not cause them to relax their exertions to get the steamer away.

We had a Yankee on board, said to be the owner of the steamer, and just as we were leaving the dock, four gentlemen joined us with their baggage, on which their names appeared as Major Redjacket, Captain Leatherneck, etc., with the letters R.A., which had been painted over, but were still visible. As soon as we left the dock I took the wheel, for the man who should have taken it was incapable, and it fell to me though it was not my trick. It was a dark night, but not very foggy, so we could sight everything well off, and were going our full speed of eighteen knots.

I thought it was time I was relieved after I had been at the wheel for considerably more than the usual two hours, and I spoke to the pilot, for he was the only one who came near me all that time. He had paid me a number of visits: indeed, I thought it strange he should hang about me so much, for we steered aft by hand-gear, and I was therefore a long way from the bridge. I afterwards perceived there had been a reason for it. He told me he would have me relieved in half an hour, which he did, and I at once made tracks for the forecastle, for the steward had told me tobacco had been served out and he had left a pound in my bunk. I had just reached my bunk and lifted the tobacco when the ship went grinding on to Lundy Island, tearing her bow-plates and frames as if they had been made of paper. I was close to the fore-peak hatch, and, lifting it off, I beheld a brilliant phosphorescence as the water rushed in with such force that this part of the vessel was quickly filled up, and the orders were soon passed along to lower the four boats.

I should mention here that I had a chum in the last brig I was in—a young Glasgow sailor, called Bob—who had joined the steamer with me, and after the boats were lowered I returned to the forecastle for Bob, as he had been on the sick-list for two days with boils on his legs and was unable to walk. I took him on my back to carry him to the boat, and when I reached it with my load I discovered that the second officer, Mr. Buntline, was in charge of her, and I was glad of that, for he was a good old sailor, well known in Glasgow. When I had got Bob deposited in the boat, Mr. Buntline told me to go to the boat-beams on the port side and fetch a quarter of beef which was hanging there. I did so, but I no sooner had it on my back than I heard, in a Yankee drawl: " I say, you drop that beef! " I paid no attention, so the voice called again: " If you don't, I shoot! " and at the same instant I felt a bullet strike the beef, but I continued my journey to the boat. I thought then, and I think now, that if it had been daylight I would not have allowed such a gross insult to pass unpunished. The Yankee was, we were told, the owner of the steamer, and would command when in American waters, but, at the time of firing, he was no more to me than any other passenger.

We left our ship when she had settled down on the rocks aft, with the water about four feet deep on the deck, and the second mate struck out a course for himself, as we did not want to keep company with the captain's boat, which carried the owners and the passengers. After about an hour in the boat we fell in with a pilot cutter and went on board and started shouting, ringing a bell, and making various other noises, which attracted the other boats, and they were soon all around us. When I saw such a crowd coming on board the small vessel I went down the little forecastle at once, and took a good cut off the beef, which I had placed there, before the others helped themselves, so Bob and I were provided for for two or three days.

About eight o'clock next morning we hailed a tug that was passing close to us, though we could not see her as there was still a little fog about. We all transhipped to the tug and returned to the wreck when the weather cleared. We went on board, for we found that we could get into some of the deck-rooms, though it was evident that only the masts and funnel would be visible at high water. We saw that someone had been there before us, for some curtains had gone from room doors, a small cask of rum and other things were missing, and the wheel and binnacle had also disappeared, but the wreckers had evidently been disturbed, probably by the tug's whistle as we slowly approached the wreck.

The captain told the second officer to man a boat and go after the thieves, who, he thought, would likely be at anchor to the southward. Mr. Buntline prepared for the fray by tying a red door curtain round his waist, and sticking therein a cutlass and a brace of revolvers, while a sou'wester gave the finishing touch to this effective rig-out; his complexion was decidedly dusky, and on this occasion he looked more like a pirate chief than an honest British tar. When I saw this bold buccaneer picking his boat crew it occurred to me that there might be bloodshed on the expedition, and as I did not want to be involved in anything of that sort, I suddenly discovered that I had business of immediate importance to attend to in the forecastle, but Mr. Buntline's eye was upon me, and he called to me to go into the boat, which I, of course, did at once. Off we went, and before we had gone far we sighted four or five fishermen at anchor, and steered for the nearest, which proved to be the best for our purpose. As we drew close I said to our second mate: "That's my sou'wester the captain is wearing, I know it by the horse's head (trade mark). I bought it in Gravesend and they are not to be got here."

Mr. Buntline boarded the fishing smack, followed by the rest of us, and accosted the man with my sou'wester. "Are you the master of this craft?" he demanded, and received an answer in the affirmative. He had laid his hand on the sword which he drew out, and gave the man a blow on the side of the head with the flat of the cutlass. "Take it off, you thief!" he said, "and give it to that man," and in an instant my property was on my own head. The second mate then returned the cutlass, and drew a revolver, which he held at the master's head. When the crew saw that, they all came aft and begged Mr. Buntline to put away the revolver, promising, if he did so, to return all the stolen articles, which they did in double-quick time. We intended to search the other smacks, but when we looked round we saw they had made off with a nice breeze. As night was setting in, we abandoned the chase and returned to the tug. When I got on board I managed to hide myself in a quiet corner in the forecastle, and when they wanted boat-keepers, I, for one, was not to be found : I did not believe in towing behind a paddle steamer when the clothes I had on were all I possessed, and further, there would be no pay for the work.

We reached Cardiff the following morning, and there was a large crowd to receive us at the dock-gates. The tug lay off a little way and we went ashore in our boats, the captain, owner and passengers being in the first. When I saw that the owner was going to be ashore before me I said to him, as he went into the boat: "I say, you're the man who fired a revolver at me; I want to see you on shore when I get there."

"Me!" he exclaimed, "what do you want with me?" I noticed him, as he spoke, feeling for something in his belt, but one of the military men caught his arm and pulled him down on the seat, and the boat pushed off. I have never seen him since.

It was low water when we landed at the steps outside the dock-gates, and the newspaper reporters came buzzing around us like bees. One attached himself to me and offered me a drink, which I declined, but I said I would take a pipeful of tobacco instead, and after I had lit up I began my yarn. I was just comfortably settled when a man, who had the appearance of a rigger, approached and asked me for a match.

"It's no use asking a ship-wrecked mariner for a match," I said.

He then opened the blade of his knife, saying: "Well, I'll take a Liverpool light if you don't mind." He then stuck his knife into the bowl of my pipe, lifted the whole of my dottle out and put it into his own empty pipe, said "Thank you," and walked away. That was the first, and last, Liverpool light anyone took from me.

We were taken to the Sailor's Home, one of the best and most comfortable I was ever in, and I wrote at once to Mrs. Boardinghouse for £5, for I had left my clothes and bank book with her. No one would think of taking many clothes on a blockade runner, " not so much as would make a bolster for a crutch," as Jack would say, so I had left the best part of my wardrobe in Glasgow. The crew, with the exception of Bob and myself, were sent on at once to Glasgow by the Shipwrecked Mariners' Society, who refused to do the same for us because we were known to have sent home for money, and also because both of us had recently thought right to discontinue our annual subscription to the Society.

In about a week's time Bob and I shipped in a Whitehaven brig with eight of a crew all told, bound to Barcelona with coal. We went to have a look at her before signing on. When we went on board the captain and mate were at breakfast, so Bob and I took a look round. I could see she was old but in grand condition; she was the shortest vessel I had ever been in, and she steered with a wheel which had a beautiful cover with the lion and unicorn very nicely painted thereon. It was evident from her model and general arrangements that she was very ancient, but everything was kept in such fine condition that she was like a vessel newly off the stocks. We noticed she had swinging booms, and knew by that that she had square lower stunsails. The captain soon came on deck, and he asked us what we thought of her, and if she would suit us. We told him we would be very pleased to go in her, and I remarked that she looked quite new. Captain Blowhard, as I will call him, replied: " She is fifty-three years old and I have been in her fifty years."

" I have been looking to see if the pump-bolts were much worn," I said, " but there are none there, and I see the pumps and delivery hole are full of spiders' webs, so they are not used much."

" I will show you the pump-bolts," he said, and then disappeared down the companion, returning in a few moments with a small parcel wrapped in thin paper which he proceeded to unfold. " Here are the pump-bolts, shining like silver," he said proudly, "they have been in my drawer for fifty years." We afterwards learned that it was a weakness of Captain Blowhard to show the pump-bolts to every stranger who came on board. The mate was a nice, quiet old chap, who seldom spoke except on business, but we all liked him, and he was one of those men who would rather do a piece of work themselves than trouble other people about it.

We joined the next morning, bent sails, took in stores, and sailed the following day. The captain was at the wheel when we left the dock gates, but as soon as the ropes were in I relieved him, and as I took the wheel he said to me, " Follow the tug." I tried to carry out orders, but I soon found it was more easily said than done ; the tug would be four points on the starboard bow one minute, and four points on the port bow the next minute, and I was powerless to prevent it. The captain seemed to look on it as a matter of course, so I supposed he was used to it, but when we let go the tug she steered rather better. We had a very fair passage across the Bay, and when we reached Cape Finis-terre we had fresh north-east breezes—genuine Portuguese trade winds. We therefore set the top-mast and lower stunsails, and then she started her tantrums. It was hard a-port, hard a-starboard, all the time, for she seemed determined to yaw a cer-tain distance, and yaw she would, in spite of her rudder, while the best helmsman amongst us could not stop her from lifting her stunsails, first on the port and then on the starboard side. The best speed we could get was seven knots, though she made as much foam as if she were doing seventeen. Captain Blowhard used to smoke a churchwarden pipe in fair weather when everything was going well, and I can remember him on one occasion leaning over the stern with his pipe in his hand as he listened to the roaring of the sea under her counters and watched the very irregular wake she was leaving behind her. Presently he turned to the man at the wheel and said: "I don't mind your making Z's, but, oh Lord! don't make round O's."

Captain Billy Blowhard was a very good sailor, but too old for sea service; he was practically blind at night, and he said, on the second day out from Cardiff, that he wanted me in his watch so that I might look out for him in the night watches, and by this arrangement I was excused from taking my turn at the wheel. He was a staunch teetotaller, but the foulest-tongued man I ever sailed with. After dark there was not a word from him, but in daylight he would uncoil it in great, long strands, usually at the boys, and I frequently heard them called such foul names that it was as much as I could do to hold my tongue, but my chance came before the passage was ended. I might state here that I have always had a rooted objection to such language. I have never called a man an improper name, nor would I allow any man to address me in that manner. One day when we were off Cape de Gata, the wind was easterly and we were working her on four hour tacks—hard-a-lee every eight bells. As I have already said, she was very short and stumpy, and very much resembled a serving mallet (flat at both ends), which was a source of trouble in steering and also in tacking, for the yard-arms would lock and the braces foul, when the order was given " mainsail haul."   Again at " fore-bowline—let go and haul," the fore brace would foul the main yard-arm.   We usually cleared them by pulling and letting go sharply two or three times till the brace jumped off the yard-arm, but on this occasion, off Cape de Gata, one of the braces had fouled and did not clear as quickly as usual.   The captain was at the wheel and he called out in his usual bosun's voice : " Lay hold of the wheel, one of you young ——, till this old —— goes up and clears that brace."

However, it cleared without his help, and as soon as she was round and the ropes coiled down, I said to the others, " Come on aft with me—I'll speak to him."

They evidently understood me, for, without another word, they all followed me, and when we were assembled I said, " Captain Blowhard, we want to speak to you for a minute, please."

" Well, what do you want ? " he growled.

" Well, sir," I went on, " we have come to complain at the name you have just called us.   I might say we don't complain at you applying it to yourself—you can call yourself what you like—but we object to you calling us by anything but our proper names, and what is more, we won't stand it."   I noticed he was getting funky so I grew bolder. " And if ever you call either a man or a boy in this ship such a foul name again, you had better get your account of wages made out ! "

Never, from that hour till the day I left the brig, did I hear him say one coarse word, and the work went on as well, and even better, than with any crew he had ever had. He very often told me so on quiet nights, when I was on watch, and he would stand in the companion-way with his head just above the companion, yarning away the whole watch. His favourite topic was the days when both he and the brig were young, and they were running to Quebec in the summer time. According to his account she was a favourite passenger ship, and he was always careful to say, in his stories about different voyages, " we were full up with passengers." I found out from his yarns that " full up " meant ten !

Perhaps it was his former position as captain of a passenger ship that had made him pompous, for he certainly was very much so in fine weather and in daylight, but he became very tame after dark.

The mate told me an amusing story about the captain. He had been on a voyage to Rio de Janeiro, commonly called Rio, and on the homeward voyage the brig was nearly becalmed between Tuscar and the Smalls, when a schooner steered close past her and the master hailed the brig, shouting, " Where are you from ? " Captain Blowhard responded with bombastic emphasis, " *Rio de Janeiro*," adding, according to sea custom, " Where are you from ? " Back came the answer in a good imitation of old Billy's style, " *Corkio de la Corkio !* "

We had a fair passage to Barcelona, where we stayed four weeks, and all went well as far as the

captain was concerned, but there was one rather
unusual occurrence.   One day I was on the quarter-
deck putting some new canvas into a sail.   I had to
ask the captain for canvas when I wanted any, for he
kept all stores locked up, and when he brought the
bolt of canvas up this day, he sat down on my bench
to wait till I had measured the quantity I wanted,
and by way of conversation, asked me how I liked
Barcelona.

"Oh, very well," I said, "but there is one thing I
don't like, and that is the beef we get to eat."

"Why, what's wrong with it?" asked the captain;
"ours is all right."

"If you don't mind," I said, "I will go and bring
you the meat that was given to us to-day for dinner."
I did so, and explained that we had had that same
cut every day.

"Well," said Captain Blowhard, "that is not
what I expected you to get.   I pay the same for
the forecastle as I do for the cabin."   But I
knew all about that little trick.   When a butcher
is trying for the contract to supply a ship he may
undertake to provide meat at sixpence a pound all
round, but good meat is from eightpence to ten-
pence, while the coarse fag-ends of flank sell at
threepence or fourpence a pound.   The butcher
therefore sends a good joint to the cabin every day
and reckons to make his profit by sending cheap
cuts to the forecastle.

The above conversation took place on a Saturday,
and next morning I told the boy who acted as cook
to call me when the butcher came.   He did so, but

before I got on deck, he had hauled the basket up from the boat alongside, and as I rushed along, the boy handed me the usual piece of meat. I called the butcher's attention to it, and the master butcher, who was in the boat, said something to the effect that it was good enough for us. I immediately lifted the meat and struck him on the head with it. He shook his fist at me and swore volubly, but in Spanish, so it "missed fire." I expected to hear more of the affair, but day followed day and never a word was said, though we certainly got very much better meat.

The following Friday was Good Friday and in the morning we set about topping our yards to please the Spaniards. This was done by topping the fore-yard by the starboard lift and the mainyard by the port lift, hoisting the topsailyards, then unlashing the starboard foretopsail lift and port maintopsail lift, taking the lifts down into the tops, and topping the topsailyards to the same angle as the lower yards, which formed two crosses. It pleased the people and assisted in getting us into the good graces of the captain of the port.

After dinner we all went on shore to see the many sights of the day. Bob and I kept together, but we had not penetrated far into the crowd when I caught sight of the butcher, and from the look on his face and the appearance of two cut-throat looking villains he was speaking to, I realised that I was on dangerous ground. Bob was of the same opinion, and I had just said to him, "What do you think we should do?" when an Englishman in the crowd

whispered to me, " Run for your life ! "   I suppose
he understood Spanish, and had overheard the
conversation between the butcher and the two
desperadoes, but he did not say another word and I
acted on his advice instantly, for the men were
within twenty feet of me.   I had to proceed
cautiously at first, not to offend anyone by pushing
too much, but when once I got clear of the crowd
my course to the harbour was down hill, which just
suited me, and I do not think my pursuers gained an
inch.   When I arrived at the boats I found that all
the boatmen were, as might be expected, up in town
and I at once took to the water, preferring that to
steel.

Unfortunately, I jumped into a bed of seaweed,
but none of it fouled my legs, so when I got clear
of the weed I turned on my back and was glad to
see the two ruffians standing at the edge of the
water, apparently with no intention of leaving
terra firma.   That was my last time ashore at
Barcelona.

After discharging, and taking in eighty tons of
ballast, we sailed for Huelva, making a very good
passage till we were abreast of Malaga, when the
wind set in from the westward and blew hard.   We
shortened sail to two close-reefed topsails, and were
under that sail for seven days, when we were driven
back abeam of Cape de Gata.   We then had a
shift of wind, and in twenty-four hours were within
eight miles of Gibraltar, when we were caught
again ; but this time close in shore where the water
was smooth, so we were able to work her down with

whole topsails and courses. We tacked every two hours, and the next day got a leading wind and sailed through the Straits, arriving at Huelva twenty-one days after leaving Barcelona. There were a number of Danish brigs and schooners laid up in the river, as Denmark was then at war with Germany, but ours was the only vessel on the berth to load, so the ore came along as quickly as it could be taken in.

We were at Huelva for a week, and then sailed for Glasgow, getting fair winds all the way across the Bay and up St. George's Channel, but when we passed Ailsa Craig the wind was strong, and the rain falling in torrents. We had two whole topsails and fore topmast staysail set (they were our summer sails, and not very good ones either), and as we were drawing close to Holy Island the mate sent us to unbend the jib and rig in the jib-boom. I went out to unbend the jib, and had just reached the boom end when a squall came from the north-west and split the main topsail, blew the staysail to ribbons, and the fore topsail split right round by the tabling, leaving about three inches, though Jack would say " it blew clean out of the bolt-ropes." The canvas blew on to the jib-stay and came down on my devoted head, knocking me senseless for a little, and when I managed to draw myself together, I found my retreat was cut off. I could see nothing but canvas, and blood gushing from a wound in my head, but in a minute I heard Bob's voice at the other side of the canvas calling, " Are you there, Harry ? " I answered, " Yes, Bob, I'm here, but get me inboard as soon as you can. I am losing a lot of blood."   As my brain cleared I saw a way of escape, so took out my knife and soon cut my way through the canvas.   I was anxious to get on deck as soon as possible, because, as I sat astride the boom, the canvas formed a bag between my knees, and into that the blood from my head was running rapidly, and I saw that it was time I was in safer quarters. I never knew what caused the wound, for there was only canvas flying about.

We always treated such wounds as follows :—If, by sitting still for a few minutes, it did not stop bleeding, we put a little pad of lint or canvas on the wound, tying it on with a handkerchief, and then went on with our work. The blood hardened on the wound, which, according to our ideas, made fine cement, and then we had to be very careful in combing our hair for a week or two afterwards.

A tug came out from Lamlash, which we engaged, and while they were getting out the tow-rope, I went below and shifted my clothes, for I was covered with blood from head to foot. We anchored for the night at Greenock, where we chalked for watches, and as I was taking an active part in this matter, the others said they could keep the watches without me, but I would not agree to this, though I thought it very good of them to suggest it.

For the benefit of the uninitiated, I will describe the ceremony of chalking for watches. When a ship came to anchor in a roadstead the usual sea watches ceased, and the men would be told to set an anchor watch, which usually started at 8 P.M., so, if the orders were to call all hands at five o'clock, that would be nine hours, and if there were ten men in the forecastle they would arrange to keep one hour watches, leaving out one man whom they called the "farmer" because he had the privilege of sleeping all night. They started by sending a boy out of the forecastle, while, with a piece of chalk, they drew a circle on the deck, dividing it into as many sections as there were men; then each of the men put a mark in one of the spaces, and when all were done the boy was called in to rub out the marks. He put his finger on any mark he chose, and the maker of it had to take the first watch; then he picked out another and the maker of that mark was condemned to the second watch, and so on till nine had been rubbed out. The remaining mark represented the lucky "farmer."

We got under way next morning and arrived in Glasgow, where we were berthed at the buoys in the stream.

CHAPTER IX

CROSSING THE LINE

AFTER my usual three weeks' stay with Mrs. Boardinghouse I shipped in a small passenger steamer, bound to Sydney, New South Wales. She was built by Inglis for the Australian Steam Navigation Company, to run between Sydney and the Hunter River, and was commanded by one of London's crack Australian packet captains, the mate being my old shipmate, Captain Pannikin, while the second mate, Tom, was a Norwegian. The captain's wife and family were going out as passengers, with the wife's brother as steward, for they were all going to Australia for good.

The vessel was brig-rigged, and she was loaded down to the sponsons with coals and stores, but she was a pretty little vessel, and the saloon, which was built on the upper deck, was the prettiest I had ever seen. The large glass windows at the sides were boarded up for the passage out, but there was plenty of light from the skylight, which was not boarded, though we were supplied with boards to protect it during bad weather. My chum, Bob, would not trust his valuable life in such a small vessel, so we parted company.

We left Glasgow on the first of September, so we had little to fear from the weather, and called at

St. Vincent for coal. We steamed across the equator, but before falling in with the strong south-east trades, we unshipped half of the floats, then turned the wheel half a turn and made all secure in the paddle-box, for we had a long way to go and some big seas to encounter before we would ship them again. We had five days' coal left when we stopped steaming.

The captain was very anxious that we should get up a " burra tomasha " on crossing the line for the benefit of his wife and family, and the mate let us know in time that we were to have a holiday on the occasion. Now, although I had knocked about a good bit, I had never been across the equator, but evidently no one on board suspected that I had not yet crossed that " menagerie lion running round the earth," as the schoolboy called it, for I was pressed to represent Neptune, which I finally agreed to do. I at once set about learning my speech, with the assistance of the mate, and the crew also offered me many suggestions as to what I should say, but they were not of much service to me as they were mostly hints for whisky. The men wanted me to fine each member of the captain's family a bottle of grog to let them off the shaving, but the mate suggested that if each of them would come down off the bridge and kiss Father Neptune, I could treat it as a sign of obeisance and it would not be necessary to shave them. That just suited me, for the family were all girls ! I got ready a very tidy rig-out and the mate helped me as much as he could. My throne was built on the gun carriage, and a boy we had as O.S. was selected for Amphitrite; a new top-gallant sail was to be hung up by the four corners and filled with water which was to be supplied by the donkey engine, and all was ready the day before we crossed.

In the last dog-watch of that day the captain sent for me and said he expected his girls would refuse to go to bed till they had seen some sign of Father Neptune, so he asked me if I could manage to hail the steamer at eight o'clock without spoiling the next day's ceremony. I said I would go and see what I could do, and would let him know in a few minutes.

I went to the mate and asked him for a blue light and a little vermillion; I then got my wig ready and hung a three-inch rope from the bowsprit end to the water, with a figure-of-eight knot on the end close to the water. That done, I returned to the captain and told him I was ready, if he would bring his family on to the forecastle when eight bells struck. "Please answer all questions I put to you," I said to him, "and when I ask you for a match throw me this piece of wood as if you were throwing me a box of matches. Then when you hear me sing 'good-night' please take the ladies away aft at once for I will be hanging by a rope at the surface of the water."

At eight bells I was at my station, and by the time the sound had died away I heard feminine voices on the forecastle, so I turned my back towards them and hailed the steamer in a low, gruff voice. I heard the girls exclaiming, "That's him,

father! I heard him then!" so I turned my face towards them and hailed in a good bosun's-mate's
voice, "Steamer ahoy!"

"Hallo!" answered the captain.

"What steamer is that?" I inquired.

"The *Tumbulgum*," was the reply.

"What is the captain's name?"

"Dick Spanker."

"Ah, good evening, Captain Spanker," said Neptune, "we have met many a time, but I understand
that a number of your passengers and crew have not
had the honour of paying their respects to me, so I
give you notice that I will be on board of the good
steamer *Tumbulgum* at one o'clock to-morrow.
Good night, Captain Spanker."

"Good night," he replied.

"Oh, Captain Spanker," I continued, "could I
trouble you for a match? Mine have got wet."

"Here you are," he said, throwing me the piece
of wood.

"Thank you," I said, and then lit the blue light,
but some of the wax fell on my bare feet, causing
me to throw it overboard rather too soon. I next
slid slowly down the rope, singing as I went this
little ditty :—

> "Good night to you all, and sweet be your sleep,
> May angels around you their vigils keep,
> Good night! Good night! Good night!"

As I rested at the figure-of-eight knot before
starting up again, I heard the captain sending the
girls aft, and when I got on deck again I found all

my shipmates were as much amused as the girls had
been. The captain sent for me to tell me that it
had been a very good show and his daughters were
highly delighted. "The mate tells me you are a
teetotaller," he added, "so I suppose you won't have
a glass of grog, will you?"

"No, sir, thank you," I replied, and that concluded the first part of the proceedings, which were
continued at noon next day when I started dressing.
I had a nice manilla wig and moustache, my face,
neck, arms and legs were painted the colour of a red
herring, and the grains (a four-pronged harpoon
which served as my trident) were new and shining.
Promptly at two bells I took my seat on the
travelling throne, and by the captain's orders the
engines were stopped for an instant, going on again
at once, but the momentary stoppage had made
everybody run on deck to see what was the matter,
and they found the procession on its way aft. I was
pulled along on the gun carriage with Amphitrite
sitting at my feet, and when we got to the break of
the promenade deck we found the captain with his
wife and four daughters, the chief engineer and chief
officer, seated there on campstools. I held forth
in this style:—"I, the great and mighty King
Neptune, have heard from my ambassador in Britain
that the good ship *Tumbulgum*, bound through my
domains, has on board a number of passengers and
crew who have not yet had the opportunity of paying their respects to me, so, like true children of the
sea, they must now come forth and be presented to
me. Then my staff will initiate them into our ways,

and after having passed through that ordeal, they will be free to travel through these realms as long as they live." My Prime Minister then handed me a roll of paper containing the names of all the people who had to undergo treatment, and the first name I read out was Mrs. Spanker. She answered by handing my Premier a bottle of whisky, and I then called upon the eldest girl, who came down and kissed me, and her sisters followed in their turn.

In the meantime the men who were to pay homage to King Neptune had been kept forward till they were sent for, and the first one called was a big, strong Highlander. He was blindfolded and led along to be examined by my doctor, who ordered him to be shaved with a No. 1 razor (a piece of hoop iron) and to take six pills. Then my two policemen led the victim up a ladder to a platform of which he knew nothing, for it had just been rigged up, and there he was directed to sit down while the barber smeared his face with lather (not made of Brown Windsor) and scraped his visage with an iron hoop. Then the pills were administered. I will not particularise, but will just say that both the pills and the lather were rather a foul mixture. When the man had swallowed his dose the police-men pulled the seat away from under him, and head over heels he went into the sail full of water beneath the platform. There were two men standing in the water ready to receive him and duck him a few times, after which he was allowed to go. Another name was called and the same performance gone through until the men were tired of it, which, as a rule, on these occasions is not very long for there are usually a few bottles of whisky waiting to be demolished. Next day the ship was back to her usual trim; she was a very comfortable vessel, with little or no growling, either amongst ourselves or with the officers, so the time passed very pleasantly.

Early in the passage the captain asked me if I would wash for his family as he had heard from the mate that I was a good hand at it, and he supposed I had learnt it in the Navy. " No, sir," I said, " my mother taught me all the branches of washing, and if I can't dress your white shirts it is my fault and not hers." He asked me if I had a smoothing iron, and I told him that I always carried one with me. He said he would pay me three shillings per dozen pieces, but I said, " No, sir, I will do the washing but I won't take payment, if you will just supply the soap." So one of the rooms on the sponsons was given to me as a laundry, and I will close this subject by saying that they took no soiled linen with them when they went ashore in Sydney.

Captain Spanker thought right to take a very southerly track, and at one part of our passage, in latitude 52° south, we fell in with a great number of icebergs. We felt the cold very much in our little vessel for it was built with very thin iron, and we had no fire in our quarters, which made the time in those latitudes very miserable for us, but we never doubted the captain's policy in choosing that track.

We were very well fed in this ship, not that we had a greater variety of articles than those contained in the usual provision list, but we had as much as we wanted, for nothing was weighed out to us, and we had coffee served out every watch during the night.

One forenoon when I had been at the wheel from ten till twelve, I noticed a beautiful albatross hovering about, and I also noticed a line and hook lying on the skylight, with which the captain had caught some Cape pigeons that morning to amuse his daughters. I did not say anything about the albatross, but as soon as I was relieved at eight bells I baited the hook and threw it over the stern; we were just moving through the water at the time and the water was quite smooth. The hook was over fifty yards astern when the noble bird swooped down beside it and I threw out plenty of line so that it should not be towed away from him. In an instant he took the bait and I had him on board before anyone knew there was such a bird in the vicinity, for it is a very easy matter to haul these large birds on board.

According to the habit of his kind, he became sick as soon as I landed him on the deck, but when he had recovered I carried him to the saloon where the captain and his family were at lunch. I carried him right in, stood him down on the carpet, and walked out, for I had no business there, but I looked back when I reached the door and I thought it was a lovely sight. The panels all round the room were hung with beautiful oil paintings in gold frames, the carpet had a red ground, and the magnificent white bird, standing there as if it were stuffed, gave the finishing touch to the picture. After I had had my dinner I went aft to see if they wanted the albatross, but found the captain had just caught another, so I took mine forward to be converted into a sea-pie, for which the steward promised me a couple of onions and a few potatoes, though our stock of the latter was low at that part of the voyage. Maybe some old "salts" who may read this will say that albatrosses are not worth wasting potatoes on, and that they are tough and taste fishy, but I will guarantee an excellent dish if they are treated in the following manner. Kill, clean and cut the bird up into small pieces in the usual way; let it stand all night in fresh water with two handfuls of salt added, and in the morning put the pieces into a large pot. Cover them with cold water without salt, bring it to the boil and let it simmer for half an hour. Then pour the water off and make the sea-pie in the usual way, with the addition of four ounces of dripping, and I am sure the result will give satisfaction.

We had no very heavy weather while we were so far south, but when we got into what we call the "roaring forties" we had very strong winds and high seas, and then we found what a nuisance the paddle-box was when running before the wind. When the big rollers came running up alongside and into the paddle-box they made such a noise that it was impossible to get any sleep, but nothing was broken and we got along all right.

One day when we were about six hundred miles from Sydney and the weather was very fine, all hands set about getting up the floats that had been stowed in the hold, and we afterwards lowered them down to the engineers who were at work inside the paddle-box. We all rendered what assistance we could to the engineers, for it was hard work, and there were only three of them. It would have been rather awkward if the weather had changed for the worse while we had this on hand, but fortunately we managed to finish the job before any really bad weather arrived, though she rolled at times and dipped a few of us right under. There was no way on the ship so we were able to hold on, and no one was washed away, but we were all glad when the last nut was screwed on and smoke coming from the funnel.

When we reached Sydney we went alongside the company's wharf, and as soon as the last rope was fast we were told to go. We thought this rather sharp because we had expected to be engaged in her again on the Hunter River Station, but we were soon told that none of us would be required in this or any other steamer in the company; they appeared to have a mortal dread of " new chums," so off we set to look for something else, and the second mate, steward, and myself took up our abode at Barry's coffee shop in George Street.

Two days afterwards Mr. Pannikin called to tell me that he had been appointed the company's rigger, and he asked me to join his gang, which I did. The company had a steamer nearly ready for launching, and our first job was to cut and fit her rigging, which did not take long, for she was a very small steamer with two masts and no square sails.

There were only the gang of rigging, and the

spans for the cargo gear to splice and serve, which lasted about a week, but the other man and myself had to do it all, for our boss had gone on the spree after cutting the rigging ready for splicing. The two of us were at the launch of the steamer, which was named the *Kennedy* and was the first to be built in Australia, but Mr. Pannikin did not put in an appearance though I had done my best to hunt him up, without success. About a week after the launch we had everything set up and finished, and the steamer was on the loading berth. Then a friend told me he had heard from the manager that I was to be discharged the next day (Saturday), so I took the hint, and when the manager paid us his usual afternoon visit I approached him and said, " Sir, now that this job is finished I would like to leave to-morrow if that will suit you."

" Yes ? " he returned ; " where are you going to now ? "

" Well," I said, " I want to go where there is plenty of work, for I don't like dodging about, filling in time."

Since my arrival in Sydney I had discovered why they would not employ new chums. They had found that, as a rule, long voyage sailors could not stand the hard work in the Australian coasting trade where the crew had to load and discharge their own cargoes, and very few of them could carry a sack of flour up a plank about eighteen inches broad, so they soon gave in. All the ship's crew were out of employment except the cook, who had been engaged as cook in Cowan's Family Hotel, Sydney, where the

Post Office now stands, and he asked me if I would join him as cook's mate, which I was glad to do, for the pay was good.

I liked the work very much, and I commenced to wonder if I should ever give it up, for the cook made things very pleasant for me by helping me along and showing me all he knew, which was very fortunate for me, because, at the end of my second week, he threw up this job for a better one, and I was asked to take his place. I knew, within myself, that I could do the work, but I was surprised at the proprietor asking me, though perhaps he thought cooking was my line of business. I was to get three guineas a week and the dripping, but I made no money out of the latter as all the servants in the hotel belonged to Sydney, and I gave them the dripping to take home. They offered to pay for it, but I let them have it gratis, and so, though I made no money out of the transaction, I made a number of friends. The proprietor was so pleased with the result of my labours that he paid me £3 10s. and told me that he would soon raise my pay again. After his kind words I decided to stick to my new occupation, but my resolution weakened and I threw away the bone for the shadow.

The second mate and steward of the steamer I had come out in called on me every day to try to coax me into going to the gold diggings with them, and they brought me the daily newspapers with accounts of the great finds people were having at the diggings. Eventually their counsels prevailed, and at the end of three weeks as chief cook, I resigned that lucrative appointment. It was a foolish proceeding, for, every Saturday night, after a week of congenial work, I had only to go upstairs to have three and a half golden sovereigns put in my hand, and yet I gave up the gold that was certain, to go and dig for that which was very much less so.

I left the hotel on the best of terms with everybody except the proprietor, who was rather annoyed at my desertion and would not believe in the glowing accounts of the results of the digging, as they appeared in the papers. "Oh, yes," he said, "you read of a man, or perhaps two men, who have made a good find, but the papers never tell you of the hundreds that return empty-handed after spending every penny they had. But there you are! If you *will* go, I can't help it, but when you return to Sydney, rich or poor, look us up."

I promised to do so, and he gave me permission to leave my clothes in the hotel, for a very small wardrobe is sufficient in the Bush. I stayed at Barry's coffee shop for a few days while we fitted out the expedition with a handy little axe, a frying-pan, a two-quart billy (which was merely a block-tin pitcher) and other useful articles. We also bought a tent, seven feet six inches long by six feet broad—made of duck, because we had to study weight, and it was hard to say how many miles we would have to carry it before we found gold enough to buy a horse. All being ready, we made a start one fine afternoon, but the adventures which befell us must be carried over to a fresh chapter.

CHAPTER X

OFF TO THE DIGGINGS

WE intended to take train to Penrith, a small township about thirty miles from Sydney, which was as far as the railway extended in those days, but when we reached the station we found there would be no train to Penrith till morning. However, there was one just going to Liverpool, a village about half-way to Penrith, and we decided to go by that, as we did not want to go back again after having set out, and camping out a night on the way would serve as a trial trip for both ourselves and our gear.

My chums were both named Tom, so it was arranged that the second mate should be called Tom, and the steward Thomas. Tom was a Norwegian by birth, but as he had attended Glasgow schools and had sailed out of Glasgow for many years, he could speak Scotch very well when he liked. He was a very nice fellow for a companion, though rather timid for bush-work, but he was what we called a level-headed man, and as I was rather impulsive, I thought he would keep me in check. Thomas was our late captain's brother-in-law, and had been a clerk in a London office which he had been asked to leave in a hurry, but

138

that has nothing to do with my story. We made him our cashier, and got him to keep a log-book: it was only a penny note-book, but I thought it might be of service to us some day.

When we were making up our swags to leave Sydney it turned out that Tom had a red blanket and Thomas a blue one, while mine was grey, but it was arranged that Tom should always carry my blanket in his swag, for I had to carry the tent, which was also made up like a swag. Thus it fell out, quite by chance, that we travelled with red, white, and blue over our shoulders, and from that fact we could be traced all over the country, as I shall show later on.

On arrival at Liverpool, we left our swags at the station while we had a look round the village for a suitable place to camp, which we found close to the station; it was well wooded, but there were no very large trees. We started just before dark to rig the tent, light a fire, fill the billy and put it on to boil, with the result that our tea, which we much enjoyed, was ready three-quarters of an hour after we arrived on the spot.

Our small stores consisted of half a pound of tea, one pound of sugar, two pounds of ham, and four pounds of flour; we could get fresh supplies at many places on the way, so we took only small quantities in order to keep down our weight, for we did not intend to make " dampers " while we could get bread to buy.

After tea we lay down on our new beds—the grass—but, as might have been expected, did not find it very conducive to slumber. In the small hours of the morning distant thunder could be heard, every peal telling us that it was coming our way. The lightning was very vivid, and when the rain came on, which it did in a very short time, it seemed as if the heavens had opened, for the water came through the tent as if it had been a herring net. If we had been favoured with a slight shower first, the duck would have closed its meshes, and I think we should have been all right, but as it was we hauled the blankets over our faces and did our best to weather the storm. The tent was well spread and it became as tight as a drum, and the big raindrops falling on it made a terrific noise, in the midst of which I thought I felt a breeze coming in at the door-flap. I pushed the blanket off my face to see what was causing it, and with the next flash of lightning saw a most unearthly sight—a bullock standing with its head right in the tent. I soon recovered from the shock when I realised the true nature of the apparition, and said to my companions, " Look at the door and wait till a flash of lightning comes." When the flash came Tom grasped my arm like a vice, but I laughed heartily and he loosened his grip, though poor Thomas fainted. I never mentioned the matter afterwards, but this little incident showed me that I should have to do the fighting if we should happen to get into a tight corner at any part of our travels.

The next morning was a lovely summer morning with a cloudless sky and a hot sun. We spread out our blankets and tent before lighting a fire and making breakfast, and by the time our meal was over, everything was nearly dry. We packed up and caught the train to Penrith, where we arrived early in the forenoon, and started our travels at once. The road we took had been made by convicts in bye-gone days, and was a very good one, well made and well metalled; I do not remember how far it ran into the bush, but I think we walked for three days before we came to the end of it.

One hour after leaving Penrith we were right in the bush, and we did not hear a human voice but our own until evening.

We could not see far ahead, for the country was so densely wooded, but we heard a voice, uttering the foulest language, accompanied by the crack of a stock-whip. We heard the string of oaths poured out continuously for some little time before we came in sight of the owner of the voice, and when we did so, discovered that he was a coal-black driver of a team of bullocks. I had heard it said that it was impossible to drive a team of bullocks without swearing fluently, and this was my first example of the orthodox style. The man's master was riding on horseback a little bit ahead, and when we overtook him we found that he was a man who had lived at Barry's and dined at our table, so we struck up an acquaintance at once. We had noticed that, though got up in style when in Sydney, his hands and face showed that he was used to hard work; we had also noticed one day that he had a very big roll of bank-notes with him, and now we learned all about him.

We camped for the night on the same ground, and had a long chat with our friend before turning in. He told us he had been down to Sydney from Yass with two drays of wool (the other dray being on ahead), which he had sold, and was now returning with stores for himself and a great many people all along the road, so that there would be very little left in either of the drays by the time he reached home. I looked round the load to see what it consisted of, and found a heterogeneous collection, including Huntley & Palmer's biscuits, Thompson's whisky, Tate's sugar, blocks of salt, shovels, picks, a box from Duncan & Flockhart, and many other articles.

I had my first lesson on cracking a stock-whip that evening, practising for an hour, and when I got up next morning I went straight for the whip, for I was determined to master it, thinking it might prove a useful accomplishment some day—as it did.

After breakfast we set off by ourselves, for bullocks can only go fourteen or fifteen miles a day, whereas we intended to do twenty-five, although old stagers would say twenty was enough. We had not been very decided as to our destination hitherto, but on the morning that we left our friend with the bullocks we made up our minds to steer for the Araluen diggings. We did not find the road very dull for the first few days, for we never walked more than ten miles without encountering something to break the monotony—a house, a small village, a well, a mail-coach, or a traveller. We never passed a house without calling, and we were always made welcome and supplied with anything we wanted, free of charge.

One day when passing through a small village about one o'clock, we thought we would try to buy a dinner from some one, for it would be a nice change from the ubiquitous tea, bread, and ham of the bush, so we approached the open door of a little cottage from which issued a most appetising smell of some kind of stew. A woman stood close to the door and I remarked, "What a fine smell! Perhaps you would be good enough to sell us some of that stew—that is, if you have any to spare."

"Come in," she said kindly. "Take off your swags and sit down."

Just then her husband came in for his dinner, and, after the usual salutations, I explained how we had been attracted to his house, that we were from Sydney and bound to the Araluen diggings.

"Just so," said he. "Well, friends, you will get a share of all that is going, so make yourselves at home. But as you are new chums I will say this to you—never talk about paying. We have all had to travel through the bush or we wouldn't be here, and I can tell you we have sometimes been sorely pressed, but my wife and I were never charged for anything we got on the road, and no traveller that comes to our door shall go away empty. It may not be much we have, but what we have you will share with us, and you will find it the same all through New South Wales."

I found that this was quite correct. If we wanted our billy filled with milk as a change from tea, we had only to ask for it at some wayside house, and, if they had it, they gave it at once. If we asked for a meal, too, we were sure to get it, but nowadays, I understand, nothing is given to travellers; I suppose it was overdone and the good people had finally to refuse all assistance.

After we had travelled about a week we were anxious to reach a township, the name of which— along with others with jaw-breaking native names —I cannot remember, but we heard it was of some considerable size, and it being then Christmas eve, we wanted to be as sociable as possible and camp there on Christmas Day.

We reached our destination as daylight faded, and found that the town of considerable size consisted of four houses on one side of the road and five on the other, but there were a few more scattered about within sight. Close to the houses, on a walled-in piece of ground, stood a half-built church which, to all appearance, had been abandoned long before, and, as there were no trees at hand on which to stretch the ridge of our tent, we went inside the four walls of the church and rigged our tent there, but we lit our camp fire without the walls. After supper we lay down, for we were very tired, but we were hardly down before we were up again and had struck a light to see what was biting us—we had lain down on an ant's nest! They were big, healthy ants, with appetites in proportion to their size, so we had to shift outside and sleep without a tent.

We were up early next morning to see what sort of a place we were in, but though the people were all about, no one called on us, as was usual, and when I walked round, passing every door, no one spoke to me.

The inn was open and a few men were sitting in the veranda drinking their morning " nobbler," for, travel where we would in Australia, whenever we came to a collection of half a dozen houses, we were sure to find that one of them was a tavern or drinking-shop of some kind, and hitherto we had sent Thomas into each for a bottle of lemonade (price sixpence) so that he might pick up any news that would be of service to us.

We had reached a hot-bed of bushranging and were on the look-out for a gang known as Ben Hall's gang, which at that time was composed of five men, all splendid shots and smart horsemen. They reserved their attentions for the mails and people with plenty of cash, and did not molest poor travellers like ourselves, but of course they were down on the police.

When I returned to the camp for breakfast Tom told me he had spoken to two men who were both very old, with a rich Irish brogue, but they were not at all sociable in spite of its being Christmas Day. After breakfast we again walked round, and from glimpses I got through the open house doors, I came to the conclusion that it was the dirtiest place I had ever come across.

During the day I spoke to a man about seventy years of age who had lived in one of these dirty little houses for thirty years, and he told me he belonged to London, had been in Australia for fifty years, but did not know the name of the ship he had come out in.   I came to the conclusion that he had had a free passage out.

We were glad when daylight broke next morning, and we marched out of that township without shedding a tear.   We were passing through a densely wooded part, about eight miles further on, when, in the stillness, we heard a horse coming along at a gallop.   It was soon up to us, and the rider, a gentlemanly-looking man, checked his speed slightly and said as he passed us, " Ben Hall's just behind me ! "

Poor Tom began to tremble and Thomas went off the road into the bush to put the money into his boots, though I said, " What are you afraid of ?   I believe he would rather give us a £5 note than take away our £5," which was all we had left.

Shortly afterwards Ben Hall came in sight and we advanced like Scotland road militia men— " altogether one after the other."   I was leading, and just as he came abeam I said " Good-morning," and he responded with a " Good-morning " also. When he was out of hearing my two friends came up alongside and remarked that we evidently had nothing to fear from that gang, while Thomas added, " I don't care now if even Morgan comes along."   It was easy to be bold when we knew that we were two hundred miles from the district infested by Morgan, the bloodthirsty bushranger ! About an hour afterwards we passed the four men belonging to Hall's gang and they also said "Good morning" in passing.

The next township at which we camped was bigger and cleaner than the last, and was called Bungunda. We camped on its outskirts, and on passing through next morning found all the inhabitants busily decorating their houses, not with flags, but with any piece of gaily coloured cloth that they could lay hands on. We enjoyed the fun and lent them a hand, for we learned there was to be a marriage among them and the prospective bride was a general favourite. She came out and thanked us for helping to beautify the place.

As it drew close to the hour when the parson should arrive to tie the knot we started again on our journey, but when we were passing the inn—the last house in the village—we saw a number of men looking along the road from the veranda, and they stopped us for a chat. They told us that the parson was coming from Goulburn by the mail, which was overdue, so they, living as they did in the heart of the bushranging country, were afraid something was wrong. They were getting out their rifles when we left. One man among them, whom they called Mac (I learned from the papers afterwards that his name was M'Lean), possessed a revolving rifle which was the only one in the country. It was newly out from home, and Mac was very anxious that the landlord should saddle a horse for him so that he might go along the road by himself to see what had happened, but we left before it was settled.

About four miles further on we saw ahead of us

a mail coach, two drays, and a lot of extra horses, and at first sight we thought there had been a collision or accident of some sort, but when we reached the scene of action, we were ordered to sit down on the grass. It seemed that Ben Hall, with his gang, had stopped the down mail, politely telling the passengers not to be afraid, for no one would injure them if they got out and sat down on the grass. They had started to ransack the mails when two drays had come along, and they were also stopped and some of their good things— such as biscuits, cheese, and lemonade—distributed among the passengers, themselves, and us when we arrived. The gang were all dismounted except one man called Dunn who acted as look-out, taking a short canter along the road from time to time to see if the road was clear.

The up mail arrived in a short time, and the passengers were ordered out to eat, drink, and be merry, while I watched my chance to tell the parson what I knew and what I had heard Mac saying at the inn. When the men had taken all they wanted out of the mails they invited the ladies (of whom there were four) to have a dance, as they found one of the passengers had a concertina, but they had just started when we heard the report of a rifle, and a bullet grazed Dunn's ear. In an instant the four bushrangers were on their horses, with their hands grasping their revolvers, and were galloping along the road in pursuit of Mac who, we could see, was retreating. We knew that they would not return, so everyone set about packing up, the dray drivers taking back what had not been opened, and the mails started at once.

We were the richer by two tins of biscuits and half a small cheese, with some other little things, so we fared very well, though we had been delayed about half a day.

On the following day we passed through the largest township we had seen since we left Penrith; it was Braidwood, one hundred and ninety miles south-west of Sydney, and it boasted two inns, a police-station and court-house, and an auction mart for horses. We bought a little in the way of sugar and tea, sugar being ninepence and tea four shillings per pound, and we camped about two miles beyond the town. All the people we met were as kind as ever, but they appeared to be very poor, which I thought to be very strange, for we were drawing close to gold diggings, and I had expected to find everyone in the vicinity rolling in wealth. They told us we were only one day's journey from the first diggings, called Major's Creek, but it had been worked out by Britishers and given over to China-men to work, for if our people gave up a creek which they thought was not rich enough, it might still be good enough for a Chinaman. We were advised to camp early, about two miles this side of Major's Creek, if we found we could not get through it before dark, as the Chinamen there were getting a bad name. We saw we were going to be late, so we camped at four o'clock, and Thomas and I walked on for a look at the diggings while Tom rigged the tent. When we lay down that night I put the axe at my head, for it was all we had in the way of firearms, but all passed quietly.

Early next morning Thomas and I went towards the Creek again to make sure of our way through it, while Tom made the breakfast, and we returned in about an hour's time. As we approached our tent we saw two horses made fast, and when we drew closer found two fine-looking troopers—a sergeant and a private. When we were near enough I shouted, " Good morning," but I received no answer, and for fear there was any mistake, I said in a loud voice, " Have you come to breakfast with us ? "

" No ! " answered the sergeant, sharply, " but I'll wait till you get your breakfast."

Tom's face was a picture of misery, so I turned to him and asked, " What's the matter with you, Tom ? "

" This is what's the matter," put in the sergeant. " You are charged with sticking up (bushranging) a man and robbing him of his money on the evening of Christmas Day. Were you at —— township on Christmas Day ? "

" Yes," I replied, for this was the dirty, miserable village where we had spent that day.

" Now, before we go any farther," said the sergeant, " make up your swags as you make them every day."

We did so, and stood before him with our usual red, white, and blue burdens on our backs.

" Now, then," said the sergeant, " listen while I read the wire I have received from Braidwood," and after reading it he continued, "Is that you three or is it not?"

There was no getting away from the fact that the description applied to us—three young men, very fair, thought to be foreigners (a Norwegian, a Scotsman, and a pure-bred Cockney!), passed Braidwood yesterday on their way to the diggings; one carried the tent, and the others red and blue swags. We could not fathom the meaning of it at all, but the sergeant gave us a crumb of comfort by saying that he thought there was a mistake somewhere. It was hard lines, we thought, to have to retrace our steps and to be seen in charge of the police by all the people we had spoken to on the road. By way of a feeler, I asked the sergeant what he would do if we refused to go back unless he supplied horses. "Oh, I would soon get the horses," he replied, "but I would put you on the horse in a way that would be very unpleasant for you. Now, don't get any evil thoughts into your head: come along quietly and I'll put your swags on my horse, but you must take them off at once if we see anybody coming, and when we draw close to Braidwood, for it is against the rules for me to do it."

He wanted to be friendly with us, but I thought it was not very easy for innocent men to respond to the advances made by a man who was marching them back as prisoners. Poor Tom's eyes were not dry all that day, and the sergeant, noticing this, spoke to me about it, so I tried to cheer him up.

" We have been made prisoners for sticking up a

man," I said. "Now, did you, Tom, or did any of us stick up a man?"

"No," he replied.

"Well, then, what are you afraid of? There is no law, either in England or Australia, that can punish us when we are innocent, so dry your eyes." That was before the Beck and Edalji cases were heard of.

"That's right, Tom, my boy, cheer up," the sergeant chimed in, "it will all come out right in the end."

When we arrived at the police station at Braidwood we were marched into the charge room, and the inspector sent for. When he came he compared us with the description, then wired for the man to be sent at once to identify us, and in the meantime I asked if he would allow us to camp outside.

"I am sorry," he said, "but I have no power to do so."

"Will you really have the heart to put three respectable people in a cell?" I asked.

"That is all I can do for you to-night," replied the inspector. "The man can't get here till about ten o'clock, and after that we will see what can be done." Then he departed and left us in charge of the policeman, who lived on the premises with his wife, and a real, fine fellow he was, both he and his wife being natives of County Down. He took us to a cell, saying, "The place is all clean and so are the blankets. I must lock you up, for those are my orders, but I don't think you are guilty of robbery, so my wife and I will try and make you as comfortable as we can. She is making your tea now and will bring it along to you in a few minutes."

The wife, a nice little woman, soon appeared, bringing us tea, scones, jam and cheese, and I got Thomas to thank her when she came back for the dishes, for he was better versed in the art of polite conversation than either Tom or myself, but I joined in and told her all we wanted was a smoke, for we had some tobacco with us.

"Well, you may smoke," she said readily.

"It's very kind of you to say so," I returned, "but I must get permission from the master first, for I like to do things shipshape—even in chokey."

"Patrick!" she called aloud, "sure, these lads can have a smoke?"

"To be sure, they can smoke," we heard the lock-up keeper answer, and we gladly availed ourselves of the permission.

I fell asleep, but Tom woke me about ten o'clock by crying out in a great state of excitement, "He's come! he's come!"

"Well, let him come!" said I, sleepily, and turned over on my other side, but Tom did not take his ear away from the little opening in the door (a hole used for passing in prisoners' meals) for about a quarter of an hour, when he collapsed and dropped down beside me crying, "Oh, it's us! it's us!"

"What's us, you fool?" I growled. "I ask you again—did you stick a man up? No? Then what are you making a fool of yourself for?"

Just then the officials came to the cell with candles to have another look at us, and, for the sake of saying something, I asked the inspector if we could go now.

" No," he answered, " not even if it was clear to me that you are innocent. When you have been put in a cell you can't be discharged till you go before a magistrate, so you are here for the night, and we will see how you get on at ten o'clock to-morrow forenoon."

After the inspector left, the lock-up keeper told us they were all sure that the old man had been on the spree on Christmas Day and had lost both his own and his master's money in drinking and gambling, and that he had then concocted the story about having been held up and robbed by three men. He thought the matter would rest at that, but we were the only three who had passed for several days and we had been remarked on account of our red, white and blue swags, so his master, with the help of some of the squatters who had noticed us, made out a description and wired to the police to stop us.

We were up early next morning, and had a walk and a smoke in the policeman's garden before being supplied with a good breakfast of Irish stew, tea and home-made scones. This was not the usual way to treat prisoners, and we had to thank the kindly Irishwoman for these concessions.

At ten o'clock we were marched into the court-yard without our swags, where we stood at attention till we were joined by six policemen, the sergeant who brought us being one of the six, all dressed in the usual bush rig like ourselves. They toed a line with us, and then a dirty, drunken old fool of a man was brought in to pick out the three men who had robbed him.

"Don't hurry yourself," said the inspector, "but take a good look and make sure you get the right men."

He crept along the line, looking up into each face, till he had passed the whole nine without saying anything, then he turned back again and when he came to the sergeant he said, "That is one of them." The inspector immediately ordered us to fall out and we waited about the yard till the magistrate arrived at eleven o'clock. In the meantime the inspector and the rest of the police spoke to us freely on the matter and pitied us for the inconvenience we had been put to. At eleven o'clock we marched into court, and I must say I felt rather cut at the difference of treatment meted out to us there (I was forgetting that we were still prisoners), for the police, and even the old sinner who was the cause of all the trouble, had chairs to sit on, while we, with our swags again on our shoulders, had to stand in a narrow strip of a prisoner's box. The magistrate with his clerk soon came in, and the police and the public stood up to receive him with due honour—the public consisting of one man, a local newspaper reporter. I never saw such a face as the magistrate's outside the gates of the Zoological Gardens, and I am sure supporters of the Darwinian theory would have considered it strong corroboration of their views. The inspector commenced the proceedings by relating all he knew of the case; then the sergeant told how he had found us by the description and arrested us; then the inspector went into the witness-box again and told of the man's mistake in picking out the sergeant; he then gave his own opinion of the case and said the prosecutor was one of the most disreputable men in the district. This concluded, the clerk read all the evidence over to the magistrate, who then turned to us and said, "Prisoners, you are discharged."

"Thank you, sir," I answered, "but what will you allow us for the harm you have done to innocent men?"

"Ah! we don't do that in Australia," he replied.

"Well, you haven't got a man in the force——" I began, but the Irish policeman pulled me down the two steps out of the box, and to drown the remainder of my speech he called out, "Order in Court!" When we got outside they told me a story of a man who had been brought back from Adelaide (a matter of about 700 miles), and when they found he was not the man they wanted, they turned him out on the road, though he was penniless, to retrace his steps the best way he could.

Our friend, the lock-up keeper's wife, made us a fine dinner of boiled pork, greens and duff, at which the sergeant joined us, and in the course of the meal I said we were puzzled to know what to do now for we would not think of going back by the road we had marched along as prisoners. They all advised us to go to some diggings that were only eighteen miles from Braidwood as there were only six hundred people on it, nearly all of whom were sailors, and they gave us all the little tips they could think of, so we set out after dinner.

The road was only a narrow track, but it was straight, and we walked our best pace, arriving on the outskirts at seven o'clock. We intended not to let our arrival be known till the morning, which was Sunday, when we would have plenty of time to look round for a good place for our tent. In the meantime I got the tent up, while Tom lit a fire and made tea, and Thomas went to the store to buy three shovels, a pick, and a prospecting dish, and to take out our licence, or "digger's rights," after which we had supper and went to bed, no one having called.

Next morning I was up early, lit the fire, and called Tom to make the breakfast while I had a look round, and when I came back Tom told me he had had visitors of the right sort who had all offered to give us anything we were short of, or to show us round, and after breakfast we went on a tour of inspection. We found plenty of friends, and on their advice we pegged out our claim, and later in the day shifted our camp to a nice place only a hundred yards from our claim and away from the other huts and tents, for we had noticed in our walk round that card-playing and whisky-drinking were the principal Sunday recreations. We learned from our new friends that they were not getting very big finds, but they were making a living and nearly all were satisfied.

They usually sold their weekly finds of gold on

Saturdays, and a number of them told us how much they had sold the previous day; they averaged about two ounces each.   We received many invitations to dinner that Sunday, but we preferred to go to our own camp so that we could chat over all we had heard.   When Thomas was at the store for our tools he asked for four pounds of steak, but the storeman laughed at him and cut off seven or eight pounds, saying, "There you are, my boy! I suppose you don't mind if it's a little more.   I won't charge you for beef till you find gold."   Beef was very cheap, but there was no baker's bread to be had, and thenceforward we had to make a damper every evening.

CHAPTER XI

DIGGING FOR GOLD

WE took our breakfast at five o'clock on Monday morning and at six we started work on our claim. Tom and I each commenced to sink a hole six feet by three feet; I saw at once that he was a good shovelman and that I should have to wire in if I wanted to keep up with him. Perhaps he thought the same of me, for he never straightened his back but kept right on. I was first to reach the bottom, and when I had cleared all the loose earth out of the hole, I went to ask one of the old diggers to come and explain the work to us, which he willingly did.

The diggings we were on were called shallow or poor men's diggings, because no machinery was required to work them, not even a hand-winch to heave the earth up. The depth of holes ran from four to six feet, the bottom being rock, and it was in the earth that lay immediately on top of the rock that gold was found. The gold-bearing earth, or pay dirt, was easily distinguished, for it was quite different in colour and substance from the earth above it. The diggers called it mullock.

In some parts of the diggings the gold-bearing earth was only two or three inches deep, but where

159

we struck bottom it was one foot three inches.
Acting on the friendly digger's advice, we started
with the pick to dig out enough to fill our dish,
taking a sample from both ends and both sides, and
took it to a small running stream close at hand.
There were a number of diggers at work at the
stream and they readily showed us how to wash our
earth. They placed the dish in the water so that
the water nearly covered the dish and the earth;
then they washed the earth by rubbing it between
their hands, squeezing the lumps, and throwing
away the stones; that thoroughly done, they lifted
the dish just off the bottom with both hands and
gave it a sharp swirl as if trying to throw out the
contents, but only the earth went, for all the gold
had settled to the bottom and was quite safe unless
they were very careless or turned the dish upside
down. Having got rid of the dirt, they lifted out
the little specks of gold and put them on a sheet of
paper, while they repeated the process with another
dishful of earth.

We soon got into the way of it, and when we had
washed all our samples and found which yielded
most gold, we returned to our holes to start crevicing
the best end—that is, making a small tunnel to get
out as much of the pay-dirt as possible without the
roof of the tunnel collapsing. The height and span
of the arch depended on the size of the man who
was working it, but they were usually about two
feet six inches. Having made the arch, we had to
work lying face downwards or on one side, scraping
the pickings as they increased into the big hole out

of the way, until there was a nice little heap, when we threw it up.

While Tom and I were at work in the holes, Thomas was not idle on the surface. All the first earth we had thrown up had to be thrown back a bit to leave a clear space for the pay-dirt, and he had to watch that they did not get mixed. Then he had to make frequent journeys to the creek to wash a dishful so that we might know if we were working in the right direction, or whether it was becoming barren. All the little specks of gold that we found were carefully picked out of the dish and deposited in a little wash-leather bag for that purpose, though the longer-established diggers threw away the result of a washing when it was very poor, but we could not afford to do that, for stores were dear and our money was all gone.

We worked from daylight till dark, day after day, collecting all our wash-dirt till Saturday, when we intended to wash it all and see how much per week we were making. When that day arrived I left my mates to wash while I went to have a look at other people's claims and to learn all I could from them. We met again for dinner, but were not very happy, for the result of our washing was very poor, though we could not say how much it was worth till we took it to the storekeeper that evening, for he bought all the gold, the place not being big enough to support a branch bank.

After dinner I asked Tom to climb up a very tall tree with me and have a look at the diggings from a height. When we reached the top we had a fine bird's-eye view of the whole of them, and they appeared to cover a space about one hundred feet wide and about half a mile long, winding in and out so as to keep in the deepest part of the gully. I drew Tom's attention to the fact that our hole was a little further out than any of the others, so we descended, drew our pegs, and tried for a new claim nearer the centre of the diggings, but as we could not find the usual eighty feet unoccupied, we started without the pegs, and touched bottom that evening before knock-off time, which was five o'clock on Saturdays. Then we went to the stores to sell our gold, and found that the storekeeper was very pleasant and appeared to know all about us, though Tom and I had never been there before. We handed him our little bag, and he began by emptying the contents on to a sheet of white paper which he held over the flame of a candle till the gold was thoroughly dried and warm; then all the fine sand which had adhered to it and another foreign body which we always found in the dish after washing (I think it was platinum) separated from the gold, and being lighter, he was able to blow it away, but, to my anxious eyes, it seemed that nothing would be left to tell the tale of our labours. After he was satisfied that all foreign matter had gone, he put the gold on the scales and pronounced the grand amount of the emolument for our hard week's work to be eight shillings and fourpence—two shillings and ninepence each, or one penny per hour.

Well, if we were long in making that handsome

sum we were not long in spending it. Sugar was ninepence a pound, flour fourpence, potatoes fourpence, ham half-a-crown, beef and mutton twopence. As I made our bread, or damper, as it was called, every second evening, I might describe the process. I have already mentioned that a billy and a frying-pan formed our entire outfit of cooking utensils. I first filled the billy with water, and then put one pound of flour (about sixteen level tablespoonfuls) in the frying-pan. We seldom had salt, but I always tried to have a tin match-box full of bi-carbonate of soda, which I measured by turning the spoon end for end and taking as much soda as I could lift on one inch of the fiddle end of the spoon. After stirring the soda into the flour I poured in a little water and mixed it carefully, for space was very limited in the pan, till it was all worked up to a stiff dough. I kneaded it into the size and shape of the frying-pan, turned it out on to the grass while I cleaned the pan of the dough that adhered to it, returned the damper to the pan and then proceeded to cook it. I spread out the fire, removing all half-burnt wood and leaving only nice, clean wood-ash, upon which I placed the frying-pan and covered over the damper with ashes, keeping the hottest for a top dressing. In about twenty minutes I turned it out, gave it a slap on each side to remove the ash, and the result was a nice, clean piece of bread about ten inches in diameter and three inches thick.

To return to the store: in making our purchases for the week we had to consider the state of our exchequer and ca' canny, and the storekeeper, perceiving our difficulty, said, " I suppose you know it is against the rule to give tick here, but I'll be happy to give it to you three fellows, because I think you are square-going chaps and wouldn't bluff me, so take away what you want and pay me when you are able."

I replied that it was very good of him to make us such an offer, but I had never worked on the credit system and did not intend to commence then, and my chums supported my views. The store was quite a Whiteley's on a small scale; it was a wooden structure—clinker built—and was guarded at night by four fierce-looking dogs, for it frequently contained a large quantity of gold. It also contained all the gin, rum, brandy and whisky in the district, for there was a heavy-drinking population to be supplied, and no other shop for eighteen miles. The drinking was carried on outside the store with empty boxes for seats and empty barrels for tables, and, of course, nothing less than a bottle was sold.

On Sunday we had sea-pie for dinner and slept as much as possible in preparation for a hard week's work, instead of calling at any of the huts or tents, for we did not approve of the drinking and card-playing that was going on in all of them. That reminds me that we had a minister at the diggings, though I do not know how he came to be there, but it shows that one may meet all sorts and conditions of men in Australia. The " boots " in the hotel at Sydney had been a captain in the army.

On Monday we started to work even harder than

we did the previous week, and kept it up at a rate which caused a small sensation in the diggings. At the end of a week's heavy labour we found we had realised barely one pound each, and I thought of my late master's advice, and declared that if we did not make two pounds each the next week I would leave the place. This spread through the diggings on Sunday, and we had a few calls from men who advised us to try our luck a little longer; one man offered me three pounds a week to work with him, but I stuck to my guns. Thomas agreed with me, but Tom did not, for which I was sorry, because I liked him and I did not care for Thomas, about whom there seemed to be some mystery.

Again we worked with all our might for a week, to find, when Saturday came, that we had made about twelve shillings each; so on Sunday morning Thomas and I left the diggings, taking with us our blankets, my ditty bag, about two days' food, and seven shillings each in cash, leaving Tom in possession of our tools, cooking utensils, and the tent. We reached Goulburn on the third day and were kindly received by the people, who told us we would find plenty of work at good wages, but I had made up my mind to go and consult with the squatter with whom we had travelled from Penrith, for I thought his advice would be worth having, and had no doubt he would provide us with work. I found that his station was about five miles from Yass, and we set out in that direction, but my plan did not suit my companion's book at all. He seemed to grow lazier every hour; if we sat down on the grass for a few minutes' rest he grumbled when I said it was time to start; in the morning I had to start without him and he would overtake me about two hours later. He talked continually about bush-ranging, and it soon became evident that he wanted me to take up that line of business, but whether on our own account or attached to some existent gang, I cannot say, for as soon as I perceived what he was aiming at I forbade him to again mention the subject to me, and when we reached Yass we parted company. Soon afterwards Thomas joined Ben Hall's gang, but before many months had passed he was captured, and suffered capital punishment for having caused the death of a policeman.

I found I could not reach the squatter's house with daylight, so camped about a mile off with the sky for a roof over my head. Early next morning I reached the house, where my friend made me very welcome, and he sat for hours listening to my account of my travels since I had seen him. Then he showed me all over his place, taking pains to explain everything, and I found much to interest me. After dinner I remarked that it was rather strange that he should go to the expense of building such a fine house and then let it stand with only the priming coat of paint, though I had noticed in one of the out-buildings a large amount of paint which appeared to have stood there for some years.

" Well," he answered, " I'll tell you how that is. The two men who built this house had, according to their contract, to give the woodwork a coat of lead-colour, which they did. Then the following year I arranged that a man in Yass should give all the woodwork a coat. Well, he brought his paints on a Saturday and I told him to leave them where you saw them till Monday. On the Sunday he cleared out to the diggings and I haven't seen him since, though that was nearly four years ago."

"If you don't think me too forward," I remarked, "I would like to tell you of another thing I noticed when you were showing me round. You have a number of tarpaulins, or covers you may call them, lying about in a useless condition. Now, if you have seven and you cut up one to repair the others, you will then have six good cloths to depend on to cover a dray or a stack of grain, or for any other purpose."

"That's quite true," he rejoined. "Would you do it?"

"Well, I *could* do it if you thought right to employ me," I replied, "but I don't wish to push myself into your service. I don't know much about handling stock, but if you like to try me you will find me very willing to learn."

"Well, I will engage you," said he, "and you can mend the covers, do the painting, and make yourself generally useful."

I assured the friendly squatter that he would not regret having employed me, and then asked him where I was to live.

"Oh, in the house," he replied. "My aunt will make up a bed for you, and you will live with us."

"I hope you are not doing too much for me," I said. "Won't your other men be jealous?"

"None of them come about the house," he replied; "they all live out in the bush beside their work, and I'm often away myself, and my old aunt will be very glad of your presence."

As he concluded by saying he would give me three pounds per week, I was very pleased with the arrangement, and started work at once by turning out the paints. I had carte blanche as to the colours, so I painted the house a light stone colour, the windows white and green, and the front door three shades of green. The painting occupied me a whole week, from daylight to dark every day, but I was well rewarded when I saw the boss so well pleased with the result of my work. When he returned from his daily round of inspection he would bring his horse to a stand about a hundred yards from the house, and sit there for some time, admiring his freshly-painted home.

I still stuck to my faithful friend, my ditty bag, which again proved its worth, for after the second week every cloth about the place was in good repair. On Sundays I use to saddle a horse and have a look round; I did not like to venture far into the bush by myself, but I saw a few of the employees and some of the stock, while at the same time I was getting practice in horsemanship. I saw that harvesting had started close to the house, and I asked one of the men to give me a lesson on handling the hook, which he willingly did, and I kept at it till I thought I was fairly proficient, when I asked the boss to let me help at the harvesting as I heard he was short-handed, and he gave his consent. The harvesting ground was four miles from the station, but I was allowed to go and come on horseback, and I got on very well with my new work. It is not such hard work as in England, where one must cut very low in order to make as much straw as possible, for in Australia they did not want the straw.

On the evening of the third day my attention was drawn from my work by one of the men shouting that my horse had broken his hobbles, and through looking up when I was just in the act of cutting, I managed to cut a slice off the little finger of my left hand. It bled profusely, and I might have escaped a lot of trouble if I had gone to the station at once and had it dressed, but either through washing it in dirty water, or through tying it up with a dirty rag, it became a badly poisoned finger.

I continued to work at the station for a few days, but my finger got rapidly worse, and I threw up my job and left, very much down-hearted at my bad luck.

In passing through Yass I stopped to pass the time of day with a blacksmith who, after seeing my finger, very kindly washed it and dressed it with Friar's Balsam. In the course of conversation I told him I wanted work to do as soon as my hand got better, and he told me of a Scotch squatter, living forty miles from Yass, who wanted a man to drive his wool down to the coast. His name was Graham, and I was to travel forty miles to the south-west and then follow a bullock track on my right which would bring me to the house. My hand was already getting easier, so I bought three days' food and started in good spirits with a small supply of Friar's Balsam and my hand in a sling, both kindly given to me by the blacksmith.

During the journey I met only one man, who was coming from the opposite direction, and we sat down together to compare notes. I found he had been to Graham's station looking for work, which he was refused, and he added, " You needn't go there, for Graham is a crusty old beggar."

However, I held on my way, walking leisurely on account of my hand, which I washed and dressed each day, carrying it in the sling till I reached the bullock track, when I removed it so that I might not be refused employment because of only one sound hand. After walking for an hour along the track, I came in sight of the house, and immediately two big curs of dogs made for me and helped themselves to my right leg, with the result that I reached the veranda minus a large quantity of blood and one leg of my trousers. To add to this encouraging reception, Graham, a big, uncouth Scotsman, appeared and said, " What were you doing here ? The dogs would never touch anybody but trespassers."

That was adding insult to injury and roused my indignation, for I knew I had passed neither gate, fence, hedge, nor notice-boards.

" Look here, Mr. Graham," I said sharply, " did the Lord make Australia for the Grahams, that a poor soul can't walk through it ? "

His manner changed as soon as he heard my Scotch accent, and he asked if I could speak Gaelic.

"No," I replied.   "I belong to Edinburgh."

"But there are plenty of peoples in Edinburgh can speak the Gaelic," he said.

"Yes—the policemen!"

I was then taken into the house, where I was supplied with all that was necessary for dressing my wounds, and also with a pair of peg-top trousers made of good, strong cloth, "heather and oakum" shade.   When I was fully rigged out, I returned to the presence of the mighty Graham and asked him if he had a spare job to fit me.   He inquired if I could drive a team of bullocks, and on my replying in the affirmative, he asked me whose team I had driven, and I gave him the name of my boss at Yass, whom he happened to know.   In answer to another query, I said my wages at Yass were three pounds a week, which brought forth the quick response, "Ah, you'll no get sae muckle here!"

After thinking it over, he informed me that he would give me two pounds and my food, and I closed with that offer.   He then explained that my first duty would be to take a load of wool to the beach, a distance of thirty miles.

There was no harbour at the place, but there was sufficient shelter for a small steamer, bound to Sydney, to call for wool collected from various stations within easy reach, and it was much more convenient than sending it by road.   Graham told me the worst part of my journey would be where the road zigzagged over a high, steep hill, but I would find a good stretch of flat country just before reaching the hill, and that I should take the heavy incline when my team was fresh in the morning. I made a mental note of all such scraps of information, for both road and work were new to me. Fortunately for me, the load was not ready for five days, for by that time my dog-bites were better, and my finger doing well.

My own countryman was not so good to me as my last boss, who treated every man as a gentleman till he found he was a rogue, but this one reversed that motto and showed it by his face. On the evening before I started I saw my load all ready, the axles greased, and my stores, blanket, bucket of water, etc., hung under the dray by the axles, while the ten bullocks I had to take were left in the paddock so that we could get them yoked and make a start with the first sign of daylight. Two men, who slept in the small bark hut with me, helped me to yoke my team, and I made a good start, keeping at an easy pace for the first day.

I reached my camping ground about five o'clock, and after I had made my tea I walked round to see if the bullocks were all right and to look for water, but they had found it before me and stirred up the mud, so I could not fill my bucket till morning. Though I had only travelled twelve miles I was quite tired out that night with my great responsibility, and the cares and worries attached to it prevented me from sleeping.

At daylight I managed to get my bullocks yoked with very little trouble while the billy was boiling, and started them off before I sat down to my tea, and then commenced the serious business of getting up the hill. For the first hour the ascent was easy and I felt reassured, but it soon became steeper, and the climax was reached when the road became a mere shelf on the face of a precipice, the rock rising high on my right and a deep gully yawning on my left. With close attention and a free use of the stockwhip I got over the difficulty, but I think the bullocks deserved more credit for their performance than I did. I soon found that it was necessary to apply the whip without stint when anything extra was required of them, for it was the only way to keep them under control. I was glad when we began to descend, and I camped on the first level piece of ground, where, to my delight, I found another team also camped for the night. The other driver and I spun yarns most of the night, for it is a great thing in the bush to meet a human being after having had nobody but bullocks to talk to for several days.

At that time the principal subject of conversation was bushrangers. We considered the bushrangers of New South Wales a very decent lot compared with Morgan, "the bloodthirsty," as he was called, for he was guilty of shooting men, women and children in cold blood—in fact he seemed to pay more attention to the shooting branch of the business than the money-lifting. On the other hand, Ben Hall's gang, although they were splendid shots, always tried to get out of a tight corner by strategy rather than bloodshed. I will describe one of their escapes, as it occurred when I was in the district.

One fine morning the gang arrived at a station a

few miles from Goulburn, where they passed the time of day with the boss, dismounted, hobbled their horses, and turned into an outhouse for a nap. Someone passed the word to the police at Goulburn, and in a very short time seven troopers and a sergeant arrived at a gallop. When they halted, the sergeant dismounted and placed his men round the outhouse, all being done by signs to avoid waking the sleepers. Ben Hall had three men with him, which made eight policemen awake to four bushrangers asleep. The troopers sat with their rifles at the "ready" while the sergeant walked up to the open door of the outhouse and called on Hall to surrender, but the only answer he got was a revolver bullet about the knee. Then out rushed the gang, broke through the police line, secured and unhobbled their horses, mounted, and rode off without a scar. Such cases as this were of frequent occurrence, so much so that there was a great deal of grumbling in Sydney and other large towns, where it was said that the police were either afraid or in league with them. The fault in this case was that the police used heavy, lumbering rifles, to aim at swiftly-moving objects at close quarters, instead of revolvers, with which they would have had six shots.

While on this subject I will tell a short story of Morgan. For some time the papers had been full of the cold-blooded murders this man had committed, when an article appeared in the Melbourne papers, charging the New South Wales police with cowardice, and saying they had had many chances of ridding the country of the pest, but had failed. Next day, one of the Victoria police—a Sergeant Perry, if I remember rightly—volunteered to bring in Morgan, dead or alive, and his services were accepted. It was arranged that he should draw stores at any store in the country and that he should go single-handed, with neither horse nor dog, but the police helped him along with traps and saddle-horses till he drew near to Morgan's district, when he became an ordinary traveller with swag and billy. In the meantime the papers were full of long and flourishing accounts of the brave man's career with all particulars of his life and his father's before him. No one seemed to realise the fact that the bushranger had the papers as regularly as any man in town; Morgan therefore knew just what to look for in his new enemy.

Perry travelled one day in New South Wales, and when dark set in he selected a camping ground, lit a fire and made his supper. He had just finished his tea when Morgan, who had been watching all day, approached within a few yards of him and called him by name. As soon as he heard the voice Perry leaned over for his rifle, but Morgan fired, and that moment the police force lost a man. I could tell many similar stories of bushrangers, for wherever I travelled in the bush I was always within the territory of one of the gangs. I met Ben Hall's gang a number of times, but I never saw Morgan—except in the waxworks at Melbourne.

To return to my story—I completed my first journey to the entire satisfaction of my employer, although, being a Scotchman, he did not say so. I had been only two days at the station when I was sent off again with a similar load, and this time I took an old horse with me, more to keep me company than to carry me. My old team of bullocks, of course, were not fit for another journey so quickly, for their hoofs got worn down, and I set out with ten of the most wilful wretches that were ever made fast to a dray. They wanted to go their own way at their own speed, and I wanted them to know I was master, but it was hard work using a stock-whip for twelve hours at a stretch. In fear and trembling I yoked the second morning, after much trouble with my team, for they would not go a yard unless they heard me shouting and cracking the whip. My left hand leader was a jet black animal called Captain; the right hand one was Spider, and he caused much trouble by continually pushing Captain over to the left. Consequently I had to walk at Captain's port quarter and apply the shaft of my whip pretty forcibly to get him on to his course again.

We soon reached the precipitous part of the road, and I found that I was walking in a very dangerous place for there was a sheer fall of a hundred feet to where some trees grew on a projection, and I did not know how far below that the bottom of the gully was. I decided it would be healthier and less exciting to walk on the other side of the bullocks, so I stood still until the dray was past, when I crossed immediately behind it and started to walk sharply up to the leaders' heads, but in that short space of time Spider had been at his old tricks, with the result that the dray wheel got too close to the edge of the cliff. The ground gave way and over went the dray, dragging the whole ten bullocks with it. I shall never forget the sound as those bullocks rolled down the face of the precipice, bounding against trees and projecting rocks, till at last I heard them splash into water at the bottom of the gully, far out of my sight. Then I turned round, and found my old horse standing looking at me with a face that plainly said, " Well, this is a pretty kettle of fish ! "

I sat down on the road to consider my position, and it did not take me long to decide that I would not return to the station, for the dray was smashed to atoms, the wool irrecoverable, and the bullocks all dead. On the other hand, Graham owed me five or six pounds which would pay him for the loss of the bullocks, and the old horse was worth practically nothing. I therefore determined to increase the distance between us.

My swag, containing three days' food, was round the horse's neck instead of being in its usual place on the axle of the dray, so I had a little to be thankful for after all. Nevertheless I did not feel very happy when I thought of the bad luck that had befallen me, through no fault of mine, and left me stranded penniless in the bush. I decided to walk back on the same track till I came to a good road, running off in a westerly direction, which I knew would take me to Albany, a town in New South Wales, on the border of Victoria. I immediately set out, and by eight o'clock next morning I was on the new road, having first allowed the old horse to stray away from me.

CHAPTER XII

ROAD-MAKING

TOWARDS the end of my first day's journey on the Albany road I heard a great shouting and cracking of whips behind me, and at first thought it was someone coming for me, but my mind was soon set at rest when two horse teams, eight horses in each, came in sight. The drays were piled up with cargo, and the drivers were doing their utmost to induce the horses to cover the ground quickly. There was a foreign-looking man riding alongside on horseback, who spurred his horse up to me and asked if I were going to the gold rush about thirty miles further on. I said I was out of work and perhaps the best thing I could do was to go and see if it was worth anything; he then invited me to fall in with them. They expected to get to the crest of the hill we were on before dark; hence the cracking of whips and shouting, but they had to give up the idea and camp for the night.

We were up before daylight and I had a good breakfast, for the boss gave me a tin of sardines to myself. He was an Italian, though he spoke English well, and the owner of the two loads, which consisted of all the necessaries for opening a store at

179

a new diggings, such as picks, shovels, prospecting dishes, plates and pannikins, blankets, whisky, and eatables.

The diggings proved to be nearer than the boss expected, for when we reached the top of the hill we could see the smoke from camp-fires down in the valley, but still a long way off. We reached our destination about two o'clock, but just before we got to the camp the boss asked me if I would work for him for a week, or till his brother arrived, and offered me four pounds and my food. I accepted at once, for I had no money with which to buy a pick and shovel until I earned some, and by that time I would know if they were getting paying gold, for my boss would buy nearly all the gold that was found. My decision proved a wise one, for no one found enough gold to pay his way.

My first duty was to rig up a large tent which was to serve as a store and living quarters, and was guarded at night by two very fierce dogs. I was so busy getting things into the tent after it was up that I had no time to ask any of the diggers what the prospects were, but I soon learned that they were finding only very fine specks. By the end of the week my boss had bought gold to the value of about thirty pounds, and that represented the findings of eight hundred to a thousand men. Some of them had been there two weeks, and the numbers were still increasing, but if the diggers suffered my boss did not. He had sold nearly everything he brought before his brother arrived with another two loads, and a report of more to follow, but after resting a night the brother was sent back to stop all supplies. The whisky was sold out a few hours after arrival, and drinking, card-playing, thieving, and drunken fights were the order of the day.

In a few days all the respectable men had gone, and those who were left had no money, so my boss shut up his store and left. The teams that the brother had brought had been kept for emergencies and we put a little in each dray and started for Goulburn.

The boss paid me eight pounds, and said if I liked to go back with them I could have my food, but, of course, no pay, which suited me very well. On the way I told him about the accident to my team, and he said he would let Graham know, as he intended going his way in two days' time, but to put him off the scent he would tell him that he met me at the new rush, which eased my mind considerably.

We arrived at Goulburn on the fourth day, and I found that I could get plenty of work, for in two days' time the Governor of New South Wales was to turn the first turf of the new railway from Goulburn to Sydney. I put my name on the books at once and had a place appointed to me where I had to be at a certain time with my own pick and shovel, as they only supplied huts for us to sleep in—twenty men to a hut—and the pay was eight shillings a day of ten hours.

I started with about two hundred others, including a large number of sailors; this I found out the first night after we had finished tea. Each hut

had its own camp-fire, and as we all sat round
them smoking our pipes, it chanced that someone
started singing. There were more sailors' chanties
sung than any other kind of song, and it was
very effective when a number of men at all the
fires joined in the chorus. I still remember what a
grand chorus was given to that beautiful chanty,
"In Amsterdam there lived a maid," while "Poor
Paddy works on the railway" was also sung with
fine effect. "Nancy Lee" was a great favourite,
but, indeed, we had a try at them all, including
"Homeward Bound," in spite of the incongruity of
the words.

There was a good store close to our camp, and
the prices were reasonable for Australia—beef fourpence, mutton threepence, potatoes fourpence, flour
fourpence, sugar sixpence, tea four shillings, and
coffee half-a-crown. Articles of clothing were also
to be obtained, but no books nor printed matter of
any kind. The work was very hard, and the fore-
men, of whom there were a goodly number, kept
their eyes on us at all times and also called the
names over four times a day, which did not mean
that we had to stop working, for we simply answered
"here!" without straightening our backs. These
precautions were necessary to prevent skulking, for
a man had only to go a few yards from his work to
be out of sight in the bush.

On the afternoon of my third Sunday at this
place some men arrived from Sydney in answer to
an advertisement for pick and shovel men, and three
of them were appointed to my hut as three of our

men had left. We made them welcome and gave them tea, for we were all anxious to hear the latest news from Sydney. When one of them produced a parcel of food wrapped up in newspaper I seized the paper and settled down to study it. I found that the great Blackwall steamer *London* had arrived at Melbourne on her maiden voyage, that she had lost a man overboard between the Cape and Australia, that they had lowered a boat to pick him up, that they had lost sight of the boat, and supposing her to have been swamped, had steamed away, arriving at Melbourne in due course. When the captain had made his report, people blamed him for deserting his boat in such an unfrequented part of the ocean, and when, seven days later, a sailing ship arrived with the missing boat's crew, public opinion rose high against the captain. According to human nature, some people sided with him, and in this newspaper I found a letter in his favour, written by one of the passengers, and signed J. Y. Moffat. That was my brother's name, and I decided that he must be the writer, though I could not understand what he was doing in Australia.

I determined to set out for Melbourne at once, so I went and explained matters to the foreman, who said I had given him every satisfaction, and he went to the trouble of hunting up the clerk to make up my time and give me a cheque for the amount due to me, to be paid in Sydney. I sold my pick and shovel, and next morning at daybreak I started on my tramp of ninety miles to Penrith from whence I could get a train to Sydney.

I was in high spirits, and covered twenty-five miles the first day, but my boots gave out and I had to carry them over my back.

I walked about twenty-eight miles the second day, and camped close to a township where the people told me I was forty miles from Penrith, and that the last train for Sydney left there at six o'clock in the evening. When I lay down to sleep that night I said to myself, " I must be in Sydney to-morrow night ! " and at four o'clock I started, taking with me nothing but a small piece of damper and ham. I knew I had a fine, convict-made road before me and I covered the ground at a rapid pace. At first I asked people on the road how far it was to Penrith, but as I found that, according to them, the distance increased instead of decreased, I gave up asking. Then I was annoyed at people stopping me to ask me why I was walking barefooted, and telling me that I would be lame next day, but I knew my capabilities in that direction.

I arrived at Penrith at five-thirty, but not a man about the station would believe that I had walked forty miles that day. About eight o'clock that evening I arrived in Sydney, a poorer man than when I left it, and I slipped very quietly along George Street and in at the backdoor of my old lodgings, where they seemed very pleased to see me. I washed and brushed up a little before proceeding to the hotel for a suit of clothes, and I was made very welcome in the servants' quarters.

I had just had a good meal at my lodgings, but they insisted on my taking supper with them, so, what with eating and recounting my adventures, "the minutes winged their way with pleasure." I finally bade them good-night and left the hotel with a suit of Sydney tweeds and a white shirt over my arm, but when I reached my lodgings I found everything shut up. I then discovered that it was half-past eleven, and remembered having heard the crusty old proprietor declare he would not open his door after eleven o'clock for his own father. I crossed to the other side of George Street, where there was a roof over the pavement, and laid my clothes down on a shop window-sill while I walked up and down, considering what I should do. Just then along came a policeman who grabbed my clothes, asking if they were mine and what I was doing there with them, and then requested me to accompany him to the police station. When he heard my explanation he said, "I have just had a chat with the girls in Cowan's Hotel, and they told me about you. If you come along and see the inspector on duty it will be all right."

I got on well with the police, for I entertained them with stories of my experiences of bushrangers, gold-digging and so forth, after which they made me very comfortable with plenty of big overcoats, and I slept well.

I found I would have to remain some days in Sydney till the next steamer sailed for Melbourne, and I called on the Marine Superintendent, for he had promised when we were discharged to give any of the crew of the *Tumbulgum* a free passage to any other port if they wanted it. I found him ready to keep his word, and he took me on board the *Wanga Wanga* and told the mate that I was to go to Melbourne by his steamer.

That settled, I looked out for a publisher or bookseller of whom I could enquire if the writer of the letter was really my brother, for he was so well known in the book trade that I was sure they would all know if he was in Australia. I soon discovered a firm of publishers with a Scotch name—Sheriff & Downie—and I walked in and asked for either of the partners. They both happened to be there, and I asked, "Was the letter I saw in the papers a few days ago, signed J. Y. Moffat, written by John Moffat of Stockbridge, and of John Menzies', Edinburgh?"

"Yes, he was the writer," replied one of the gentlemen, "and who are you, pray?"

"I am his brother," I replied.

"Oh, then you will be Henny Moffat!" he exclaimed.

"Yes, and you are Mr. Downie of Dean Street Church," I returned, for I had recognised him when he spoke.

I went home to dinner that evening with Messrs. Sheriff & Downie, and they told me that my brother's health had broken down, and that he had been ordered by the doctor to take a trip to Australia. They were able to tell me that he was coming to Sydney, but not for several weeks, so I kept to my plan of going to Melbourne. They also showed me a copy of the Illustrated London

News containing a picture and account of the S. S. *London*.

The morning after that dinner my attention was attracted by an advertisement in the paper for six smart young men, good shots with revolver and rifle, and good horsemen, with a knowledge of the bush, to run in bushrangers. I thought that would be a good thing, and I made off at once to the address given and was interviewed by a gentleman who explained his ideas in the following manner :—

"I suppose you know," he said, "that Government has offered three hundred pounds a head for the Ben Hall gang, dead or alive, and you will agree that that is a ridiculously small amount for the risk you would run and the expense you would be put to, buying rifles, revolvers, horses, etc. Now, if I can make up a gang of six, myself being the seventh, I will make an offer to Government to run in the gang if they will pay us a thousand pounds a head."

I quite agreed with his views, so he asked me to call that afternoon to see if he had been able to make up the number he required. When I called I learned from his wife that he had chosen his men out of about fifty applicants, and had gone to make his offer in the right quarter, but she expected him back every minute and she was able to tell me that I was one of those chosen. He soon returned, not very well pleased, for the officials thought his price too much, but they told him to call the following day for their decision. He did so, and passed all the afternoon discussing the matter with them, but the most they would agree to was a thousand pounds for Ben Hall and three hundred pounds for each of the other members of his gang; the whole affair therefore fell through. As events proved, the bush-rangers were becoming so bold that Government would gladly have paid the amount we asked to be rid of them, but we were all scattered in a few days.

The day after that affair was settled I joined the *Wanga Wanga* and sailed in the evening for Melbourne. Just as we were on the point of sailing the steward was carried down dead drunk, and the old manager called out from the quay as we backed astern, "Make that young man from the *Tumbulgum* steward; don't trust any of the under-strappers, for I think they are all drunk."

I affected not to hear this, for I was dressed in my best suit of Sydney tweeds and I intended to be a gentleman of leisure for three days, but before we reached Sydney Heads I was dressed in working garb and flying about like a full-powered flunkey. Our cabin passengers were a rough lot, mostly diggers, who went to dinner and to bed in the same clothes; everyone played cards, and money changed hands fast and furiously, but we had no disturbances. My hardest work was dealing out brandies and sodas, shandy-gaff, and so on. I was relieved by a new steward as soon as we arrived at Sandridge, and the captain thanked me for my services and gave me two pounds. I had made three pounds among the passengers, and had left Sydney with another three, so I arrived at Melbourne with eight pounds in my pocket.

I left my chest and bag at a store on the quay, and walked up Elizabeth Street till I noticed the *Argus* office, where I went in and asked if they could give me Mr. Moffat's address. They said he was living at St. Kilda, but they referred me to the bank across the street for the full address. Having obtained it, I went to the railway station, but as I had no idea how far distant my destination might be, I hesitated to buy a ticket until I saw a man, who had asked for a return ticket to St. Kilda, getting change out of a shilling. I then obtained a ticket and was soon at St. Kilda. Having found the house I had been directed to, I was informed that Mr. Moffat had gone for a walk along the beach. I followed him up and soon sighted him coming towards me, reading a book in which he was so absorbed that he did not see me till I walked right into him, as if by mistake. It was a great astonishment to him, for, as I had not written home for a long time, he had no idea in what part of the globe I was to be found.

We passed the day together and he advised me not to remain in Australia, but I thought that, being in Victoria, I would like to have a look through it, as I had done in New South Wales.

John was very anxious that I should go home in the S. S. *London*, and he gave me a letter to the chief officer to introduce me. Next day I went to have a look at the steamer, but as soon as I saw her I said I would never risk my life in a vessel of that build. One of the things to which I took exception was the very large engine-room skylight, all glass on top, which was only two feet high, while the bulwark was about five feet high; sailors will know what that means. I offended my brother very much by my criticisms, especially when I said, " She will go down into the cellar with the first breeze she gets into," and my prediction was fulfilled not long afterwards, for she foundered in the Bay of Biscay and many lives were lost, including that of Booth, the tragedian.

About this time the Confederate cruiser *Shenandoah* arrived in Melbourne and reported that she had something wrong with her screw, and the Government gave her permission to dry-dock under certain restrictions, such as, no increase to be made in her speed, no munition of war to be supplied, no British subjects to join her, to coal and be out of port in eight days. A Royal Proclamation was stuck up in the town warning all British subjects of the consequences of joining, but for all that the cruiser was offering eight pounds a month for A.B.'s, and eight pounds bounty, so I, with about fifty others, went down to Williamstown and joined her. To avoid trouble they shut us up in rooms on the orlop deck and supplied us with everything except a walk on the upper deck.

In a day or two a rumour went round Melbourne that the *Shenandoah* had sunk ten merchant vessels on her passage out, and when it was confirmed, the people who had been feasting and entertaining the captain and officers, refused to acknowledge them in the street. A cordon of police was placed round the ship in dry dock, and when the captain asked to be allowed to remain another day, his request was refused. The time appointed for floating was four o'clock on a Saturday afternoon, but we had just finished dinner when down the after-ladder came the tread of heavy footsteps, and when we looked out we saw what appeared to be the entire police force of Melbourne. There was no way of escape for us, so we marched up single file, and when we reached the upper deck we found a detachment of soldiers standing there with fixed bayonets. We had to pass on shore and stand at attention there while the ship was searched, and then we were allowed to go, after giving our names and addresses, but a man and a boy, who had been found stowed away, were marched off in custody.

The case was tried in the High Court on a very busy day, and it was late in the evening when the sentence—six months' imprisonment—was delivered. The two prisoners were removed into captivity, but the police were apparently not very anxious to find the rest of us. I had every reason to believe that we were all in court, but I did not know the others, nor did I want to, and I slid out very quietly.

I had noticed in the papers an advertisement for pick and shovel men to make a road at a place thirty miles from Melbourne. Next morning, before daylight, I was on the outskirts of the city, steering a new course.

At noon on the second day I arrived at the appointed place, saw the foreman, and started work at once. The working regulations were much the same as in New South Wales, the pay was good, and they took the value of it out of us. If a man wanted to straighten his back for a minute, or to light his pipe, he had first to make sure that the foreman was not in sight.

I thought that the part of the road I was at work on was by far the prettiest place I had seen in Australia; at the time I joined the squad they were making a road along the side of a high, well-wooded hill, and about thirty feet above a beautiful, clear, running stream. A little above us were men building a bridge across the creek, which we would reach in about a week, when our gang would cross over and start a zigzag road over the hill on the other side of the creek. The road was a Government one leading to a town called Woodspoint, and I believe this hill, or mountain, was one of the Hume Range.

I had fallen in with plenty of snakes on my travels, but that creek beat all other places for numbers, while the scorpions outnumbered the snakes; most of our spare time was devoted to killing all we could find. On one occasion one of the men in my hut was bitten by a snake on the calf of the leg, and immediately all hands went to the rescue, but as I was a " new chum " in that respect I stood aside and watched the old colonials' method, which was as follows:—They turned the victim over on his face, and one man lit several candles, holding them all close together in one hand while with the other he held the handle of the frying-pan in the flame. When he thought it was hot enough one man sat down on the injured man to keep him quiet, while another held the leg, then a third man with a sharp jack-knife cut a notch in the leg and scarified the wound with the handle of the frying-pan. I never was afraid of snakes till after that, and even then I think it was not the snake that frightened me so much as the frying-pan handle. About two months afterwards I met the injured man in Melbourne, walking with the aid of crutches, and he told me he had suffered greatly with his leg.

I had been working there only one week when our foreman said to me one afternoon, " Moffat, come to my hut to-night, I want to speak to you." When I made my appearance he explained to me that, the number of men increasing daily, he found it was impossible for him to call over all the names and to watch the skulkers, and he wanted me to assist him. I had held my new appointment for three days when one of the surveyors called to tell our foreman that their cook had gone on the spree and they wanted another one at once. He asked the foreman if he knew of a steady man who could do bush cooking and make himself generally useful for three pounds a week; then, turning to me he asked if I knew anyone.

I answered jokingly, " Oh, I only know myself."

" Well, can you cook ? " he asked.

" Yes, I can cook," I replied, " but I don't happen to be out of a job just now."

Just then someone took away his attention for a minute, and the foreman whispered to me that this surveyor was the boss of the whole concern and that I should not have said I could cook. Then the surveyor turned to me again and said, " Well now, you will have to come with me ; the pay is good and the work not hard. Go and get your swag ready and meet me at the store. I want you to lay in a stock of stores for two weeks ; here is a list of all the stores we could find this morning after the cook cleared out."

I took the opportunity while at the store of obtaining some nice little things such as the average bushman never thought of. I had a horse to carry the stores up to the camp, and as I passed all the men I had lately been working with, I heard many remarks on my change of work. Most of them said " Well done, Scottie ! " but one voice said, " A Scottie, is he ? That accounts for it ! He'll be a surveyor in a month, mark my words." It was impossible for me to pick out the owner of the sneering voice so I ignored the remark.

When I arrived at the camp I found a young lad making the tea ; his work was to look after the horses, but he had had to take the cook's place for that day. There was a small tent for the two of us and the stores, and I could see there was everything I would require for my work, which was to cook for five people, the boy and myself making seven. We had to shift our camp every three or four days, and it was my work also to unrig and rig the tents while the boy got the horses along to a new grazing ground, which was not always easily found with the works on a very steep hill. There was a horse for each of the bosses, two for the tents and stores, and one for the cook to go to the store when necessary. I got on famously, for my bosses were well pleased with my efforts, and they used to say I never gave them the same dish twice in one week, but I did, though it appeared in disguise under another name. My *chef d'œuvre* was Scotch scones *à la* bush; I made them in the usual way, but, having no girdle, I put them on an iron plate and covered them with hot ashes.

One Saturday afternoon, when I had been acting as cook for about four weeks, I went down to the store for a fresh supply of food and there found that the proprietor's family, consisting of his wife and three daughters, had arrived from Melbourne. The wife and eldest daughter assisted in the store, but the two young girls and I went off for a romp in the paddock, where I was so absorbed in turning skipping ropes and rigging up a swing, that I paid no heed to the time till, all at once, I noticed it was getting dark, and I knew I had a bad road before me. I ran into the store and asked for my goods to be sent up next day; then made a rush for my horse, unhobbled him, and rode off as fast as possible.

The new road was soft and heavy for the horse, but he was fresh and went through it well till we got beyond it, and then I had to reduce speed for we were right in the bush and it was quite dark. My horse had confidence, so I let him go and was thinking we were getting on very well when all of a sudden he came to a dead stand, and over his head

I went. He had been brought up by a large tree lying across the track, which had been cut down after we had passed in the afternoon. I sprained both my wrists in my fall, and the pain was so great that I had to walk the rest of the way to the camp, where I had my wrists bandaged and kept dipping them into cold water all night. All Sunday I walked about, watching the boy doing my work, but when evening came I went to the head surveyor and told him I must start for Melbourne at daylight. They all said they were very sorry I had to leave them, but they could not ask me to stay when I was suffering such pain, though they hoped I would return to them as soon as I could. The surveyor gave me a cheque for twelve pounds for wages due, for I had drawn nothing, as they kindly gave me all I required, including tobacco, and he also gave me a sovereign to keep me on my way to town, though I was not penniless, for I had four or five pounds sewn into the waist-band of my good old pegtops.

I took four days to reach Melbourne, where I called on a doctor, who cheered me up by telling me there were no bones broken and he thought I would be fit for work in ten or twelve days. For two weeks I spent my days exploring Melbourne, with occasionally a run to Sandridge to see the shipping and watch the passengers land.

The *London* had sailed and another noted ship was in her berth, the *Royal Standard*, auxiliary screw, a very large ship with a very small captain. There had been a long drought in Victoria, so work in many of the diggings was at a standstill for want of water, and a great many sailor-diggers went down to Melbourne to try and get a ship for home. I heard that there were many bush fires and, thinking I would like to see the bush on fire, I made inquiries as to where I should go. I was advised to take a trip to Ballarat, and as the state of my exchequer allowed it, I set off. We were soon in sight of the fires, and as we drew nearer it became very hot in the train, till at last we came to a stand, for on both sides and in front of the train everything was blazing. The guard and engine-driver had a consultation, with the result that we backed a little and then went full speed ahead till we were safely past the fire.

When we arrived at Ballarat I had a look round the diggings and found plenty like those I had worked at, but the majority were much deeper, and they were heaving up with a single winch. I fell in with some very nice fellows, who wanted me to start digging, but my wrists were not strong enough for shovelling, though they were getting better very quickly. I stayed two days and it did not cost me a penny; indeed, I think they would have kept me a month if I would have stayed. The line was reported clear of fires, and I returned to Melbourne, seeing on the way the black line the destroying fire had left on the greenness of the bush.

CHAPTER XIII

AFLOAT AGAIN

A WEEK after my trip to Ballarat I shipped as A.B. on one of the first ships belonging to the White Star Line, then in ballast, bound to Moulmein, her registered tonnage being 1,067. She had brought out three hundred single women, and was at anchor off Williamstown when I joined her. Four of the outward crew remained, and three of them belonged to the genuine " packet rat " class, while the fourth was an old naval pensioner. The new hands were a strange lot to look at when they arrived, dressed in the clothes they had been digging in and all well coated with dried mud. A number of them brought their swags over their shoulders, and I was the only one who had a chest and bag—I have the same chest yet. We left the next morning, all sober, and some of the men looked quite respectable after they had washed their faces. In picking watches I got into the mate's watch, and he appointed me to join the apprentices, who worked the mizzen-mast; there were six of them and all fine young fellows. The mate put me through a string of questions first, for in those days my youthful appearance told very much against me and made people doubt my knowledge of seamanship. Among other things he asked me if I knew how to make all the knots, such as man-rope, Matthew Walker and Turk's-head.

"Yes, sir," I replied, "and a lot more, such as rose-knot, ground swell ——"

"Oh, that will do!" he broke in, seeing that I knew my business. "They are all nice young fellows, and I will expect you to conduct yourself in a proper manner." These young lads were strictly forbidden to enter the forecastle and I was the only one allowed into their quarters. The first job I had to do in my new position was to send down the mizzen royal yard while the watch was sending down the fore and main royals, and we had ours down on top of the ballast and all the gear with it before the next one had reached the deck.

When I was aloft for the first time and looking down on my new ship I thought she was a strange model, for she looked as square as a tea chest. She was of North American build with a high, full poop, and the top gallant forecastle was also very high which gave the crew nice, airy quarters. The look-out man could walk close to the knight-heads, for she was nearly as broad there as at the break of the forecastle, and her stern showed as much surface to a fair wind as a square lower stu'n-sail.

The captain never interfered with the conduct of the work, and the chief officer was the actual director of affairs. He was a real gentleman and never used bad language to the men, though he insisted on strict discipline, and he managed to gain his ends in a very quiet way. This was my first voyage in a ship with double topsail yards, and we used to bless the inventor with every breeze of wind we had, but when we got into calm, hot weather, we left him alone and started on the man who introduced three quarts of water per day for seamen.

The mate gave me very few orders about the work at the mizzen so I was anxious to have everything up to the mark. We were in a heavy gale off Cape Leeuwin, but had fine weather after we got round, and arrived off Amherst, at the mouth of Moulmein River, in the month of May, 1865.

The rainy season had just started and all hands were at once employed to unbend sails, unreeve all running gear and to send down from aloft everything that could be sent down; even the signal halyards were stowed away in the fore cabin. Then we started to house the ship in with bamboos, of which a good supply had been sent on board. We put whole bamboos from the ridge spar to the pin-rail, and split a large number into four pieces each, which we placed fore and aft about one foot apart, while on top of that we tied the usual Hooghly dunnage mats.

We had not long been thus secured when the rain increased to an extent I had never before—nor since—seen equalled. There were five ships in port with us, and I think the demand was too great for the timber-yards to keep up a steady supply, as we had been in port two weeks before our first raft of teak-wood arrived.

The coolies stowed the cargo and the crew had

only to assist in mooring each raft as it came alongside and to work the winches, of which there were two, placed one on each side of the forecastle deck, while a rope with a running eye was passed over the bow for tipping up the end of the logs to the bow port. There was also a rope rove through a. block at the end of the jib-boom down to the raft on each side, and when a log was wanted a coolie on the raft would put the running eye round the log, the crew would haul away till it was far enough forward to let the after-end clear the stem, and then they would slip on the tipping rope. Our officers took care that we got a good percentage of large logs, for they refused any under twenty inches square, and the bulk of our cargo was made up of logs two feet square.

This work, and the weather combined, soon told upon the health of the crew, and there was nothing whatever to break the monotony except the arrival of the mail steamer every fourteen days. The first serious case of illness occurred in the midshipmen's quarters, and the subject of it, although the youngest member of the ship's company, was one of the strongest, but an attack of jungle fever carried him off, after twelve hours' illness. The next to go was the steward, and then a boy who was suffering from poisoned mosquito bites and had been sent on shore to the hospital for treatment, but caught jungle fever and died there. I got permission to go on shore to see him the day he caught the fever, and when I saw the hospital I thought there would be little wonder if he contracted any vile disease under the sun. It was a primitive structure, built of bamboos and mats, and the floor was mother earth with numerous hollows suitable for the accumulation of pools of water. The patients could lie in bed and watch the frogs disporting themselves in the pools. That visit satisfied me that it would be preferable to die in the forecastle than in that dark, dirty hole.

The next to die from fever was an A.B., and that was the only fatal case in the forecastle, though we had a number in a very bad state who only just managed to pull through. A doctor called every morning at eight o'clock, and those who were ill went aft to see him, but that was of very little service in a number of cases for, with the rainy weather and the type of fever, there was time enough between the doctor's visits to catch the fever and die, and even to be buried. My health remained good, so I was frequently appointed to night watches, and I can remember that the dose prescribed by the doctor was a brown mixture to be given every two hours. Before long the crew fell out with the doctor, and as the trouble had been brewing for some time, it was much worse when it finally broke out. It started with one of the "packet rats" going to consult him about some trouble—I forget what—but the doctor, without waiting to hear him out, said, "Oh, there is nothing the matter with you. Next, please!" But never a "next" came, and no one from the fore end would go to him or speak to him. He eventually left the ship and, strange to say, so did the jungle fever. I have spoken to people who have been to Moulmein of late years and they tell me it is now one of the best and healthiest ports in India.

Early in September we started to throw our roofing overboard, for the weather had become drier, but we were all very pleased when the last raft came alongside and we sailed, after a stay of three months. After two days at sea we picked up a log of teak-wood, thirty feet by one foot eight inches, and we got the long saw to work and cut it up to the carpenter's requirements. Then he and one of the crew, who was also a carpenter, fitted a new rail round the poop, after which they made a very handsome ladder to replace one of very old, soft wood.

Now that she was well down in the water our ship proved to be a very dry vessel, and the daily work went on smoothly, but the food was very far from satisfactory. After our long stay in the rains our biscuits were full of maggots, and the flour was as bad, so we tried all ways of dishing up the biscuits to make them more appetising. Just before meal times one of us would dip a dozen biscuits into water for a few seconds and afterwards put them in a hot oven, by which means the intruders were rendered invisible to our eyes. In the last dog-watch we would break up a bucketful of biscuits, rejecting all maggots we came across, but to make sure of killing the remainder we would pour some boiling water over the biscuits and pour it off after they were well soaked. Then we would stir in what we considered a sufficiency of chopped salt beef or pork, and an onion, if obtainable, and bake it in the oven for half an hour. This concoction was a very common breakfast dish for sailors in those days and it was known as cracker hash. Another dish which was only made on pea-soup days (three times a week) bore the extra-ordinary name of "Dog's Body," and was prepared in the following manner. A few biscuits were placed in a piece of canvas and beaten to a fine powder which was then stirred into the pea-soup which had been left over from dinner, along with some chopped pork, and baked for half an hour. Our most *recherché* dish figured under the euphonious appellation of "Dandy Funk," and it was considered the height of extravagance to make it on any day but Sunday. It was made of powdered biscuits and dripping, moistened with water, and flavoured with half a day's allowance of lime-juice and sugar to taste. Saturday's dinner was a poor one, being only rice, and Jack showed his opinion of it by calling it "Strike-me-blind." Rice cooked in the shore style with milk, sugar and spice, and served as a finish to an already substantial meal is all very well, but it is another story when it is boiled in water with a little salt, as we had it, and forms the entire meal. Once a week we had for dinner what we called "Sky Blue." It is made by putting a small quantity of barley into a large quantity of water with a little salt, and boiling it for two hours—a very good mixture for hospitals and sick-rooms, but poor stuff on which to box-haul yards.

If the biscuits contained maggots there was no

fear of any getting into the salt beef, for forty-eight hours after it had been boiled it became a good substitute for mahogany. There was a Swede among the crew who was very handy with his knife, and he made some very pretty ornaments out of the meat. The one I admired most was a frame for the companion clock, the design being a waterlaid rope round the clock, finished with a true lover's knot, and all cut out of our beef.

When the salt beef was brought into the forecastle for our dinner it was placed on the centre of the floor and a little ceremony enacted in lieu of grace. One of the sailors would approach the brown, hard nugget, plunge his sheath knife into it as far as it would go (which was not very far), turn up his eyes like a dying duck in a thunderstorm, and repeat as follows :—

> " Salt horse, salt horse, what brought you here ?
> You've carted stone for many a year
> From Belfast quay to Ballyhack,
> Where you fell down and broke your back,
> Then they did you sore abuse,
> They cut you up for sailors' use.
> The sailors now do you despise,
> They cut you up and d—— your eyes."

I cannot say that they lived very much better aft than we did forward, for they had their share of the maggots, but they acted very meanly on one occasion. We had two very large pigs on board, one of which was killed off the Cape, but not an ounce of it came forward and there was a lot of grumbling about it. I happened to hear one of the "packet rats" saying, "I'll be upsides with them for that—they won't dirty their mouths with the other one," but I paid no attention to him at the time. In the dog-watch, however, I saw him under the bowsprit hard at work, as I thought, breaking holy-stones, but when I looked again I saw it was a glass lime-juice bottle he was pounding up into powder, which he collected and saved till next day. It was pea-soup day and a lot of our soup was always given to the pig, but on this particular day I noticed that the "rat" emptied his powder into the soup before taking it to the pig. The latter gentleman soon put it out of sight and lay down for his afternoon nap, but he was soon up again, coughing and sneezing and with blood running from his nose and mouth. The captain and the steward were brought on the scene and they decided that the pig was suffering from rapid consumption so the former ordered it to be killed and thrown overboard. Then the wily "rat" stepped out and said, "We'll take it and eat it"—which we did, and enjoyed it too.

The same man frequently secured a fowl for our dinner, and this was the method he used. When the watch went aft early in the morning to wash decks the first thing to be done was to pull out the bottom boards of the hen-coops, wash and return them. This would cause the hens to put out their heads and our friend would adroitly catch one of them by the beak and run a pin or a needle through its head with the result that in a very short time it turned up its toes. When the steward came along to look after his stock and throw the dead ones overboard, there would be someone at hand to say, " Give it to me, steward."

We all did our best with the bad food, for in many ways she was a good, homely ship, but by the time we reached St. Helena scurvy broke out in the forecastle; then it attacked the apprentices, and before we reached the Western Islands the second officer had it badly. We were bound to Cork for orders, and before we arrived at that port nearly all hands were down with the disease. There being a strong westerly breeze on our arrival, the captain sent the pilot cutter on shore for our orders and kept the ship outside for four hours till they returned with orders to proceed to Liverpool. When the news spread even the sick came out to square away for Liverpool and I noticed one of the " packet rats " drop a tear when he heard of our destination. The poor fellow lived only three days longer. We had a good run to Liverpool, and as soon as we got into dock two doctors came on board to inquire into all the cases. I was heaving on the capstan when the mate told me to go down to the doctors, so I went down and was examined in my turn. They pronounced me to be the only man on board with no traces of scurvy, and said they would like to see me next day. I told them I would be at the Sailor's Home, and next day I received a visit from three medical men who asked me to attend at a certain hospital at a certain time, but I drew the line at that and said I intended leaving Liverpool as soon as I received my money.

On our first evening in port two of us joined in a little frolic. Although the night was cold and wet we went for a stroll along Paradise Street, where we noticed a slop-shop displaying the usual intimation, " Sailors' advance notes cashed here," and in the doorway was a pile of " donkeys' breakfasts," which were labelled " *Good sailors'* beds, ninepence." We took that as an insult and immediately started to drag the beds through the muddy street, and when Mr. Abraham came out to rescue his goods we treated him in the same manner. When the police appeared on the scene my chum and I made off to our rooms at the Home, where we quickly changed into our best clothes and marched off through the crowd to the theatre. Being home-ward-bounders with a good pay-day close at hand, we made our way to the dress circle, but we were very much annoyed by everyone directing opera glasses at us throughout the evening.

When we returned to the Home, the night watchman said, " You were lucky to have gone to the theatre to-night, away clear of the row that has been going on in Paradise Street. They say some of our boys dragged the contents of old Abraham's shop through the mud, and jumped on them. Someone told the police that the men who had done it were in Dan Lowrie's, and the police went there and tried to take up people who hadn't been in Paradise Street to-night at all, so the row broke out afresh."

Of course we said we were indeed lucky to have been safely out of the way, and then, like two innocents, we went off to bed; but next day we got another idea. We bought two big sheets of cardboard, a bottle of ink, and a pennyworth of paste, with which articles we manufactured two pairs of dummy opera glasses about two feet long and coated them with the ink. In the evening we went again to the same theatre, and as soon as the opera glasses were levelled at us we returned the compliment by pointing our long tubes at the offenders. In five minutes every glass was put away.

We were paid off on the fourth day, and before closing with this fine old ship, I might say that it was not the fault of the captain and officers that scurvy spread to such an extent. The so-called lime-juice was served out, and double allowance if we wanted it, but the veriest novice knew it was not lime-juice at all. It was more like stale vinegar, and that was the only ship I was ever in where I refused to take my allowance of lime-juice. Being very fond of sweet things, I laid in a stock of sugar at every port, and at Moulmein I also expended two rupees on yams and shalots, to which fact I attribute my immunity from the disease that attacked the rest of my shipmates.

CHAPTER XIV

ROUND THE HORN

I SHAPED my course from Liverpool to Mrs. Boarding-house in Glasgow, and remained there for five weeks, when I shipped as A.B. in the barque *Starlight*, Captain Diable, bound to Callao with a cargo of coal, and from there to proceed to the Chincha Islands to load for some home port. Before signing the articles I went down the quay to have a look at the barque, accompanied by my old chum, Bob, who had also agreed to join, and we were both pleased with her appearance. She was a new ship, having made only one voyage, and had been built at St. John's, N.B.

I have given the captain a French name which describes his character, but he was a Welshman, and so were the mate, second mate, and carpenter, all hailing from the same town in Wales. The rigging and transporting were being carried out by an old friend of mine, who congratulated me on getting so fine a ship with such a nice, fatherly-looking old man as captain. The riggers left us at Greenock, and we proceeded in tow to Ailsa Craig, having previously set all sail, with the wind north-east. Just as we finished hauling in the tow-line, at four o'clock in the morning, we heard the captain's voice at the break of the forecastle: "Come this way, all hands, get the royal gear up." The mate had just said, "That will do, the watch," and naturally we were making for our bunks, but Diable was after us, saying, "There will be no sleep in this ship till the royals and stu'nsails are set." When we had all the gear on deck ready for going aloft, the cook called out, "Coffee," but Diable was again at our heels; "You will get your coffee when all sail is set." Daylight was in by this time, and we were able to have a look at the man who was disturbing our peace, and he was certainly not a "thing of beauty." He was wearing a very dirty discoloured suit of clothes, full of creases, and his face, which was naturally very dark, was covered with a good coating of coal dust, for the coal still lay about the hatchways as she had finished loading, while to add to these embellishments it was easily seen that he carried a full cargo of whisky. It was eleven o'clock before we were allowed to go to our breakfast; we were then off the Calf of Man, and our last meal had been a pannikin of tea and a biscuit between Dumbarton and Greenock.

The crew consisted of two Kanakas (South Sea Islanders), and one Italian, who could speak no English, two East Coast fishermen, an old Highlander, an old man from Ayrshire, Bob and myself, also a boy from the Isle of Man and one from Manchester. The Italian and Rory, the Highlander, were good sailors, and the latter's language was at least as intelligible as the Welshmen's. Old

Jack, the man from Ayrshire, was considerably over seventy years of age, and we never let him go aloft if we could help it; he was in my watch, and we made the arrangement that if there was any climbing to be done when I was at the wheel he was to come and relieve me. He was a good old sailor, and well-read, though he had given way to drink, but when he was at sea out of the way of temptation he was a clear-headed man. Very early in the passage the mate appointed me sail-maker, but I seized an opportunity of finding him alone to suggest that old Jack would be the best man for the sails and that I was more fit for the harder work about the deck. He replied in a whisper that he was only carrying out the captain's orders, and he added, "Take my advice and don't try to alter any of his arrangements or it will send him mad. He is an awful man, I can tell you."

These few words from the mate let the cat out of the bag, and assured us that we had made a great mistake in joining the *Starlight*.

Before we were out of the Channel we were put on our allowance of food and water, and we could have managed well enough on that if it had been honestly done, but we were cheated in every weight and measure. For instance, the three-quart measure for the water was stamped, according to the law, about half an inch under the rim, the type being about half an inch in height, and Captain Diable insisted that the water should just touch the mark; we were therefore cheated out of an inch in each day's allowance. Four and a quarter biscuits went to the pound, but we had four served out to us daily for one year (the length of the voyage), which meant that each of us were swindled out of twenty-two pounds, and for the whole crew the shortage would amount to two and a half hundred-weight. That may not seem very serious to the uninitiated, but those who have lived on the bare scale sanctioned by the Board of Trade will know that it is small enough without any roguery.

One could not expect much of the quality of provisions served under such a master, and as a matter of fact the only good article on board was the biscuits, or Liverpool Pantiles, as we called them. The beef and pork were so antiquated that it would have been fruitless to have tried to find a man alive who had been present at the killing or packing, but none of it went to waste, for Diable gave us to understand that the bone had been weighed out to him and that he would weigh it out to us, with the result that some days our allowance was practically all bone. An important article of food with us was split peas, but never in my life, on board or on shore, in stores or in fowl-houses, have I seen such dirty rubbish masquerading under the name of split peas. Instead of being composed of the usual peas split in two, it was a heterogeneous collection of small particles, of which a large percentage was dirt. Charitably disposed persons might suggest that it was the sweepings of a bin, but there was far too much foreign matter in it for that explanation to hold good.

I will leave the food question for the present and

introduce another shipmate whom I have hitherto omitted to mention. His name was Jack, his colour white, and his breed bull-terrier; which sums up the most ferocious dog I have ever fallen in with, and a fit companion for his master. He usually slept at the captain's door, which was beside the man at the wheel, and when Diable came out the dog would stand at attention—he had neither ears to prick nor tail to wag for they had been cut off short. At the door stood a tin dish containing water with a piece of sulphur in it for the dog's refreshment, but we took good care that the dog should not be pampered with such luxuries; we looked on that dish of water as a perquisite for the man at the wheel. When we had a big piece of work on hand, such as " about ship," the captain would go on top of the after-house to give his orders while Jack went to the main-braces, and if we did not run in the slack sharply he was on to us. When we made fast and ran to the fore-braces the dog would follow up and get hold of the last man with dire results to the unfortunate. I do not suggest that the dog acted thus from his own knowledge of seamanship; he was directed by signs from his master. The poor Kanakas had by far the largest share of bites. As soon as we got to sea we found we were not allowed oil to burn in the fore-castle, even for the first few nights, while the cook was collecting slush (dripping). After a few days we had enough fat to start with, and we had a light for three nights only, when the captain gave the cook orders not to let us have any more slush as he would require it all to coat the ship's side on the homeward passage.

Here was a nice state of affairs; bound on one of the longest voyages a ship can make and to be daily cheated over our food and water, and even to be robbed of the boilings of our own beef which had already been dishonestly weighed, being lifted straight out of the pickle on to the scale, covered with rock salt. As a matter of fact we got only fourteen ounces to the pound. The first night we had a slush lamp we spent the evening discussing what steps we could take to improve matters, for they seemed to us to be unbearable, and old Jack took the chair, but we did not come to any decision that night. Afterwards, when we had to spend the long evenings in our bunks without a light, old Jack, whose bunk was next to mine, used to entertain me with stories of the City Line of ships that sailed from Glasgow to Bombay and Calcutta. He used to say to me, "If you are spared to get home you must try them. The ships are well managed and they feed you well, nothing weighed out, but just full and by"—that is sufficient without waste. "They never keep you up in your afternoon watch, and they are able to about ship with the watch." Other good things included a bottle of oil per week for each watch and a bucket of water for each watch to wash in weekly. Altogether he gave me such glowing accounts of the City Line that I there and then resolved to try them when I got back to Glasgow again.

We thought it was the last straw when, after one

week at sea, the order went forth that we were to have no afternoon watch below. A special meeting was held that night (in the dark) to discuss this latest injustice, but, angry as old Jack was, he counselled us to lie low for we were weaker than the after-guard. "The poor South Sea men are no use," he said, "for they can hardly walk along the deck; the Italian doesn't know a word of English, Rory and I are too old for any rough and tumble work, and the boys are too young, so you see the strongest party is aft."

During the day I was sailmaking on top of the after-house with no one near me, but the captain called at times to see how I was getting on, and I soon found that he knew exactly my rate of progress. One day the second mate had called me to help them to set the topmast and lower stu'nsails, and when Diable came up after his afternoon nap he turned over my sail to examine it. He evidently saw there was not sufficient work done, for he turned his black, scowling face to me, and demanded: "What have you been doing this afternoon?" I explained how I had been called away, and the poor second mate had to bear the brunt of it, and I had an evil look for my share. I tried to say no more than "Yes, sir," or "No, sir," to the captain whenever possible, for I noticed that he did not like to be spoken to by such inferior animals as we sailors. He also objected to us speaking to each other during working hours on deck, and if anyone ventured to start a song in the forecastle in the evening it would bring down fresh wrath on our devoted heads. One night I had a quiet, confidential chat with one of the officers, in the course of which I asked, " Have you any more like him in Wales ? "

" Yes," he replied, " the captain's brother was as cruel to his sailors as our man is. On one voyage his crew mutinied, secured him by a rope made well fast to him, threw him overboard and towed him astern till he asked for forgiveness and promised to do better in future. He finally had his certificate cancelled."

This furnished me with food for thought during the long evenings in my bunk without a light.

We were about three days clear of the south-east trade winds, when one evening, just as it was getting dark, the order was given to set the main-top-gallant stu'nsail. The man who had gone aloft to shake out the sail called out from the main-top to let go the down-haul, and Bob, who was standing beside it, let it go. The captain on top of the house repeated the request, thinking no one had heard it, and Bob, thinking it was the man in the top speaking again, answered sharply, " It's all gone ! " The captain flew into a great passion, jumped down and into his room, and in a minute was out again with a cutlass in his hand, shouting, " Bob, come here ! " By this time we (the watch below) were all at the forecastle door to see what was happening, for the roars of the captain might have been heard a mile away. Bob had come forward, but I said to him, " Go on aft, Bob, he won't use the cutlass," so he went.

As soon as he was near enough Diable raised the

cutlass and brought it down with all his might on the back of Bob's head, making a great gash about four inches long, from ear to ear. Of course Bob dropped on the deck, and by the time I reached him he was lying in a pool of blood. I stooped to examine the wound, but seeing that bright steel blade still in the hands of a madman, I stood up and said, " Put that sword away, please ! "

He dropped it at once, and with the same hand quickly snapped up an iron belaying pin from the main fife-rail and gave me a terrific blow on the left side of my head. When I recovered my senses I found that the captain had left the scene of slaughter, and old Jack and the mate were trying to patch up my head. The captain soon returned and ordered the watch to carry me to his room, which they did, thinking I was to be taken there for treatment. So I was, but it was bad treatment. As soon as they had all gone out the captain lifted the lazaret hatch which was in the middle of his cabin floor, and ordered me to go down, but it was impossible for me to execute that order. I found when I tried to speak that my mouth would not open, and I was in such pain that I did not care what happened to me next. Diable then called in the mate and ordered him to put me down, which he had to do, though most unwillingly, and he did his best to avoid hurting me, but by the time I reached the bottom I had collapsed again.

By and by the captain came down, and, making me stand up on a flour-barrel, he handcuffed me with my hands behind me, and with a gasket, traced my hands up to the beams. My feelings throughout the night can be better imagined than described, and it did not even ease them to hear that the captain was suffering as much as I was, though in a different way. He had delirium tremens so badly, that it was a wonder he did not jump overboard to get away from his imaginary tormentors. It would be hard to say what would have happened to me if the ship had given a roll that night, but I should probably have lost both arms.

Next forenoon Diable released me, telling me to go forward, and not to forget that he was captain of this ship. When I reached the forecastle, I found old Jack had my coffee ready, but to eat was out of the question, for my scalp seemed to be full of broken bones, and the most I could do was to suck a biscuit after it had been well soaked. Jack held up a little looking-glass for me to see my face, and then I understood why the old man was crying as he attended to me. When I looked in the glass, I saw the ugliest face I had ever seen: it was all the colours of the rainbow, with a few odd tints thrown in, and the left side of my head was swollen so much that my nose appeared to have shifted over to the right side. My arms were of no use to me for several hours, through having been bound up all night. My head gradually healed up, and I was never off duty, but it was a long time before I could eat a biscuit in its hard state. Bob recovered before long, for, in his case, the damage had been a clean cut.

The captain disappeared from our sight for a few

days, after he had thus distinguished himself, and when he did come on deck again, he was very tame, but that soon wore off. About the middle of June we were close in to the land at Staten Island—not a very desirable position for us in the dead of winter in a ship without a bogey or a lamp. We went a long way south, and saw a great number of icebergs, which are very beautiful things in the daylight, but very dangerous at night. It was dark from 4 P.M. to 8 A.M., but although it was very trying to be so far south in mid-winter, we had no very bad weather in those latitudes. We had two slush lamps rigged in the fore-cabin, where we had to side-stitch our fine weather sails, for we had still to work in our afternoon watches, and by the light of our own fat.

I wonder how many sailors have been set to side-stitch the summer sails in their watch below in winter off Cape Horn, by the dim glimmer of a slush lamp. My share of look-out duty was given to the two Kanakas, who could not handle the palm and needle, so that I might have more time for the sails. In due course we bore away to the northward, with the prospect of warmer weather before us, but first we had to encounter the "roaring forties." Just as we were drawing near them, we got into a very heavy gale, and the cold seemed greater than ever. We were furling the foresail one forenoon when the gale was increasing rapidly, and the cold was so intense that we found it a very difficult matter. Everybody was on the yard except the captain, and old Jack at the wheel, and we had made several attempts but had failed. The stu'nsail booms were traced up, and I was in at the bunt with the mate and second mate, getting ready to try again, when I looked out at the port yard-arm and saw the two Kanakas looking as if they did not care whether we picked up the sail or not, so by the help of the stu'nsail booms, I walked out to liven them up a bit. When I reached the first man, I asked him what was the matter, and he looked up at me with a most pitiful face, letting go his hold of the jackstay and showing me his hand. All the flesh of it was sticking to the jackstay, and the other Kanaka was in the same plight. Those were two severe cases of frost-bite, causing us to lose the services of two members of our already too small crew. Before we reached the deck, we noticed a very big, broken sea, close to the weather bow, and at that moment the ship took an unusually heavy, weather roll, with the result that the sea broke on board, and filled her fore and aft. What a sight to look down upon? I could see nothing but the heads of the towing bits on the forecastle, and the galley funnel. My first thought was for the man at the wheel, but I saw his head just over the house, and knew he was safe. The captain was nowhere to be seen, and I was just about to say " Thank the Lord ! " when I discovered him up the mizzen rigging.

Here we were on a ship completely engulfed in a full-sized Cape Horn sea, not knowing what damage she had received, nor if the main-hatch could stand the pressure, and not caring, for she was such a floating hell to one and all of us. When the deck was clear of water, we came down to see the extent of damage the ship had sustained, but we found she had behaved well, and only a few odds and ends had gone overboard, the captain's dog being one of them. After we had put things shipshape and hauled in the ropes, for all the running gear had been washed overboard, I asked the mate if he had told the captain about the two cases of frost-bite, to which he replied in the affirmative, but Diable did not come near the forecastle for two days. We lifted the Kanakas into their bunks with their clothes and oilskins on, just as they came down from aloft, but we were unable to comfort them with any warm food, as our dinner had been washed out of the galley, and it was well on in the afternoon before we could get them a pannikin of tea. Our day's allowance of pork and the pea-soup had all disappeared, and of course *we* had to suffer the loss—not the captain : he could not be expected to provide a second dinner !

We missed our pork for more reasons than one, for we each used to cut off a piece of fat about one inch square, reeve a small piece of rag through it, stand it on our chest lid and light the rag, and so got a faint glimmer of light while we took our tea. As soon as tea was over we would blow out the light, unreeve the rag, and put the fat into our mouths by way of a delicate finishing-touch to the meal !

When at last the violence of the gale had decreased, I was sent up to loosen the foresail, and I saw the flesh of the Kanakas still adhering to the jackstay.

After the foresail was set, the captain came forward for the first time to see the sick men, bringing a candle with him, for it was a very low, dark forecastle. I held the candle for him while he examined the men, and he opined that if they would get up and wash their hands they would soon be better, but he did not offer them the water to wash in. I called his attention to the state of their legs and ankles, and when he asked what caused it I replied that they were dog-bites. The venemous scowl he bestowed on me lives in my memory yet. Nothing resulted from that visit: neither water to wash, ointment to dress, nor bandage to bind the afflicted men's hands was ever sent forward.

We soon encountered another gale, and all hands were called to take in the foresail, the second mate going on to the forecastle to let go the fore-tack, but he found that it was made fast on the capstan and had fouled. He called us up with capstan bars to heave and lift the pawls, walk back the capstan, and clear the tack, but when the pawls were lifted the capstan took charge, and everybody was knocked head-over-heels, for Cape Horn gales in the dead of winter are not conducive to alertness. However, we all escaped injury except the second mate, who received a blow on the side of his head from a bar. For some time it appeared to be very serious, and he was unfit for duty till the day before we arrived at Callao; thus we had an officer and two men on the sick-list in a half-manned ship, and we were not yet half-way through the roaring forties. The fore-cabin had been filled with water during the first gale, so that put an end to the side-stitching.

We eventually got through the stormy latitudes, but when we reached mild weather we had another trouble to contend with—the foul smell arising from the frost-bites. Those who have had no experience can scarcely imagine what it is like, and it cannot be described. We had finally to leave the forecastle and sleep on the deck, but even there and at the wheel the obnoxious smell reached us, and as the weather grew warmer it became worse. There the poor fellows lay without any attention from aft, and all that we could do was trifling, but they never seemed to complain, though they might have waxed eloquent had they been able to speak our language.

I acted for the second mate while he was laid up, and I noticed that the captain grew more gracious every day—no doubt because the whisky was done —but nevertheless we had resolved to report him to the British Consul at Callao.

CHAPTER XV

FIGHTING AT CALLAO

IN due course we arrived at Callao, and on the morning after our arrival we all went aft and asked for permission to go on shore to see the Consul. Captain Diable recommended us to go back to our work, but we insisted that if he did not allow us to go we would hoist a blue shirt on the fore-lift. There were two British frigates in the port and he knew they would answer that signal promptly, so he thought better of it, but, though he granted permission for four of us to go, he added that we might be away from ten till twelve and if we exceeded our time he would have us arrested. Then, seeing we were on the war-path, he hurriedly got into a boat and reached the shore before us, but we did not realise then the little game he was playing. He went straight to the Consulate, and though we did not know what took place there, it was a well-known fact that, in those days, the gift of a ham or a cheese just out from home was sufficient to turn the scales of justice in the captain's favour.

When we made our appearance before Her Brittanic Majesty's representative he inquired what ship we came from.

" The *Starlight*, sir," we replied.

" Well, what do you want ? " he demanded.

Old Jack led off with his log-book in his hand, but he had barely started when the Consul jumped to his feet, and pointing to the door, said, " Go on board your ship, or I'll send you to jail for six months ! "

That closed the loop-hole for escape in that direction, but we had another shot in the locker. As we returned to our ship we determined to go to one of the frigates for assistance, and when we drew alongside of the *Leander*, I was pleasantly surprised to see my old master " Paddy " on the bridge. The master-at-arms came down to the boat to ask our business, and we gave him an idea of it. He went up to report, and returned to tell us we were too late for that day, but we should come back next forenoon at seven bells. We knew that would be impossible, for Captain Diable would not allow us to leave the ship again, but our time was up, and we returned to the *Starlight*.

That was one of the greatest mistakes of my life, for if I had insisted on seeing " Paddy," Captain Diable would probably have received his deserts and we would have escaped from the indescribably cruel and fiendish treatment we had endured for over four months. It may be said that I should have been justified in running away under such circumstances, but it was contrary to my nature to throw up anything I had undertaken because it did not come up to my expectations, and, moreover, I was Scotch and had twelve pounds of wages owing to me! When we returned to our ship we found that the two Kanakas had been taken to the hospital while we were on shore.

Callao at this time was in a great state of unrest; the Spanish fleet was expected every day, for Spain and Peru were at loggerheads, and it was known that a number of Spanish ships of war had rounded the Horn. There was a great demand for labourers to fill bags of sand to protect the men working the guns which had been placed all round the bay, but principally along the low beach at the head of it. There were then in the bay four English sailing ships, as well as the two frigates, also two American ships and one American corvette or frigate. We had been in port only a few days when it was reported that the Spanish fleet was close at hand, and up went the price of men to man the guns on the beach, the best price—one hundred pounds for the engagement, or bombardment—being offered to men who could pass the examination in gunnery. When I heard of this I asked Captain Diable to let me go in for it, saying that he could not work cargo while the town was being bombarded, and I would come back when it was all over, but he would not hear of it, though he was not drinking then and was in the best of humours because he had scored a victory over us at the Consulate.

One afternoon a small Spanish vessel came into the bay under a flag of truce, and asked all the ships to shift their anchorage clear of the town. We at once hove up the anchor and let her drop out of the bay, clear of all guns, to patiently await the morrow.   After tea, we were all sitting on the forecastle, chatting and looking for the fleet, but Bob and I had something up our sleeves.   If we could only reach the beach, we could walk back to the town and offer our services, and we thought that when we returned, the captain would be glad to see us, for Callao was what Jack calls " a Shanghai port."   At this particular time the boarding-masters were so concerned about the probable bombardment of their town, that they had never come near our ship, or we would, doubtless, have had a smaller crew.

As soon as the captain and officers retired to their rooms, Bob and I set to work, assisted by old Jack. We first got up the long hold-ladder and lashed on two cross-bars near each end, like a painter's stage, and then we got four deck planks out of the 'tween-decks.   We next got the ladder overboard, and I went down on to it with some lashings, though it was, naturally, a very unsteady platform for me to work on.   The planks were lowered down to me, one at a time, and I placed them with their ends resting on the cross-bars, two on each side of the ladder, and lashed them there.   When I had finished I called to Bob to come down, and half an hour after we had started our raft building, we were paddling for the shore, our paddles being two bottom boards out of our bunks.   We reached the shore safely, but not dry-shod, and hauling our raft up on the beach, we covered it over with sand and shingle, and made off for the town as quickly as we could, so as to arrive there before everyone had gone to bed. But when we reached our destination, we found there was no thought of sleep in the town that night; carts were driving ammunition to the guns, numbers of people were removing themselves and their valuables out of the zone of danger; shopkeepers were barricading their doors and windows; everything was bustle and excitement, and we saw no idlers about.

We were directed to the office of the Captain of the Port, but when we found that gentleman, we discovered that he could not speak a word of English. An interpreter was called in, and we were at once passed over to a man-of-warsman to be examined in gun-drill. He had no ribbon on his cap, but I concluded he belonged to one of the British frigates, because he was too clean and tidy for an American. I was well up in my gun-drill, and he was satisfied in two minutes, so I spoke up on Bob's behalf.

"My friend here," I said, "is not well up in his drill, for he was only in the R.N.R. one year, but if you can manage to place him at a gun with me, I will knock something out of him."

"That's all right," he answered, without asking Bob any questions, "but he will only get fifty pounds." After making his report, he brought us out a copy of the contract, and another naval man was then sent with us to show us our gun. It proved to be an ancient thirty-two-pounder, probably belonging to one of the Peruvian ships which were too old to bring into action. We undertook to be at our gun at daybreak, and made sure of that by lying down beside it, under the lee of the sand-bags. We emptied two of them to sleep in, and though very wet when we lay down, we got up quite dry after our sleep.

Soon after daybreak great squads of men came marching along under charge of two English petty officers, who told off eight men to each gun. They were a miscellaneous collection of sailors, soldiers, cow-boys, street-sweepers, and various specimens of the genus "wastrel." I considered myself lucky in getting one dressed as a man-of-warsman, but I soon discovered that his rating was "Jack in the Dust," and all the gunnery he knew was harmless. I might explain that this name is given to a man, usually an ordinary seaman, who is appointed to assist the purser's steward to serve out bread, flour, and other stores, so that he is usually very dusty.

As soon as I got my complement of men, I started to drill them a little, but it was a difficult matter, for I knew no Spanish, and they knew no English, but with the use of signs, and an occasional application of my spare trigger line, we proved as good as our neighbours. I soon noticed that I was the only man in charge of a gun who was not in uniform, and I was surprised that I had been taken on at the top figure. At noon the first Spanish ship hove in sight, rounding San Lorenzo, and before long there were five in the bay, but our order to fire was not given until the Spaniards had opened fire on the town. Our guns, of which there were about eighty or a hundred, were all ready trained, and our first round wrought considerable destruction among the fleet. We continued firing as fast as we could load, occasionally receiving orders on which ship to lay our guns, but we had to use our own discretion very much as to that, for there was only one man who could speak English to us. I would have liked to watch the progress of the engagement as sails were rent, and yards and masts came crashing down, but I was too busy watching the loading, for my "greenies" were quite capable of putting in the shot without the powder if I took my eyes off them. Plenty of shot passed over our heads without striking our sand-bags, and very little damage was done in the town, as the buildings were of mud. The largest ship came close up to our guns at my part of the beach, but her marksmanship did not improve, the elevation being too great, which was a blessing to us. By three o'clock we noticed the outside ship to be broadside on, with her jib-sheets to windward, which told the seafaring portion of us that she was going to show us a clean pair of heels.

At four o'clock the "cease firing" was sounded, though we had still to stand to our guns, but I was very anxious to hear what damage our side had sustained, so I told Bob to go along towards the town, and to come back as soon as possible with his report. It was long after dark before he returned, but when he did make his appearance, he had much to tell me.

When the enemy sent the first broadside into the town, the people were panic-stricken, and thousands rushed to the railway station, where they took tickets for anywhere, the clerks passing them out as quickly as possible, taking the money but giving no change. The people, however, soon discovered that the Commandant had stopped all trains, and they started to walk to Lima, a distance of eight miles. The road between Callao and Lima had never been so busy as it was that afternoon, and there were hundreds toiling along, footsore and weary, who owned horses and carriages, but in their excitement had completely forgotten the fact. Others, again, with fewer worldly possessions but more *savoir faire*, seeing the horses and carriages standing idle, coolly borrowed them for the day and drove in comfort past the rightful owners as they made slow and painful progress on "Shank's pony." The shop-keepers who had not taken the precaution to barricade their premises the previous night were seized with panic at the sound of the first shot, and hurriedly fled, leaving their shops open and un-protected, no matter how valuable the stock.

Now Callao contained a very large number of the lowest dregs of humanity, including beach-combers and sailors' boarding-house keepers, who were fully alive to the advantage (to them) of such a state of affairs, and they "grasped the skirts of happy chance." I think I might safely say there were hundreds of such men absolutely penniless before the bombardment began who, three hours after-wards, were wealthy men ready to book as first-class passengers by the next mail steamer as soon as the Pacific Steam Navigation Company's office opened its doors again.

Bob was very fond of a "wee drappie," and after

he had finished his yarn I remarked, "The pubs are open, anyway; I can tell that by my nose."

"Of course," he said, "the pubs are like the other shops; they have been opened by the public for the good of the public, and I had a drink, like other people. I think the best thing we can do is to clear out of this and take a share of the good things that are going."

"Shut up, and go to sleep!" was my last order, and I proceeded to set them a good example by jumping into a hole I had dug for that purpose before dark. I awoke at daybreak to find that someone had covered me with a soldier's coat, which no doubt accounted for my sound sleep, and I crawled out of my hole to rouse my companions, but to my astonishment they had all vanished. I walked along to several of the other guns but found them all deserted, and I hardly knew how to act under these new circumstances, which were not very agreeable to me. At last I resolved to take back my gun stores, cutlass, etc. to the office of the captain of the Port, where I had obtained them, and then to return to my ship. Breakfast was out of the question, for the cooks, in common with others in much higher appointments, were all looking out for plunder, but the scene had changed by the time I arrived in town, for people were crowding back from Lima to find their premises empty or being emptied, so a free fight was soon in progress, and sticks, knives and revolvers were all pressed into active service.

I made my way to the office, where I found only a

lad in charge, and as his entire knowledge of the
English language was comprised in the one word
" yes," I was not much wiser after the following conversation :—

" Have you dismissed all the men from the South
Fort ? "

" Yes."

" What have I to do now ? "

" Yes."

" There's the lock, sight, priming wire and this
box of tubes; will you take them from me ? "

" Yes."

" I would like something to eat. Do you know
where I could get it ? "

" Yes."

" Well, where ? "

" Yes."

" Oh, go to Jericho ! " I exclaimed, and banged
out of the office in a rage.

To reach my raft I had to traverse about a mile
of streets in a rather shady locality, and found " the
battle raging loud and long," as I picked my way
along like a cat at a dog show. I saw numbers of
men spread out on the streets, some suffering from
wounds, others from wine, and later on I discovered
Bob suffering from both causes, but he was too
drunk for me to take him along with me.

At last I got safely on to the beach at the other
end of the town and found my raft just as I had
left it. There was a light air of fair wind to take
me off, and I was well received by the mate and
second mate ; Captain Diable, fortunately, being on

shore. The mate told me in confidence that he thought the captain would say nothing about my escapade if Bob turned up all right, but if he were Shanghai-ed Diable might blame me for it.

"I know where Bob is," I said. "I'll go for him as soon as I have had a biscuit and a drink of tea."

"No, no," said the mate, "I can't let you go. We must trust to his following you."

The captain arrived about two hours later and I was glad to see Bob in the boat with no bones broken, though his figure-head was cut and carved like a Maori chief. The captain's first orders were to heave the anchor up to go back to our berth in the bay. There was a very light air of wind off the land and we set all jibs, staysails and spanker, but it hardly moved her, so we ran a small kedge out and by midnight we were anchored in our old position in the bay.

We had just turned-to next morning when news came from the hospital that both the Kanakas had died during the night and would be buried that afternoon. On hearing this four of us went aft to ask the captain for permission to attend the funeral. Old Jack, acting as spokesman, pointed out that although our late shipmates were of a dusky hue they, like ourselves, were strangers in a strange land, and all we could do for them now was to show this little bit of respect to their memory.

Captain Diable, with a grin on his evil face, refused point blank to let any of us attend the funeral, but he evidently got a fright for he did not venture out of the ship till evening, when the funeral would be over, and he watched us all day like a cat watching a mouse. No doubt he had a guilty conscience, and I hope the spirits of those dead men haunted him for the remainder of his life!

If Jack and I had been allowed to go we would have interviewed the doctor as to the cause of death, for we were convinced that the primary cause was dog-bites. The men's ankles and hands had been bitten over and over again and they were covered with open sores that cold morning off the Horn when we were kept so long on the fore-yard, and it was not to be wondered at that the frost nipped them.

Work went on as usual for a few days, till one morning, when we were all sitting at breakfast, I heard some one making a rattling noise on our cable, but I paid no attention to it, though others in the forecastle did, for it was a pre-arranged signal from a boarding-master that a boat was under the bow to take the crew on shore. The result was that only the two East Coast fishermen, old Jack and Rory, and myself were left, for Bob went with the others, after vainly trying to persuade me to accompany him, and that was the last I saw of him for a number of years. I met him only once more, so I will describe our encounter and then let him drop out of my story.

On a cold, winter evening about five o'clock I was returning to my lodgings in Paisley Road, Glasgow, from the Navigation School, and during a heavy squall of hail I ran into somebody coming up with a fair wind, who said, " Hello, Harry, is that you ? "

" Why, Bob ! " I exclaimed, " where did you spring from ? " Then, noticing that he wore uniform, I added, " Have I the pleasure of addressing Captain ——— ? "

" Yes," he said, " you have. I'm the captain of the six P.M. down express to Ayr ! "

He explained that he had left sea, and had received very good promotion in the service of the Glasgow & South-Western Railway. I have never seen Bob since.

To return to Callao — when the five of us responded to the mate's call of " turn to " after breakfast he asked where the others were. " Gone ashore, sir," we replied. He reported to the captain who, along with the second mate, accompanied him forward and they went into the forecastle, taking old Jack with them to point out the bunks and belongings of the men who had left, but they were too late. Our mates had not left much behind them, but what they did leave was shared out between us before they had been gone ten minutes. All I claimed was Bob's surplus biscuits and a cold weather bed-rug which I had made for him as a present a number of years before, and which he had left behind him because it was too bulky for him to carry away.

After three or four weeks at Callao we sailed for the Chincha Islands for a cargo of guano, and arrived there about week later. We shipped three

Peruvians for the run to the Islands and back, but none could speak a word of English and their knowledge of seamanship was absolutely nil. Two of the original crew had died, and four had deserted, leaving eight of us forward—just about half the requisite number.

CHAPTER XVI

OUT OF THE WORLD FOR THREE MONTHS

THE Chincha Islands lie about ninety miles south of Callao, and are three in number, being named North, Middle, and South Islands, according to their position. The guano on North Island was nearly finished when I was there, on Middle Island it was half worked off, and about two-thirds still remained on South Island. The channel, or anchorage, between South and Middle Islands is about one-third of a mile in width, and between North and Middle it is half a mile. Most of the ships anchored there, but the *Starlight* took up her berth in the narrower channel.

When a ship arrived she would anchor about a mile off and furl sails, and by the time that was done all the ships that were in port would have sent a boat to assist in towing the newcomer to her berth. The mate would then pass a tow-rope over the bow, a number of boats would get hold of it and pull away on their oars, and if the boats were very numerous they would pass out another rope. The work was done well and quickly, for the weather was always fine about the Islands, and there were no shoals.

When a ship had finished loading the crew would burn a tar-barrel, or some other kind of bonfire, after dark, and make as much noise as possible by means of ringing bells, cheering, etc., till their throats were dry, when the captain would give orders for the main-brace to be spliced. All this commotion gave notice to the other ships to send their boats at daybreak to tow the first ship out from her anchorage.

There were only three small ships near the *Starlight*, and a large American, named the *Harry Bluff*, but she lay at some distance seaward and was really out of the channel. We were very close to the loading shoots, the nearest being only five hundred yards from the ship, and they were all in sight, except one called the " Cape Horn," which was round a point on the weather side. The sea was never very rough, except at the full and change of the moon, but still it was always a ticklish job to load a boat at " Cape Horn." On our passage down from Callao our carpenter had raised the gunwale of the long-boat six inches to give her more carrying power, for until Captain Diable could hire or buy something in the boat or barge way, our long-boat was all that we had to start work with.

We had not enough men to man the winch handles, so a horse and a quantity of hay were brought us by boat from the mainland, which was twelve or fourteen miles distant. A great number of the ships had a horse, and they were all, like ours, called Charlie. The men who brought our Charlie told me he had never done any other work in his life, and he certainly understood all about it, but he was a mere bag of bones and the date of his birth was lost in the mists of antiquity, for his teeth had long since departed. The guano was hove up in tubs with a single rope, the hauling part being rove through a block and made fast to the middle of a yoke that hung across Charlie's stern. When the tub was hooked on, the mate at the gangway would call to Charlie, who would then proceed along the deck at a funeral pace which all the rope-ends in the ship could not alter. He always came to a stand when the bottom of the tub cleared the rail by a quarter of an inch, and nothing would induce him to go a step further.

We received only one boat-load the first week—about ten tons—and we badly wanted a barge to carry about fifty tons. About this time Captain Diable heard that a Yankee ship, which had just finished loading, had a barge for sale, so we manned a boat and took him to the ship, and while he was in the cabin, striking a bargain, we had a chat with some of the crew. We found that she had been what Jack calls a very hot ship, with plenty of fighting, for their captain had been a great bully, but death had removed him three weeks previously, and they had buried him on North Island.

"Tell me his name," I said, "and I will have a look when I go there. I suppose you put up a wooden cross with his name on it?"

"Oh, no, my boy," said one of them, "there is nothing of that sort here. You just take the corpses up on top of the hill, over towards the north-east end, and lay them down. There isn't enough earth on the island to cover a mouse."

Then they told me the true story about how they had treated their captain. The carpenter built a big, strong coffin with inch and a half pine (the captain weighed twenty stones and measured six feet two inches), and all the crew went to the funeral except the mate—now captain—and the cook. When they arrived at the proper burial-place they unscrewed the lid and threw the body over the cliff into the sea—a fall of from eighty to a hundred feet—as the last little bit of spite they could show.

"Did you bring the coffin back?" I asked.

"No fear!" they replied, and one of them added, "See here, sonny, if you want a good serviceable box for your old man I can recommend that one. It's well made with inch and a half pine and secured with four inch brass screws."

This was said by way of a joke, but I had an eye to business, so I asked, "If I managed to swim to North Island to-night do you think I would find the coffin all right?"

They explained that a nigger who had charge of that island had taken possession of the coffin, but they were sure he would let me have it for one or two dollars. Just then Captain Diable reappeared on deck and we jumped into the boat. On our way back to our ship he said, "After you put me on board you will return to that ship and tow their barge to the *Starlight*."

When we got alongside our ship I said to my

boat-mate for the captain's edification, "I'm going for a drink; I'll be back in a minute."

I hurried to the forecastle for three dollars, running back again at once, and away we went, but before going to the Yankee we paid a visit to North Island to see about the coffin. Within five minutes I was in possession of the whole sixty-four shares of my first venture in ship-owning. It was dark when we reached the Yankee so they did not see what we had in tow, and when we returned to our own ship we hoisted up the boat, leaving the coffin to be hauled up and stowed down the fore-hatch after the officers had gone aft. We secured the barge to the swinging boom with a rope, alongside the long-boat, rove a topsail sheet (chain) through the rings of both, passed both ends on board and locked them. Desertions were so frequent at the Chincha Islands that all the captains agreed to lock their boats and barges every night, but the sailors were always on the look-out for any little departure from the agreement, and were ready to seize the opportunity when one presented itself.

Boats from all the ships were sent to the shoots at six o'clock every morning, and lay there waiting till their ship's name was called out by the man in charge of the island, which might happen at any hour of the day. A ship of nine hundred to a thousand tons would have from ninety to a hundred lay days, and the man in charge took care that she did not get her cargo in full before the lay days expired, but he was always ready to make arrangements with a captain who wanted to get away

sooner, provided the latter was willing to pay dispatch money, which was at that time a good round
sum.   In each boat there were two sailors and an
officer, and as we had to wait about the shoots for
hours we had plenty of time for spinning yarns.   It
was there that we heard all the gossip of the fleet,
and there that plans were frequently made for a
grand decampment.

A well-planned flight took place shortly after our
arrival.   A large Yankee ship from San Francisco
had a fine boat which had been built on her deck on
the passage down, a boat after the style of a whale-
boat, sharp at both ends, and carrying forty tons.
One night two of the Yankee crew, after breaking
the lock, made off with this boat at midnight;
pulled to another ship for a steward who had
promised to have some eatables hanging over the
bow; then to the next ship where the men had two
stu'nsail booms over the bow; then to another
where two top-gallant stu'nsails were ready for
them, and, of course, a few men from each ship
slipped into the barge at the same time.

When the news went round in the morning that
a barge had been stolen and twenty-five men were
missing, a meeting of captains was held on board
the Yankee, the mate of which had gone aloft with
the telescope and discovered something like the
missing boat about ten miles to the southward with
two lugsails set, but as it was impossible for them to
recover their property, the meeting soon broke up.

Our barge crew was composed of the second mate,
one of the East coast men and myself.   Our meals

were sent to us at the shoots, but sometimes we pulled alongside for our food, which would be passed down to us, and we would return to our station and eat it there.

We made many kind friends among the men in the other boats when they saw our miserable fare—biscuits and coffee for breakfast, biscuits and salt horse, or pork and pea-soup for dinner, and not much of any of them. We always asked other people for a drink, as ours was the only ship at the Islands that served out a bare three quarts of water, and the majority of them were not put on their allowance at all. Of course all ship's crews had to be careful, for there was no water at the Islands, but only a few served it out, and they allowed a gallon and an extra bucket every Sunday morning for washing. We never had a pint given to us on any day of the week with which to wash our faces, and we certainly could not afford water for ablutions out of an allowance of three quarts per diem, for we were in the tropics and employed on very dry, dusty work. Our friends in the other boats, and particularly the crew of the American ship *Harry Bluff*, gave us many savoury tit-bits, and we always saved some of the good things for old Jack and Rory.

On the next Sunday after I had acquired the coffin, the captain seemed to be in a very good humour, so Jack and I approached him to ask for a loan of the boat that we might call on some friends in the other ships. He was quite pleasant—for him —and said that he did not think either of us would

run away, so he would have been pleased to let us
have the boat, but there was an agreement between
all the captains in the port that they should not
lower boats except for their own use. He added
that, though he must abide by the agreement, he
would allow us to go to see our friends if we could
get a boat to take us, and I seized the opportunity.

"Well, sir," I said, "if I can build a box big
enough to float me, you won't have any objections?"

"Certainly not," he replied graciously.

We returned to our own quarters and I soon had
the coffin hauled up out of the fore-hatch and
launched under the name of *Harry Bluff*. I had
previously nailed the lid to the bottom to give
buoyancy, and I had also made a double ended
paddle out of the bottom of a discarded bread
barge, but, my wood being scarce, the hold-waters
were not exactly oval, as they should have been.
When they went in to dinner aft at one o'clock the
launch took place, and I paddled off at once that I
might be in time to dine on board the big *Harry
Bluff*. All hands, including the cook, were on deck
watching my arrival and they threw me a rope which
I made fast. I then jumped out, and they hauled
my boat off to the swinging boom. The second
officer met me at the gangway, for the discipline in
the ship was perfect.

"What is your business?" he inquired.

"I have just called to see some of the crew," I
replied.

"What ship are you from?" he asked.

"The *Starlight*."

He made his report to the chief officer, who approved of it, and then told me to come aboard. I had been standing on the top step of the accommodation-ladder, but now I stepped on board and, saluting the quarter-deck by lifting my cap, I walked forward, where I received a hearty welcome from one and all. After a splendid dinner we all adjourned to the top-gallant forecastle to enjoy our pipes and a chat, and I soon discovered that they knew a good deal about the *Starlight* and Captain Diable's cruelty to his crew. Two of the men told me they had been at Bombay on the previous voyage, and they heard there that Diable had managed to get a number of his crew put in prison for trying to take charge of the ship on the passage out, but the Bombay people had afterwards discovered that it was the captain, and not the men, they should have imprisoned. Diable, however, was cunning, and was always on his best behaviour while in port.

In the course of the yarn-spinning the carpenter invited me to his room, which was in a large deck-house, between the main-hatch and the foremast. The house also contained the galley, bos'n's room, and a workshop, and like every other part of the ship, it was all perfectly clean and tidy. The carpenter had served his apprenticeship on the Clyde with Tod and M'Gregor, but had gone to America as a young man, and at this time he could " guess and calculate as well as the next one."

" I noticed as you were coming alongside in that dugout of yours that she wasn't just up to the mark," he said. "It won't be very safe for you to go far in her."

"True!" I returned, "but I don't intend to go so far that I couldn't swim ashore if she happened to empty me out."

"Well," he said, "I was thinking that if you would leave her with me for two or three days I could fix her off for you."

I agreed to leave her till the next Sunday and swim back to my ship, so I asked a few of the men in the forecastle to help me to get her on board, which they willingly did. I jumped down and hooked her on to the fore-yard guano whip (a rope for hoisting the guano), while the others hooked on Charlie, but he evidently had conscientious objections to Sunday labour, for he refused to budge an inch and no amount of whipping would alter his mind. However, we got the coffin up, and placed it at the carpenter's door. Then I called on the cook and had a look at the galley, where everything was spotlessly clean and shining. I was particularly taken with the large quantity of loaves of bread which were arranged on shelves as in a baker's shop, and I asked if they used no biscuits.

"No, sonny, no biscuits here," replied the cook, who was a nigger.

"I wonder if the day will come when they will feed us on soft tack," I remarked.

"It should," he said, "for it's as cheap as biscuits, but the trouble would be to find cooks. You know, sonny, the owners don't want you to spoil all the flour and throw it overboard, and then fall back on biscuits, because then they would have both to pay for. Your English cooks are no use; the best of them can only make pea-soup, and duff like a bullet, and you get "Strike-me-blind" every Saturday, sometimes as hard as gravel and sometimes burnt. All they have to do for breakfast is to boil the coffee-pot, and for tea to boil the water. If you fellows want cracker hash or dandy-funk you have to make it and cook it yourselves, because the cooks think those little dishes are extras, and they are too lazy to help you. But it's not like that on board this packet, sonny; I can do all the cooking here and no man would try to come inside that door, but mind you, if our boys want anything they just come and tell me, and I fix it up for them."

He held forth in this strain for nearly an hour, and afterwards, in the forecastle, they assured me he was one of the best cooks they had ever sailed with. They wanted me to stop for tea, and they also wanted me to take something to old Sinbad, as they called old Jack. They had taken a liking to him when he came to the shoots with our food, and whenever they gave us a share of their meals they would say, "Don't forget old Sinbad." Unfortunately I had to refuse everything on this occasion, even a big loaf of bread which the cook offered to tie on my head, for I knew I was too deep-draughted at my best to allow four pounds dead weight to be added.

I hurried away at last that I might be back in time to signal my safe arrival before it was too dark, which I managed to do. Tea was just ready when

I arrived, and I was glad of the hot drink after my swim. I had plenty to tell my shipmates that night after tea, and to think over after we were in bed. To say the least of it, it was not soothing to think how many men there were, well-fed and comfortable, in ships that were like "homes from home," while we were dragging out a miserable half-starved existence in a den of torture, without a drop of water to wash our faces, not to speak of our clothes. We were all carrying cargo at the same rate of freight, but some shipowners were so mean and grasping that they would half-man their ships, fit out with food not fit for pigs, and supply ship furnishings, ropes and sails to correspond.

I have never been able to find out where they bought such rubbish as I have seen put on board for a long voyage, but I am pleased to think those days are past, though the change is due to the increased liberality of the shipowners as much as to the improved regulations of the Board of Trade, whose grandmotherly protection has done more harm than good to the genuine sailor.

It must be clear to every reader of the daily papers that in nearly all "sailor *versus* captain" cases which appear before the magistrates, the verdict is given in favour of the seaman or fireman, as the case may be. It must not be supposed that I am down upon Jack, but I certainly bear no good-will to the drunken, good-for-nothing men who form a large percentage of the crews on board our ships and steamers of the present day. Instead of a knowledge of seamanship they take with them an endless stock of assurance and impudence, as an illustration of which I will describe one case which occurred shortly before I retired from sea.

One fine morning we were bowling along between Malta and Port Said with all sail set, and the sails that were not drawing were drying. When I came up from breakfast I left the promenade deck for a walk round the ship to see if all was right, and when I was clear of the fore-trysail boom, I looked up and noticed that the gaskets on the port yard-arm were hanging down abaft the yard. I saw there was a man in at the bunt, so I shouted, " Fore-yard there ! "

" Hallo ! what do you want ? " was the answer.

" Make up the gaskets on the port yard-arm before you come down," I called.

" What are you shouting at ? I can't do two jobs at once," grumbled the man in a low voice, but still loud enough for me to hear, so I called him down and sent for the chief officer. Then I put the man through a few questions.

" Do you consider yourself a seaman ? " I asked.

" Yes," was the answer.

" How long have you been at sea ? "

" Three years."

" Then let me tell you you are no seaman, for all seamen know how to address their officers in the usual course of their duties. Now, sir," I added, " I will test your abilities. Take hold of the wheel from the quarter-master."

" I can't steer," said the man.

" Well, do you know what this is ? " I asked.

" Yes, it's a heaving-line."

" And what are all those marks on it ? "

" Oh, it's a lead-line ? "

" What mark is that ? "

" I don't know the marks."

" Now, there is a strand of three-inch rope and a block," I said. " Make a grommet strop for that block. Sit down there and take as long as you like about it."

He set to work, and a beautiful mess he made of it. At eight bells the strand had become a bunch of rope yarns and he had lost all the turns of the strand. He was forced to admit that he knew nothing about it, so I asked—

" Can you strop it with a short splice if I give you a piece of rope ? "

" No, I can't splice," he replied.

" As far as I can see, there is only one thing you can do," I said, " and that is to address your master in a disrespectful manner. You shipped in this steamer as A.B.—a rating you are totally unfit for, so you are now disrated from A.B. at three pounds five shillings to O.S. at two pounds, and that amount is a great deal too much for such a useless fellow. Pipe down ! "

That was the last punishment I meted out to a so-called sailor before I left the sea, and it is a fair specimen of many such cases.

After this long digression I must continue my account of our adventures at the Chincha Islands.

CHAPTER XVII

TO CALLAO AND HOME AGAIN

TWO ships at the Islands had a plan of their own for securing an extra load of guano, and of course the *Starlight* was one of the two. The idea was to send their barge to the shoots at three o'clock in the morning in order to obtain the first load, for which the men in charge did not call a ship's name, as they were pleased when their Chinese slaves could make an early start—say about five-thirty A.M. Many a time we were alongside our ship with thirty tons before six o'clock, and we had to make this early start every morning under very unpleasant meteorological conditions. There is no rain in that part of the world, but the clerk of the weather sends a dew as a substitute. Everyone has heard of slight dews, heavy dews, and even " mountain dew," but not one of them is as wet as a Chincha Island dew, and the most disagreeable job we had was going in the barge at that early hour.

Every day I received a loaf of bread from the black cook and some good square meals from the men in the *Harry Bluff's* barge. They also treated me to plenty of chaff about my boat, and I could see they were up to some little game, by such jokes as " Will you have a figure-head or a straight stem ? " and " Mind you bring a bottle of lime-juice to the launch." On the following Sunday a boat called at our ship with some grass for Charlie and a bag of sweet potatoes—an unwonted piece of extravagance for Captain Diable—and I asked them to take me to the *Harry Bluff*, which they did.

The second officer was at the gangway as usual, but this time his face wore a smile as he said, " Good morning, Harry."

" Good morning, sir," I replied, and went forward to be introduced to my boat in her new guise. I found her lying where I had left her a week ago, but there was a vast change in her appearance. The carpenter had made two triangular, water-tight boxes, one of which he screwed on each end of my boat, making her three feet longer than before, so she was now ten feet over all. The men had painted ports on her, and her name—*Harry Bluff*—appeared at one end; they had also eased up all the screws and white-leaded the seams. The carpenter found that the lid, which I had nailed to the bottom, was a fine piece of wood which he wanted, so he took it off and replaced it with a piece of wood the whole length, which he cut so that it projected three inches on each side in place of rolling chocks.

I felt as proud as Lucifer and wanted to leave at once, but I had to wait for my dinner and a smoke, and then all hands came out to see the launch. For the first and only time I was glad to get away from the *Harry Bluff*, and I made off at once on a visit to one of the Aberdeen clippers between North and Middle Islands, on board which I had often been asked to dine on Sundays. I caused a great sensation when I arrived within sight of the ships, for all the sailors in the port had heard about the coffin, and they had mustered on the forecastles to see me paddling along. Many and various were the comments they made.

" Well done, Scottie ! "

" Go at it, Harry ! "

" Ship ahoy ! Where are you from ? Where are you bound to ? "

" Do you stop out all night ? "

" I say, Harry, how many guns has she got ? "

" Hey, Scottie, there's a rat in your main chains!"

" Hoist your ensign, Scottie ! "

When I boarded the Aberdeen ship I was much impressed by the comfort of the crew's quarters. The bunks and ship-side were painted stone colour, the roof white ; an oil lamp hanging on each side indicated that there was no stint of light ; and charts, sextants, and books in beckets overhead showed that there were navigators at both ends of the ship. Lying outside the forecastle door was a thrummed ponch mat, inside was a thrummed canvas mat, and everything was as clean as a new pin. I passed a very pleasant two hours with them, and everyone spoke to me, from the captain to the cook, but I could see there was no lack of discipline. The captain told the steward to give me two tins of preserved beef, remarking, as he gave the order, " I understand you are not very well fed on board the *Starlight.*"

He did not get that information from me, but I

suppose he had heard about me, so I thanked him very much for his kindness. The steward brought me two four-pound tins, and I really felt ashamed to be always walking away with eatables, but we certainly needed food, and they seemed to know that in the few ships I visited. I stayed to tea with my Aberdeen friends, and was regaled with a portion of a seal sea-pie. They had caught a seal the previous day, which they had made into a sea-pie, and as they had expected me to tea on Sunday they had kept some and warmed it up for me. I spent every Sunday in this way, having dinner on the Aberdeen ship and tea on the Yankee, or vice versa, but though I called at several other ships I never stayed to a meal on board them.

I sometimes lent my boat to men I could trust, but she did not seem to like that, for she invariably tipped them out. The secret was, in going into her, to be very careful to step right in the middle, or over she would go. On one occasion I went to North Island to see the cemetery, and as it happened to be surf day—full moon—I had to be particularly careful to sit low and keep the sea end-on. I reached the island safely, and found a strange sight in the cemetery.

As I have mentioned before, there was no earth to cover the dead, so the bodies, which were principally Chinese, were simply laid down in rows— eight or ten in a row—and I was astonished to find them all in a first-class state of preservation owing to the action of the guano. They were all quite natural, except that the eyes had gone; but for that, they looked like a lot of men resting, for some of them were sitting up. I went towards the first one I saw in that position, thinking it was a visitor come to look at a friend, but I found it was a corpse drawn up by the sun.

While passing Middle Island on my way back I was obliged to put my boat broadside on for a short distance, with the result that she emptied me out. I was close in shore, so a few strokes put me on the beach, and the boat soon followed me. That was the only time in three months that she turned me out, and as it happened just after dark, no one saw my misadventure, and I kept the fact to myself.

Week after week passed, with the same daily routine and my little bit of amusement in my boat on Sunday, till at length our last boat-load arrived alongside. The Aberdeen clipper had left a fortnight before, and the *Harry Bluff* followed a few days after us.

On the Sunday before we sailed I was taking my last cruise in my boat when someone hailed me from the *Fearnought*, and on going alongside I found that the mate wanted to see me about my boat. They had been in the port only a few days, but long enough for us to hear at the shoots that this famous Western Ocean Packet had changed her manners as well as her trade, and from being the wildest ship trading across the pond, she had become one of the quietest and best ships afloat at that time. The result of that visit was that I sold my boat to the mate for five dollars, and I was only sorry afterwards that I had not asked for ten, as I could easily have got it. Our barge was sold to another ship, and we understood that Captain Diable obtained fifty dollars more than he paid for it.

There was neither cheering nor bonfire on board the *Starlight* when the hatches were put on, and only eight boats put in an appearance next morning. It was customary for the crews of the boats to come on board when the ship was far enough off the Islands to hoist the top-sails, and when that was done a glass of grog was served out to every man. They then returned to their boats and gave three cheers as they pulled away, but our send-off was a very half-and-half affair. Most of the visitors refused the grog because none was served out to the ship's crew, and the cheering was very mild; indeed, had it not been for the presence of an officer in each boat, I think the cheers would have been replaced by groans.

On the following day we arrived at Callao, for we had to report there before sailing for home. All ships bound for the Chincha Islands for guano had first to call at Callao, where they would receive a visit from two or three officials who, after examining the ship and asking numerous questions, would nail a small strip of zinc on the ship's side to show what depth she might be loaded to. I think the position of the zinc was not decided by the questions put and the measurements taken, so much as by the liberality of the captain, but as our captain had none of that commodity in stock, the zinc was tacked on as they thought fit.

During our first night at sea the captain and the mate went over the side on a stage and shifted the zinc up four inches, which meant about two hundred pounds extra into the owner's pocket without the expenditure of any " liberality."   They thought we were asleep during this manœuvre but " we're no aye sleeping when oor een are stickit."   On leaving the Chincha Islands all ships had to return to Callao to be re-examined by the officials, who first ascertained if the ship was loaded to the zinc mark (our captain had obliterated all traces of the transfer by means of paint) and then sealed up the pumps for twenty-four hours, at the end of which time they returned to see how much water she had made, and if all was right she was allowed to proceed on her journey homeward.

On our arrival at Callao it was arranged that we should each have five dollars of our wages in advance, and a day's holiday the next day : a plan which suited me exactly for I wanted to go ashore to settle up with the Captain of the Port, though I did not expect to come off very well, for I had heard some time before that there had been an entire change of Government.   Five of us landed together, and the others waited outside the office of the Captain of the Port while I went in and explained my business to him.   To my great astonishment he allowed my claim, and smilingly handed me a cheque for over four hundred dollars.

I thanked him, and we all went off to a café where we had a good feed.   I asked the proprietor how much my cheque was worth, but after looking at it he looked at me to see if I were trying to take a rise out of him, and then said in broken English that it was worth nothing: an answer for which I was partly prepared. Then, as he could speak a little English and could understand it very well, he sat down beside us, and explained the state of the country and its financial position.

The President who had signed the cheque had been hanged by the crowd, and it was daily expected that his successor would share the same fate. I offered to strike a bargain with the proprietor of the café, and though he fought shy of the little piece of paper at first, he afterwards said he would give me ten dollars for it as a curio. But he suggested that, as we had expressed our intention of going to Lima, I should take the cheque with me and try to find a purchaser in that city; if I did not succeed he would give me the ten dollars that afternoon when we returned.

So we set off for Lima by train—a most primitive concern, which took nearly an hour to cover the distance of eight miles. The railway ran through some of the streets in Lima, and there the train could only creep along, for in spite of whistling and ringing of bells, the drivers of vehicles would persist in crossing our bows. The engineer or fireman had to get out and walk ahead, and frequently they had to do a little fighting with the drivers. However, we got there eventually, and after a walk through the city we visited the cathedral, which, we had heard, was worth looking at, and indeed we found it was a very grand building.

There was a large marble font close to the entrance, and I noticed that everyone who came in went straight to it, dipped their fingers in and crossed themselves. I drew Jack's attention to it, and just then Rory came up and remarked that he was very dry. In a joking way Jack said, "Take a drink out of that basin," and Rory made straight for it. There being no drinking-cup, he had to drink like a horse, and as his beard was long and shaggy, it also was being refreshed, when in came a very grand dame who walked up to the font, but when she discovered Rory's head in the basin she gave a scream and dropped on the door-mat. In an instant the whole of the cathedral staff were making for the entrance, so I exclaimed, "Run for it, Jack!" and made off down the street as fast as my legs could carry me. When I got tired of running I amused myself by looking at shop windows till it was time for our return train. I found Rory waiting at the station, and he told me he had given a man who had overtaken him a dollar to let him go, and say no more about it. Jack was there too, but he had managed to get into a grog-shop in my absence, and I found him about "three sheets in the wind."

When we arrived at Callao I went straight to the café to settle with the proprietor, and found him willing to fulfil his promise, but as it was then time for us to return to the ship I would not have the opportunity of spending any of the money, which would be of no use to me at sea. I explained that to the man, who said I might go into the shop next door, which was his property, and select goods to the value of ten dollars. I went in and found it to be a very large store dealing in all manner of things, from a needle to an anchor.

The first thing I put my hand on was a Panama hat, and the proprietor said he would let me have it to settle the bargain, though its price was twelve dollars. But I also wanted a basket of oranges, one of onions, and ten pounds of sugar, so we were at a deadlock for a while. Eventually I got all these articles and arrived on board only one hour late, with Jack half-seas over, and Rory vowing vengeance on all Roman Catholics because his drink of water had cost him one dollar.

The following morning our new hands—three men and a boy—arrived in charge of a boarding master—all of them so drunk that they had to be hoisted on board. We hove up the anchor at once, and I have no doubt we made a very poor show of seamanship in leaving the bay, for, even if we had had the help of the three drunk men, we were only half-manned. We were quite unable to hoist the topsails by hand, and had to take everything to the capstan.

By the time everything was set, and I had time to look around, we were nearly out of sight of the land, but in that part of the world there is no bad weather worth mentioning, so we were safe so far. Next morning at eight o'clock we were all called aft to be picked for watches, and then saw our new hands for the first time: three fine, strapping fellows, but the boy was very small.

While we were all standing aft the mate suddenly

said, "Who is that forward there?" and on looking round we saw, to our surprise, a sailor in man-of-war clothes, which were covered with guano. He was called aft to explain his presence on board, which he did by saying he had deserted from H.M.S. *Topaz*, and had stowed himself away down our hold. I do not know how the captain received the news, but the rest of us were very pleased to see the stranger, who was a big, strong lad with two years' service in the navy, so he was likely to be of some use. I was pleased when he was put in the mate's watch, along with myself and one of the newcomers, who was an Italian and a splendid seaman, but he could not speak a word of English, and had had no experience of England or of English ships. We became good friends and he showed me the contents of his chest, which included one of the finest-looking daggers I ever saw, and a revolver with three chambers loaded and two empty. If only he could have spoken English he might have told me what had become of the two cartridges, but, anyway, I saw that Captain Diable would be well advised to keep his cutlass out of sight that passage. The other men, a Russian and a Swede, were also good sailors though unable to speak our language, but the Swede, although healthy in appearance, proved to be fit for light work only, owing to the condition of his lungs, and he could not go aloft.

Captain Diable, having no further use for our slush, kindly allowed us to utilise it for the purpose of illuminating the fore-castle, and we were so pleased that I am afraid we frequently burned our lamps after the sun was on duty.   I passed a lot of my time experimenting with lamps to see which gave the best light, and found that the best results were obtained in the following manner :—I cut a clear glass bottle in halves by means of friction and used the neck end.   I whittled a piece of wood about twelve inches long till it was about half the thickness of a pencil or less ; pulled the threads out of a piece of canvas till I thought I had sufficient ; wound them round my four fingers till I had a wick as thick as a finger ; marled that bunch of threads on to one end of the stick ; put a cork into the bottle ; made a hole in it with a roping needle ; made a fine point to the splint of wood, and pushed it down through the hole in the cork till the wick was level with the top of the cut bottle.   That done, I hung the bottle up to a beam, poured in the fat in a liquid state, and it was ready for lighting.

However, that lamp being of glass, it was suitable for fine weather only, so I had to contrive another for bad weather.   I cut a preserved meat tin in halves, and obtained a piece of zinc about the same size as the tin, to make a false bottom.   Then I drove a nail as long as the depth of the half tin through the zinc and put it in the tin.   To make the wick, I wound a narrow strip of canvas twice round one finger, tied it with a slack turn of twine, slipped it off my finger, and placed it on the nail, when it was ready for the fat to be poured in. The worst of this lamp is that it smokes very badly, on account of the nail in the middle of the wick, while in the other the wooden splint burns as the fat burns down, and so causes very little smoke.

We approached the "roaring forties" this time with less dread than on the outward passage, for we had longer daylight, which was as good as another two men in the watch, and our forecastle could be kept a little warmer with two lamps burning. One evening when we were in latitude 45° we were staggering along with the whole topsail set, expecting every minute to be called out to tie the first reefs. If the force of the wind had kept steady she might have been able to stand the whole topsail, but we were having some very strong squalls of wind and hail that made everything crack again. We were not called out, and she had just to stand it, but after midnight the squalls lessened, so the main-top-gallant sail was set when daylight came in, and we soon set all sail with hopes of better weather. I went aloft to loosen the main-royal, but when I reached the cross-trees I found they were slued round a long way from athwart. I called to the mate to look up, and after thinking it over for a minute, he let go the top-gallant halyards. In the meantime I had a look round to see where the mast was sprung, and in a few minutes the captain and the mate came aloft, but none of us could find the damage, so it was evidently under the spider band—an iron hoop three inches broad, and about two feet below the cross-trees—which meant that the fracture was a serious one, putting "fishing" out of the question. All hands were called : my watch to send the yards down, and the other watch to assist the carpenter to cast loose the spare spar to make a topmast. Neither sending down yards nor handling a spare spar was comfortable work, for she was rolling very much and shipping a quantity of water. I did not leave the mast-head till we had her dismantled, and from my post of vantage I could see the poor carpenter cutting the new mast when the ship was steady, and holding on for all he was worth when the ship took a big roll, which made me think that we aloft had the best of a bad bargain.

It was dinner-time before we were allowed down, and all the afternoon I worked with the carpenter, old Jack taking my wheel, until daylight failed us, when I, as well as the carpenter, was allowed to go below till daybreak. At noon the next day the mast was ready for going aloft, and I went back to my station at the mast-head. The Italian was a great help to me although he did not know a word of English, but sending a mast aloft is the same all the world over, and he knew it all thoroughly. Soon after dark we had the upper topsail set again, and the top-gallant mast up, but the weather had become so bad that we were allowed to go below till daybreak. Next day we set the top-gallant sail, but the royal was not sent aloft till we had rounded the Horn.

Sailors in well-found, well-fed, and well-disciplined ships would say the loss of a topmast was nothing to talk about, but it meant a good deal to us, for there had been no alteration in our stores, except that the beef and pork were about a year older, and the biscuits were showing signs of life. We were still being robbed of our measure of water and everything else, but fortunately there was no sign of grog throughout the passage home. I have omitted to mention that we were bound to Cowes for orders.

When we got into fine weather again the usual cleaning, painting, and scraping was the order of the day, and a very tall order it was, for all the yards, masts, and blocks were bright, so everything from the truck to the deck had to be scraped. My part was to make a mizzen staysail, and Jack worked with me when he was not at the wheel.

One day when we were crossing the N. E. Trades there were three men and a boy aloft scraping yards, the boy being at the lee main-top-gallant yardarm. Suddenly he fell from aloft and struck the main-yard, falling from that to the rail, which he struck very heavily, and then fell overboard. We knew he must be killed, but we put out a boat which proceeded to what we thought was the right place, but they could see no sign of the unfortunate boy, so they returned to the ship.

All went on as usual till we were close to the Western Islands, when we were told that the coffee was done and the tea so short that we could not have an extra allowance to take the place of the coffee. Two days later we were told that the tobacco was done, but that did not trouble me much, for I always had a pound in reserve for such an emergency. It was a more serious matter to be bound in-channel in the month of February with no coffee and only lively biscuits for breakfast. Fortunately, I had saved up about thirty pounds of my allowance of biscuits, so I proceeded to make a substitute for coffee. I baked the biscuits in the oven till they were a dark brown colour, then put them in a canvas bag and pounded them with a mallet till they were crushed into a fine powder, which took the place of coffee for the rest of the voyage. It was not exactly Mocha, but we thought it was better than nothing. When I was in the little brig with old Captain Blowhard he told us on one occasion that the coffee would soon run out, and I suggested that he should add some biscuits, which he did. It turned out to be quite an improvement on the pure article, and if only they had given us notice in time in the *Starlight* we could have made her coffee spin out in the same manner.

CHAPTER XVIII

I LEAVE THE *STARLIGHT* AND JOIN THE CITY LINE

WE had a very fair passage in-channel, and ran in through the Needles just as the wind began to strengthen. We anchored off Cowes about seven P.M., and we all rejoiced at the knowledge that within a few days we should gain our independence. We chalked for watches, and I had the good fortune to get the first watch, which was from eight to nine-thirty, so I promised myself a fine long sleep, but "the best-laid schemes of mice and men gang aft," as the Baboo said. When I was relieved by Rory I made straight for the forecastle, and was in the act of undressing when the cable gave a sudden jerk and the bight fell on the forecastle deck—a sure sign that the cable had snapped. The captain and mates came running forward to see what had happened, and then called us out to let go the second anchor, which was soon done, but to everyone's great astonishment it had taken only part of the chain that had been ranged when we discovered that the second anchor had gone the same way as the first. We lashed the two kedge-anchors together, and lowered them over the bow with a hawser fast to them. The next order was for all hands to go down the hold and dig for the spare anchor which we knew to be about

six or seven feet deep in the guano. That would
have been no hard task if only we had had a place
to throw the guano as we dug it up, but, as it was,
we did not get the anchor over the bow till breakfast
time, when we found that we were very close to our
original berth.

The captain went on shore to report his arrival
and the loss of two anchors, with sixty fathom of
chain, and returned in the evening with the news
that we were bound to Rotterdam, but we would
have to wait some time for the anchors, as the forge
men were out on strike. The next day he again
went on shore and returned in the evening with
Mrs. Diable, which was a happy event for us, for
from that hour we received better treatment. The
fresh-water pump was free to us, beef and biscuits
were supplied ad lib., and there was not a word of
complaint heard among us, although we were still
kept without coffee. Some ill-feeling sprang up
again a few days later. For three days I had been
at work on a stage over the stern, painting the
ship's name, port, and some scroll work round about
it, when one of the East Coast men came over on
the quiet to see how I was getting on. I was
sitting on the middle of the stage, putting on the
finishing touches, and I could neither see nor hear
what was taking place on deck, but, as my friend
was standing, his head just reached the mooring
pipe, and he heard Mrs. Diable say to her husband,
" What is that nice smell ? "

" Oh, that's the smell of the pea-soup blowing
along from the galley," he replied.

"What, William!" she exclaimed, "do you give that to the sailors?"

"Yes, my dear," answered Diable.

"'Deed to goodness! There's well off they are when they get such a fine savoury dish to dinner."

When the story was told in the forecastle neither the pea-soup nor the woman who had praised it received a blessing. The peas were really done, and our soup was made from the dust and maggots at the bottom of the cask, so Mrs. Diable might with advantage have taken a hint from the Geordies— "A' ye that knaw nowt should say nowt."

On the second morning as we lay off Cowes, the ship that had loaded close to us at the Chincha Islands, and which we had left about two-thirds loaded, arrived at Cowes, got her orders for Rotterdam, and left the same day.

On the tenth day we received the anchors and chains and proceeded to our destination, which we reached three days afterwards. It was dark before we anchored, but nothing was said to us about leaving, which disturbed our peace of mind very much, for we noticed, for the first time, in looking over our articles of agreement, that, if the captain liked, he could take us to a loading port. Our fears were set at rest at six o'clock the next morning, when the mate came forward and, after asking if we were all there, said: "We are done with you now; you can pack up and leave. You will be paid off at the British Consulate to-morrow morning at ten o'clock."

For a while we did nothing but cheer (though if

the Diables had shown face they might have been saluted with groans), and I thought that was the happiest day of my life, but soon spite held full sway in the forecastle. The sick Swede set the ball a-rolling by throwing six handspikes overboard, the Italian followed suit with a large top-block, and another man bent the bos'n's chair on to the end of a four-inch rope and stuck it out of the bow mooring pipe. When the chair caught the tide, away went the rope overboard till we heard the end go plump and then all was still.

Soon after daylight came in we all went on shore, the Scottish contingent keeping together, and I called at the Leith steamer, where I arranged about passages for the four of us. My only trouble now was to keep hold of old Jack till we reached Glasgow, so I restricted him to three glasses a day till we got on board the steamer, when I reduced it to two, giving the other one to Rory.

We all mustered at the Consulate at the appointed time. I was the third to be called in, and when I arrived at the pay-table I found Captain Diable standing behind the pay-clerk. He turned on me one of the sour distortions of his face which did duty for a smile, and said, " Well, Harry, how are you going home ? "

Just then the pay-clerk passed over my discharge with thirty-eight pounds lying on it, and I observed that Diable had given me " Character for ability V. G. ; Conduct G.," so I answered, " That is none of your business ; I will pay my way wherever I go."

Under those circumstances I saw the last of the most cruel-hearted tyrant a sailor ever sailed under, but before I drop him out of my story I will tell the last I heard of him. It was in Colombo thirteen years after the above incident, and I was in command of the S.S. *City of Cambridge.* I had gone ashore for two hours to be out of the way of the coal dust, called at the agents', and then went to the dubash's office, where I could sit in the cool veranda and see my steamer lying in the bay. I had been alone for some time, when the dubash came in, followed by a captain whom he introduced to me as Captain Bills of the ship *Nemo.*

" How do you do? " I said. " Sit down and have a chat."

He sat down, and his first words were, " Well, Harry, I see you don't remember me."

" I do not," I said, with some surprise.

" Well, well, there you are, you see! Now that you are a steamboat you don't know us poor fellows in sailing ships," he protested, humorously.

" Well, if you know me," I returned, " you will allow I am never too proud to shake the flipper of an old whale. But tell me where we have met."

" I was mate of the *Starlight*," he answered.

I jumped to my feet and seized both of his hands, and an hour later he did not think I was too high-minded to acknowledge an old ship-mate. We had all liked the mate, for he was a nice fellow, but, like myself, he had shipped in the wrong ship that voyage. He said that both he and the carpenter had tried to make Captain Diable believe that the gear off the deck had been stolen by harbour thieves, but I told him it was all done by the foreign sailors, and that I would not have stopped them if they had gone aft and collared the captain. I also told him that, if it had not been for my intervention, the Italian would have come down from aloft when we were sending the new topmast up and given Diable a few inches of cold steel.

Captain Bills told me how the next crew had brought Diable up by the round turn, with the result that he stopped on shore and bought a public-house, which he managed till he died, not long afterwards.

If this story should ever reach Captain Bills' eye, I hope he will communicate with me for auld acquaintance sake.

In due course we arrived in Glasgow from Rotterdam, and I parted with old Jack, never to see him again. Readers may think that we should have taken strong measures to keep our captain in order, but I must remind them that this happened just about the time that seven sailors were condemned to death for the *Flowery Land* murders. The crew of the ship *Flowery Land* had been so badly treated that they mutinied, and eventually killed the captain and officers, with the result that five men were hanged at the Old Bailey and two were transported for life. There was only one alternative—to report the matter to the Consul—and I have described what happened to that attempt.

The old sailors used to say : " When a dungaree jumper is seen coming into the court, Justice flies out at the window," and that was very true in those days, although matters are very different now.

I had made up my mind during this voyage to have no more to do with sailors' boarding-houses, so I left my chest and bag at the railway station until I found lodgings, which did not take me long. The boarding-house or sailors' home is a necessity for men who spend all their money, but I never worked that way. After each voyage I made I added a little to my account in the Savings Bank, and when the voyages became longer ones I arranged with myself that ten pounds should go that way every voyage until further notice.

I was most happy and comfortable in my new lodgings, and before I left Glasgow I coaxed two other fellows to try my plan, which they did, with the same result. I was honoured with a visit from Mrs. Boardinghouse one evening. She had become so frail that she had to come in a cab and be helped upstairs by the driver. She tried to coax me back to her house, first by scolding, then by crying, and in one part of her lecture she said, " I have always been very pleased to have you, and now I am getting old and near the end you must come back, and I will do something for you."

She meant that she would remember me in her will, but I objected to sporting about on money made out of homeward-bound sailors, and outward-bound sailors' advances, and she had to leave me when she found she could not turn me out of the tack that I was on. I had seen some very shady work in the boarding-house from time to time, although I must admit I was always well treated. Up to that time I had never taken an advance note from any ship I had been in, but I had seen men go into the kitchen to report to Mrs. Boardinghouse that they had shipped, and to hand over their advance notes. Jack would be invited to sit down, the whisky would be produced, and half an hour later some of the other boarders would be called in to carry Jack to his bed. He would see no more of that month's advance, but perhaps when he was going away Mrs. Boardinghouse would say, "Where's your bed, Jack?"

"I haven't got one," would be the answer.

"Oh, but you must have one. Mary, run down to Mr. M'Snuff's and buy Jack a bed—hurry up. Come away into the kitchen, Jack—she'll be back in a minute."

Then the benevolent lady would give him a small bottle of whisky, containing a gill and called a "bosom friend," and Jack would go off quite happily, saying what a good friend to the sailors was Mrs. Boardinghouse. Nevertheless, she had only expended about five shillings on Jack in return for a month's pay.

Although I was taking my ease at my new lodgings I was also keeping my weather eye open for a "City" ship, and after I had been there two weeks I took my first walk down to the shipping office to see an old friend who kept the sailor's reading-room. In the course of conversation I told him I had determined to ship in a "City" liner if I had to wait a month for one, and he said the *City of Shanghai* had put back to the Tail of the Bank for some unknown reason, so if I called next day he might be able to tell me more about it. I called the following morning and he told me the City Line superintendent had been down to the ship, with the result that the captain had been discharged and the crew, sailor-like, had all left, though there was nothing wrong as far as they were concerned. I also learned that a new captain had been appointed who would be at the shipping office at ten o'clock next morning to sign on a new crew, and I knew that there might be some trouble in getting men, as the reason for her putting back had been kept very quiet, so I went straight home, turned out my chest to see what I required for another voyage, bought the usual odds and ends, and packed my chest and bag again—so sure was I of getting a berth.

Ten o'clock next morning found me at the shipping office, and very soon afterwards the newly appointed master of the *City of Shanghai* arrived— Captain Richard Soden. The men hung back a little at first, but before long we had enough, and I had signed on in the City Line, not to leave it, as it turned out, for thirty-eight years.

We joined the ship next day at Greenock, and left in tow at daybreak on the following morning, with a large crew and all sober. The mate and second mate were fine officers, and I was favourably impressed with their civil manner of addressing us. Before we were down channel as far as the Tuskar, I was so pleased with my new quarters that I could hardly contain myself, for there was plenty to eat, and it was all of a good quality. The after 'tween-decks seemed to me to be nearly loaded with potatoes and onions, and I found I had said good-bye to salt horse, for the City Line did not carry that article. The beef was corned—not salt—and the pork was also first-class; in fact, I had never seen the like of it since I went to sea, and all the other stores were of the same excellence. I soon found out that the quality was very closely watched by the marine superintendents—Captain James and Captain Francis Brown—the two best friends to seafaring people I have ever fallen in with, and that without flourishing of trumpets, but in a quiet, unostentatious way.

The crew were not only large in numbers, but they were also the heaviest men I had sailed with, the majority of them being " big, braw Hielan'men." They were not exactly experts in seamanship, but they were all willing, hard-working fellows, and it was a pleasant change to sail with so many of my own countrymen.

The ship having worked down channel, and having sailed back and down again, it had told on her sails very much, and an assistant was wanted for the sail-maker, who had more work than he could manage. The mate asked me if I could turn my hand to sail-making, and as I said I could, he set me to repair a top-gallant sail that had been blown away during the night. I brought my tools aft, arranged a plank across two buckets for a bench and overhauled the sail with the sailmaker, who gave me a bolt of canvas and left me to cut for myself. The mate called him back to cut the canvas, but I heard him reply that it was unnecessary to cut for me. Towards evening the mate asked me if I was a sailmaker, and I answered, "No, I'm a sailor."

"But you must have a liking for that branch?" he said.

"No," I replied, "I never liked a sitting job, but I try to do as I am told. If you want me to keep at this, of course I will."

"I want you to sleep in at night," he said, "and work all day till the sailmaker is able to do it himself."

The sailmaker was a fine young fellow, and we got on well together. He gave me a few wrinkles, and perhaps he learned a few from me, for he had had only six years of that work, while I had been at it for ten years, off and on.

Our captain was an Englishman, and a thorough gentleman. He did not interfere with the general work of the ship, although he was always about, and when we got into fine weather he started a navigation class for the apprentices from ten to eleven-thirty, every forenoon. He also invited anyone from the forecastle who liked to attend—a chance which I was very sorry to miss. It came to the mate's ears, and after speaking to me about it, he kindly made arrangements for me to attend the classes. By way of return for his consideration I spent half of my breakfast and dinner hours at the sails, and so made up my time.

I had a quadrant and Norie's Epitome with me, for I had made up my mind that I would rise in my profession if I could. I was fortunate in having a splendid master to start with, and it happened that none of the apprentices had had such an opportunity before, so we all started on the same footing. None of them had a quadrant, and I lent them mine every Sunday to take the altitude of the sun at noon; I remember how pleased they used to be when their reading agreed with the captain's.

On that voyage, and many succeeding ones, a considerable portion of my time was spent in teaching the apprentices seamanship, and some of them were very quick in picking up knowledge about knots, plaits and sennit, turning in shrouds, seizings, etc. They also learned to heave the lead without dropping it inboard about the fore-rigging, and in the last dog-watch every evening I told them as much as I knew. Captain Soden used to come along and stand at the door to watch what was going on, and the mate also took a great interest in our proceedings. If we wanted a skein of marline or house-line, or some other article, I got one of the boys to ask the mate for it, and he never refused. Of course some of the articles we made in our own time were given to him for the ship's use; such as belts for heaving the lead, and sword-mats for boat-lashings.

I had fine young lads to deal with, and passed many a pleasant hour with them, asking such questions as :—If you are looking in the sail-locker for a foresail or mainsail, how can you tell the one from the other? The mainsail has three bowling cringles and two bowling bridles, while the foresail has two bowling cringles and one bowling bridle; but very few, even experienced, sailors can answer that off-hand.

Another very simple question, which has floored many a one, from apprentices to ship-masters, is:— How many points are there in the compass? The answer invariably given is that there are thirty-two points and sixty-four half-points, but as a matter of fact there are thirty-two points, thirty-two half-points, and sixty-four quarter-points.

My first passage in the City Line was such a grand change from the previous voyage I had made that I thought nothing could tempt me away from it, and I felt that I could not do enough to serve them. There was only one drawback: our cook was lazy, dirty, and stupid, and he did not know whether to boil a potato for three minutes or three hours. It was quite common in those days to take a man if he said he was a baker, but that was not a safe guide, and his efforts to make soft tack frequently meant a mere waste of flour. The one we had in the *City of Shanghai* had passed himself off to the captain as a baker, but what he did not know about baking would fill a book.

On one occasion we were put to the painful necessity of trying him by court-martial for carelessly burning a sea-pie nearly to a cinder. As was customary in the *Cities*, a pig was killed when we were south, running down our longitude, one-half being kept for the cabin use, the other half given to us, so we made a famous sea-pie. We peeled the potatoes, stowed the bones and onions in the ground tier with meat and potatoes on top, laid a deck of dough (which I had made), stowed more potatoes and meat in the 'tween-decks, and finished with an upper deck. Pepper and salt, of course, were added, and water poured down the hole in the deck till it was full up. A small pot was filled with prepared gravy to feed the pie during the two and a half hours' boiling it required. The big pot, containing the pie, and the small one, were taken to the cook at eight o'clock, with full instructions for him to add the gravy as time went on, and on no account to let it boil dry. When the bell struck at noon two men went to the galley for the pie, while the rest of us smacked our lips in anticipation of a grand dinner, but when the big pot was brought in and the lid lifted off, a change came over the spirit of our dream. A vile smell first greeted us, and examination showed that everything was burnt black except the upper deck and that had a horrible taste. We found on a visit to the galley that the liquid which had been supplied to feed the pie was still standing where we left it and had not even been put on the fire to boil. That was a clear case against the cook, and when the dinner was over and the galley cleared up, the culprit was summoned to the forecastle to stand his trial. He had no defence to make, so he was strapped over the body of the windlass and received twelve cuts with a rope-end.

That is an example of many dinners which that man spoiled for us during the passage. "God gives us food but the devil sends the cooks," said the old sailors. But I liked my ship, and in spite of a bad cook I lived better than I had done since I went to sea. So time wore on till we arrived in Calcutta, after ninety-two days, and were appointed to the moorings abreast of where the Sailors' Home now stands.

CHAPTER XIX

ADVENTURES IN CALCUTTA AND AFLOAT

THE ship *City of Vienna* was in Calcutta with us, and in the evening, after work was done, some of us would visit her, and some of her people would come to our ship, and we passed the time with songs, and playing on such musical instruments as we possessed. One evening we went on shore with all the instruments we could muster, which comprised a flute, concertina, tin-whistle, and bag-pipes, the latter being played very creditably by the cook of the *City of Vienna*. We formed up just abreast of the Bank of Bengal, and marched down the Strand Road to Eden Gardens, which we reached just as the band played the National Anthem. We waited till it was finished and then the cook struck up a reel. The Scotch people sitting in their carriages caught the infection of the music at once, and leaving their seats, they started dancing on the lawn. Our party contained six or seven apprentices dressed in uniform, which helped to give us a respectable appearance, and when the police finally asked us to stop, it was done politely, and with the plea that it was after music hours.

We were so elated over our little bit of fun that, instead of returning to the ship, we marched into the town, entering by Old Court-house Street, with the flute, whistle, and concertina doing duty till we reached Tank Square, when the piper struck up again, and we marched round and round the square. The verandas were soon filled with our countrymen, who could not continue to sit at dinner when their inspiring national music was being played in the street. On our second round turn we noticed that an unusual number of native police had collected, but we continued our frolic in happy ignorance of the fact that we were breaking the law. As we passed the Scotch Kirk for the third time, the police, headed by a European inspector, stopped us and took us in custody to the floating police station close to our ship. A few of our number bolted in the dark, but I did not intend to try, for I could not see what harm we had done. The instruments were taken from us and we were lodged in the lock-up, but in a short time we were called on deck to muster before an official. A number of gentlemen —Scotch, no doubt—were in attendance to vouch for our good behaviour, and in a few minutes we were dismissed. Open-air meetings and processions were forbidden in India from the time of the Mutiny till the Salvation Army commenced to take a good hold some years ago.

I did not learn who our deliverers were till nine years afterwards, when I was chief officer of the *City of Carthage*, homeward bound from Calcutta. As we had a fair number of passengers a concert was held one evening, and a certain gentleman was put down for a reading. When the time for his contribution arrived he related some of his Indian experiences, among which he told the story of the sailors walking round Tank Square, headed by the bagpipes, and afterwards being locked up, whereupon he and several friends left their dinner-tables and went to the magistrate to get them released. When he had finished speaking I went over to him and heartily shook his hand, telling him I was one of the party he had rescued from imprisonment.

The next piece of fun took place on our liberty day, when we had received an advance of money. Four of us—two apprentices and two from the forecastle—had arranged to go ashore together, and the first thing we did when we got there was to strike a bargain with a ghurry wallah (cab-driver) to drive us about the town for six or eight hours. Of course, the ghurry that is on the look-out for "Liberty Jack" does not belong to the A1 class, but to the very lowest order, and is called by Jack a "rope-yarn ghurry," as it is usually held together by string or rope-yarns, the horse being on a par with the carriage. The usual hire is three rupees—though of course the man asks for four at first—and it must be paid in advance, for he knows, from past experience of Jack, that a bird in the hand is worth two in the bush.

Having made our bargain we drove off to the Bazaar, feeling as happy and proud as if the whole place belonged to us, when suddenly, and without the slightest warning, the bottom of the ghurry fell out. Fortunately we sustained no damage, as the horse was jogging along very slowly, and the first thing we did after picking ourselves up was to ask for the return of our money, but the ghurry wallah declared he had given it to his master, and he did not know where to find him. The man, of course, wanted to return home, but we saw the matter in a different light and wanted some value for our money, so we arranged that one of us should sit up beside the driver and one stand up like a footman on the stern-sheets, while the other two should go inside and walk. In this order we arrived at the Bazaar Chundahchok to do our shopping, and quite a crowd watched our progress.

As we made our purchases we placed the parcels on the seats which were still in their original position but were not strong enough to bear our weight. From the Bazaar we went to Baboo House, and from there to a native refreshment house for our dinner, which, of course, consisted of curry and rice. After dinner we went to the China Bazaar, where we had a great crowd round us, wondering why we were walking inside our ghurry, and then we made tracks for the ship. When we reached the ghat the ghurry wallah started the usual bowing and scraping for "backsheesh," but we did not give him a copper, for we believed it was a planned affair.

A week later an illustrated paper told the story of the jolly tars going shopping in a bottomless ghurry, and gave a picture depicting our progress. So far so good, but they spoiled the account by saying we were drunk, when, as a matter of fact, none of us had drunk anything but lemonade all day.

In search of some of our mates we peeped into a

few of such noted houses as "The Hole in the Wall," "The Numbers," and "Smoky Jack's," but that slight look—the only one I have ever had—was quite enough, and it helped to account to me for a good deal of illness among the crew after liberty day. Cholera was rife in those days; we were still drinking river water, and it only required a little carelessness in diet, or a dose of Flag-Street-made brandy, to send a man to Circular Road (the cemetery). We invariably left Calcutta minus one or two of our original crew, and on one occasion we left five behind. I blame the men far more than the climate, for those who took care of themselves, and did not touch native grog, very seldom had any sickness, while for my own part, during my twenty-five years in the Indian trade, I never had a sore head nor missed a meal through illness.

But on one occasion, when I was chief officer of the *City of Edinburgh*, I met with a severe accident which necessitated treatment by a surgeon. We were moored at No. 7 Jetty in Calcutta, discharging cargo at full power one forenoon in the month of May, when I noticed that a Rangoon package had been discharged on to the jetty instead of going overside into the boat. I immediately jumped up on the bulwark and sprang towards the jetty, but, unfortunately, my foot slipped on a brass coupling on the rail, and I fell overboard between the ship and the jetty. When I recovered my senses a few minutes later I found myself sitting on one of the cross-beams with my right hand lying on my knee, palm upwards, and blood running down my sleeve.

By this time a big crowd of natives and the crew had come down to help me, and I at once asked a native to give me his head-dress—a long, white cloth—with which I had my arm bound to my side with my hand across my chest, and then told them to get a ghurry to take me to the hospital, where I was treated by the best surgeon in India—Dr. Partridge. The news had spread rapidly, and a number of friends came to see me, even before the doctor, who, on his arrival, could hardly get to the bedside for my friends, several of whom—fortunately for me—were also friends of the doctor. My injury proved to be a compound comminuted fracture of the upper arm, the lower third of the bone being broken into about twenty-four pieces, and it appeared to be a case for amputation. However, the doctor ascertained from one of my friends, who was also his friend, that I bore a good character for sobriety and general good conduct, so he, with two assistants, put me under chloroform and proceeded to put the bone together. To the doctor's satisfaction my recovery was so rapid that he allowed me to leave the hospital after thirteen days, as my ship was then sailing, and the captain engaged a fourth mate to carry out my orders, for I had to keep my watch sitting on a camp-stool.

So far as I know there was no place in Calcutta in those days where sailors could pass an hour on shore in the evenings, but some years afterwards some friends of the sailors started a reading-room which was very convenient for those who wanted to write letters home, as it was almost impossible to do so on board on account of the mosquitoes. It had, however, in my opinion, one great drawback—it was situated at the corner of Flag Street and Dalhousie Square, within a few yards of "The Numbers." I am no great advocate of sailors' rests and reading-rooms in foreign parts, for they tend to make Jack dissatisfied with his home on board ship, where as a rule the quarters are fairly comfortable if only the men will look after them as they should do, but when they have a reading-room to fall back on many of them become too lazy to scrub out their quarters, trim their lamp, and keep the place in order. For my own part I always stayed by my ship at night in all ports, and I was able to take stock of how others fared who spent their evenings ashore.

There are a number of good, Christian people in Calcutta who have done a great deal to make Jack's stay in port pleasant, but there are also a number who are very poor hands at it. I remember two missionaries, one Church of England and one Dissenting, who used widely different methods. The Dissenter always called at our ship at eight o'clock in the morning, and first walked aft where he would be invited to join the captain and officers at breakfast. After breakfast he would steer for the forecastle, but the men, on noticing his approach, would pass the word along that "Holy Joe" was coming, and when he reached the forecastle he would find it empty.

On the other hand, the Church of England padre called soon after six o'clock when the men were having tea, and went straight to the forecastle, where

he greeted the men in a cheery manner.   Then he
would sit down amongst them and talk of the country and the natives, their customs and religion, till
the men had finished their tea, when he would say,
" Now we will read a chapter of Scripture," and proceed to do so, explaining and expounding as he went
on.   I know for a fact that he stopped the men from
going ashore many a night, and of course they all
had invitations to Sunday service, or Wednesday
night meetings, at the Seamen's Floating Bethel, of
which he was in charge.   On those occasions the
padre was always at the gangway to welcome the
men, and at the close of the service he doffed his
surplice and returned to his station at the gangway
to shake hands as they departed.

After a stay of three weeks in Calcutta we had an
uneventful passage home.   In those days the City
Line ships discharged their cargoes in the Shadwell
Basin, London Dock, and I stayed at the Sailor's
Home in Wells Street till we were paid off.   I then
returned to my lodgings in Glasgow and stayed
there for two weeks, when I decided to join the
R.N.R., and I put in a month's drill in H.M.S. *Lion*
at Greenock.   I found very comfortable and cheap
lodgings in Greenock, and as my pay was a guinea
per week, I got on very well.   I put in the full
month at drill because I had my eye on a fine new
" City " ship—the *City of Edinburgh*—and I had to
wait two months for her.

I remember the day when I applied to Captain
Dick for a berth as A.B.   He looked me over and

said, " You are very young; how long have you been
at sea ? "

" Over ten years," I replied.

" Have you ? " he said, still doubtfully.

" Yes, sir," I said, " and those two men ratlining
down the fore-rigging were shipmates with me six
years ago."   (The ship was still in the hands of the
riggers.)

" Well, you must be older than you look.   Give
me your discharge "—which meant that he had
accepted me.

We sailed from Glasgow in February, 1868, and
had a good hammering down channel, and by the
time we reached the Tuskar our rigging stood much
in need of setting up, but we had to keep on three
days longer till a fine morning set in, when we
started reeving off tackle.   The contents of the
bos'n's locker were turned out, and when the tackles
were aloft and all ready to start we began to take
off the seizings.   Just then the captain came along
hanging a marline-spike round his neck, and saying,
as he jumped up to the forward lanyard of the main
rigging, " Now we'll see who are sailors and who are
not."   This had the effect of making nearly all
hands scurry away to the other side, where the mate
was master of ceremonies, but having started at the
second lanyard I was not going to show the white
feather, though, of course, I did my " speedy utmost," like Tam O' Shanter's horse.

During that forenoon the captain gave a few of
the men a piece of his mind on the matter, but he
did not once speak to me, either for good or evil.

I noticed from the first that the *City of Edinburgh* was not such a fast sailer as the *City of Shanghai*, and my opinion was confirmed when we fell in with some well-known clippers, but we found that she could run well and was fairly dry. Our three best days' work running our easting down were 305, 305, and 320 knots on consecutive days, and on one of those days we passed an American ship hove to under a close-reefed top-sail. We signalled her, and found she was bound to Calcutta with ice. She arrived in Calcutta on the day we sailed, and she might have been much later if her agents had not sent a tug three hundred miles down the Bay of Bengal to look for her and tow her up, because the stock of ice in Calcutta had run done.

We sailed in the height of the S.W. Monsoon and were a long time getting clear, but she was such a comfortable ship at sea that it did not matter much to us. Blow high, blow low, watches went on regularly, and, having plenty to eat, we were quite happy. One evening when we were crossing the N.E. Trades we saw a ship coming along in our wake, overhauling us fast, and took her for a tea-clipper, till she passed under our lee, when, to our great astonishment, she proved to be the *City of Dublin*. She had arrived in Calcutta two days before we sailed, and when we reached London we found that she had arrived four days before us.

On the day after our arrival in London I asked the Captain for a reference, as I wanted to pass the Board of Trade examination for second mate, and he gave it to me at once, though he was usually very sparing with his references. I was offered a run round in the *City of Dublin*, which I was glad to accept, for I would save my train fare and get three pounds ten shillings into the bargain. The *City of Dublin* proved her speed again by over-hauling and passing several steamers on her way down Channel.

I went back to my old lodgings in Glasgow, and after a few days' holiday, attended a Navigation School for three weeks before going to Greenock for my examination. I got through all right, and then went into the country to spend Christmas and the New Year with my married sister. As soon as that was over I returned to the ship to see if Captain Dick had an opening for me, but I found he had given up command to Captain John Scott, late of the *City of Dublin*. However, I met Captain Dick on board, and after asking me if I had passed, he took me down to the cabin and said to the new captain, " Look here, John. Here is a young man I can recommend to you as bos'n."

" He looks young," was the inevitable answer.

"Never mind that, John. He's a sailor, and you won't find a better man for the job."

During this colloquy I felt more uncomfortable than I did under examination, and I was pleased when Captain Scott said he would take me and I was pleased to go. I did not like the way people remarked on my youthful appearance as if it interfered with my knowledge of seamanship.

Sailing day came, and I worked the oracle as well as I could to get all the men on board sober, so that when we reached Greenock the permanent pilot for the City Line, Mr. M'Kelvie, congratulated me on the men and on the way the work was done. The wind was then beginning to blow hard, and by the time we reached the Cumbraes it was blowing a strong S.W. gale. The tug was quite unable to tow us through the Heads, and, after remaining on the same spot for two hours, she turned round and towed us into Rothesay Bay, where we remained for four days till the gale moderated, which was a good opportunity for me to get everything into apple-pie order. We had a very rough time in channel, but we got through it without the slightest damage.

No unusual incidents occurred on the voyage until we lost a man overboard in the Indian Ocean. We were about the latitude of Mauritius, going along with a fine, fair wind, and carrying just as much as she could stand, when, with short notice, we got into a very rough sea, and, as she was plunging heavily, the topsail yards were lowered, but still the sea increased. One of the men in the mate's watch went on to the jib-boom for some purpose when a big roller came along, the jib-boom went right under, and the man was washed off. We got out a boat, for there was no broken water although the swell was high, but we saw nothing of our ship-mate.

As soon as we got the boat up and started on our course again we passed a ship hove to under her lower main-topsails, and when she saw us coming close to her she showed a black board with the following words: " Have had heavy cyclone ; sails blown away." She was the *Pride of Denmark*—a noted tea-clipper—and she arrived at Calcutta three days after us. We had very little of the wind but a good deal of sea from the cyclone, and, the remainder of the passage being fine, we arrived at the Sandheads, ninety-two days from Rothesay Bay.

We had a very hot time in Calcutta and there were always about half the crew on the sick-list; we had two fatal cases of cholera. Sailing day came round, and we sailed with two lady passengers and their two children. When we got to the Sandheads we encountered strong S.W. Monsoons, which seemed to blow new life into us, and were soon employed shortening sail. During the middle watch of the first night at sea the second mate was reported to be down with cholera, and within a few hours both ladies were attacked by the same disease. The second mate died after six hours' illness and was buried at once, but the ladies pulled through, though they did not fully regain their strength till they reached home.

When things looked so black in the cabin we removed the children to the boys' house, and the new second mate (promoted from third), and I, each undertook the charge of a child. I wanted the two-year-old girl, because I had a natural preference for girls, and the other child was a boy four years of age, but the second mate also wanted her, though from another point of view—we would have to carry them about with us a good deal, and the boy was twice the weight of the girl. We tossed for it, and the boy fell to my lot. The children would not stop in their bunks when we went on deck, and we had to tie them on to our backs with shawls and carry them wherever we went. The second mate was better off than I, for he could keep his watch on the quarter-deck, but I had to cruise round the deck to see that the gear was all right. When the weather improved we were able to set our burdens down if we wanted to do a piece of work, but it was weeks before we were relieved of our charges.

Fifteen years later, when I was in command of the *City of Venice*, outward bound, I happened to tell this story to a passenger who appeared to be very interested in my yarn. When I had finished, he asked me if I would know the boy again if I saw him, and I replied that I would recognise him by a birth-mark. The gentleman then took out his pocket-book and showed me the photograph of a fine-looking young man, saying as he did so, " That is my son—the boy you carried on your back."

On our arrival at London we were ordered to dis-charge at A Jetty, Victoria Dock, and so commenced the occupation of A Jetty by the City Line, which continued for over thirty years.

My next voyage—my last in a sailing ship—was as second mate of the *City of Benares*, Captain John Smith, and it was the happiest voyage I had made. Captain Smith had long been noted for carrying on ; he knew he had a good crew, and although the weather might look stormy, he would keep all sail set as long as the ship would stand it, and when the time came to drag the sails off her, the captain would be up to his neck in water, manning a buntline or clew-garnet. In fine weather he did his best to prevent any wind from escaping past his ship without being utilised, and carried numerous extra sails.

There were the usual skysail, topmast, lower top-gallant and royal stu'nsails, and the bull-driver or head water sail, which was set from the whisker end to the jib-boom end, the tack being hauled out to the martingale end. In addition to these we carried a water sail under the lower stu'nsail swinging-boom —a well-behaved sail, for, as the wind increased, so the square lower stu'nsail topped up the boom and kept the water sail from dipping. We also carried a ringtail with a water sail under it, and on the deck we had sails called "save-alls" set under the foot of the courses. Thus every hole by which wind could escape was closed. Captain Smith evidently considered it our principal duty, night or day, to push the ship along, and we made the round voyage in seven months and eight days, without "springing a rope-yarn," as Jack would say.

On this voyage I saw something new to me : every Sunday morning and evening the church-bell rang out its invitation as regularly as on shore, and we had prayers every evening during the week from half-past seven to eight o'clock. The captain looked well after the apprentices committed to his charge, morally, physically, and professionally, and he was nobly assisted by Mrs. Smith when she occasionally accompanied him on a voyage. When the sailors of bygone days found themselves in a tight corner, or were called upon to perform some not very pleasant task, they frequently exclaimed, "Who wouldn't sell his farm and go to sea?" They meant it sarcastically, but after my voyage in the *City of Benares* I could say it with all sincerity.

During this voyage the Suez Canal had been opened, and though the traffic at first was trifling, everybody seemed to think it would become the great ship-way to the East. On our arrival at Glasgow we learned that the City Line had started to build four large steamers, but I thought the Canal would never be a success, and made up my mind at once to stick by the sailing ships and the Cape route.

When the sailing day for the *City of Benares* drew near I called on Captain Smith, but found, to my astonishment, that he had been appointed to the command of S. S. *City of Cambridge* (building), and that if I liked to wait he would find me an appointment. Some time after that he wrote asking me to call and see him, and when I did so, told me the owners wanted all the officers to have master's certificates, and to have had previous experience in steam. That closed the door against me, but Captain Smith kindly offered to take me as quarter-master to gain steam experience. I asked him to take me as bos'n, which he agreed to do, after I had assured him that I knew how to use the bos'n's pipe.

We sailed in January, 1871, and all went well till we reached the Suez Canal, when our troubles began. It was all new work to us, and also to the Canal pilot, and groundings were frequent. No doubt we were partly to blame for urging the pilot to go quicker, but after a little more experience of Canal navigation we altered our opinion about greater speed being best for steering straight.

The Canal was very narrow and the bottom and banks very uneven, which made it impossible to steer a ship well. Another great drawback at that time was the large number of dredgers at work, but we got through without damage, though on the passage home we lost two and a half blades off our propeller. With the help of the sails, and a blade and a half, we reached Alexandria, where we dry-docked, and shipped our spare propeller, which had only two blades, for these were the days of solid screws—no shipping and unshipping of blades.

I had made two voyages as bos'n when I was promoted to third mate, and after another two voyages I was made second mate. Three voyages later I was appointed second mate of the new steamer *City of Carthage*, under Captain Smith, Mr. Barnet being mate, but after making one voyage Captain Smith retired from sea, the mate was appointed captain, and myself mate—having first obtained two days' leave to pass my examination for chief officer.

When I had made seven voyages in the *City of Carthage* I asked permission to stay ashore for a time, which was granted, and after I had been at home for three months, and had obtained a master's certificate, I reported myself to Captain James Brown as ready for any appointment. He told me to join the *City of Edinburgh*, which was then building, but was to be launched a few days later.

Captain Anderson was by her, and had been for some time, and I went down to pay my respects to my new captain.

I made another seven voyages as mate, and was then appointed to the command of the *City of Cambridge*.

On my first voyage in command I took a number of passengers and a little cargo to Colombo for the Rathbone Line. At that time there was no breakwater at Colombo, and we anchored off the town where we got plenty of rolling. I sailed for the Duke Line next voyage, calling at Madras, and there, as at Colombo, there was no breakwater, so we anchored off the coast.

My next voyage was for the Castle Line to the Cape ports, finishing at Natal, where I received a wire from the owners to proceed to Rangoon, and from that port I returned to Liverpool and Glasgow to load for Calcutta. I had made six voyages in the *City of Cambridge* when I was appointed to the *City of Venice*.

Some time after I joined the *City of Venice* I attended the Free School "tomasha" in Calcutta with the gentleman who had been chiefly instrumental in saving us from the consequences of playing bagpipes in Tank Square, and with whom I had become very friendly. We drove to the fête in my carriage, which was a single brougham, and when we were leaving later on my friend encountered another Scotch friend whom he invited to come with us, but there was some difficulty in packing ourselves into the brougham. My friend said he would drive and the coachman could get up behind as syce, but I said it was *infra dig.* for a gentleman in a white " tile " and gold spectacles to drive, so he offered to go inside and let me take the reins.   I agreed, but first asked if his life was insured, and he, seeing that I did not know much about driving, pushed me inside with his friend, jumped up on the box, and drove off.   As a bit of revenge, when the Bishop of Calcutta and other personages were driving past, I opened the door, stood on the step, and with my watch and chain started to heave the lead.   My friend did not notice my game till I called in a loud voice, " By the mark, five ! " and then he looked down.   Tableau !

CHAPTER XX

WORK ASHORE

I REMAINED in command of the *City of Venice* for nearly eleven years, and then decided to leave the sea as my hearing was failing, for it is absolutely necessary to have good hearing in foggy weather when the ears have to do duty for the eyes. I have gone from Dungeness to the Codling Light-ship with the ear and lead alone, and a blind man might do the same in a fog. I gave up command in March, 1891, and my officers and engineers presented me on that occasion with very handsome silver-plate.

A short time after I came ashore I tried for the appointment of harbour master at Ayr, but was un-successful, a local man being chosen. Some time after that my late owners offered me, and I accepted, an appointment in London to superintend the work-ing of their steamers while in that port.

This post was no sinecure, for the City Line had taken over the discharging of their own steamers from the Dock Company, the great dock strike had lately finished, and the men were rather troublesome, although they had gained the day over the Dock Company by the Mansion House agreement. They had agreed to return to work at sixpence per hour,

and a number of shipowners, including the City
Line, had advanced the pay to sevenpence, but in
spite of that there was a great deal of trouble for a
year or two. If there happened to be any coal-dust
about the men would ask for " dirty money," which
was an extra shilling per day, or if some of the
cargo was stowed in an awkward place, such as side
wings, under tanks, lazaret or fore peak, they would
deliberately stop work and come in a body to ask
for " awkward money." That was the state of
affairs when I went to London in November, 1891.

The City Line agents in London were Messrs.
Montgomerie & Workman, who now became my
masters on behalf of the owners, and I could not
have fallen into better hands. They had full confidence in me and gave me a free hand, while if I required help or advice they did their utmost for me.
I am pleased to say, after working under them for
thirteen and a half years, that we never had a cross
word, and I should be very ungrateful if I neglected
to say that not only the principals, but also the office
staff were kindness itself to me, so that a visit to the
office was a pleasant change from the worries of the
dock, which was not a bed of roses.

The discipline, amongst the dockers, if there had
ever been any, was conspicuous by its absence, but I
fought against all their bad habits and encouraged
them in their good ones, till at last I was able to
say that I had two or three hundred men working
about the ship and quay, on whom I could depend
to do their work well, and with a civil tongue: the
latter qualification being a great improvement.

When the Dock Company did the discharging the working hours were from eight A.M. till four P.M., but I altered that to seven A.M. till six P.M. summer and winter, which hours have now become very general.

Occasionally I had a sailing ship to put through; sometimes to discharge and ballast, sometimes to discharge and load outward, and alas, sometimes to hand over to new owners, for the City Line were selling their sailing ships as fast as they could find buyers.

As the dockers settled down to their work, so my appointment became more pleasant, and nothing worth chronicling took place until the Boer War broke out.

The *City of Cambridge* was offered to the Government as a troop-ship and was accepted, being fitted out in Glasgow, and the *City of Vienna,* which had just arrived from Calcutta, was also offered. We went on discharging the cargo at the usual hours till the second day, when the news arrived that Government had accepted the ship, and then we worked night and day to get her ready. On the third day she was fully inspected by Captain Pitt, R.N., who was accompanied by his draughtsman, shipwright, and a number of others to take his orders, and I had the orlop and 'tween decks swept down and electric lights burning in all dark places to facilitate the inspection. I also accompanied Captain Pitt, and was much impressed with the quickness of his eye and the ease with which he grasped the arrangements of a strange ship. In less than an hour he had completed his inspection and had given orders relative to every horse-stall, mess-table, storeroom, latrine and cook-house. He told us we were to be ready to receive troops on board that day week, and that our ship was to carry 350 men of the 12th Lancers and their horses, the S.S. *Mohawk* taking the remainder of the regiment.

Now began the busiest time of my life. We had to finish discharging the ship, dry-dock her, take forty water-tanks on board and stow them in the main-hold, take in 1200 tons of Thames shingle ballast and trim it all round the water-tanks to secure them. The supply of labour was much under the demand and wages rose in consequence. There were between four and five hundred tradesmen working on board; every deck was full of them, with lamps, candles and forge-fires everywhere, and many city gentlemen came down to see the sight. The ship was like a bee-hive, and the work done in her from Saturday to Saturday was really marvellous.

Saturday, the 21st of October, 1899, was the appointed sailing day, but one of London's choicest fogs descended on Friday and wrapped us in its embraces for five days. The troops arrived on Sunday, and men and horses were all shipped, but the fog was so very dense that we could not even find our way to the dock-gates. Monday still found us fog-bound, but at ten A.M. we left the berth for the dock-gates, and there we lay for an hour as the pilot would not venture to take her out. There were seven large steamers in the Basin waiting for us to start, and the pilot would not go, but I persuaded him to change ships with our second-on-turn pilot who told me he would go if the change were made, and he did. As soon as they let go the ropes the ship was out of sight and we could learn of her progress by the sound of her whistle only. She was followed by the S. S. *Mohawk*, but no other ship ventured out that day. When I could hear no more of her whistle I set off by train for Tilbury, and when I reached there, after much delay caused by the fog, I found that she had passed all right, but she took twenty-two hours to reach Dover—a distance she should have covered in five hours.

I soon left Tilbury and proceeded to my home, where I had not been for nearly a week. Neither had I been in bed all that time, and when I did reach my moorings I slept soundly for ten hours, which was a long watch-below for me.

We had the *City of Vienna* home again in April, 1901, but on this occasion she loaded oats and other stores for Government. The *City of Cambridge* also came to London with a large quantity of Government property saved from the wreck of H.M.S. *Sybille* on the Cape coast, and she had to be thoroughly cleaned and painted to again carry troops to South Africa.

In June, 1901, we were compelled by the Dock Company to give up our berth at A Jetty, Victoria Dock, so we had to shift our quarters to Tilbury Dock. There seemed to me to be considerable difficulty in the way of the change as far as I was concerned. When I thought of all the trouble I had had to get the men to do the work as it was then being done, and that I would have to leave them behind me, go to Tilbury and start afresh, I felt very much inclined to give it up, but my employers persuaded me to try it. They gave me a free hand to try to get my men to follow us, so I called them all together, put the case before them and asked for a show of hands from those who were willing to go to Tilbury.

I got only twenty-five volunteers to start with, but I took down their names and lent some of them a few shillings to assist in removing their household goods. By and by the others who had hung back at first came and asked me to put their names down on my list, and I soon found I had enough, but I had to leave behind some of my best men who had sons and daughters at work in the neighbourhood, and could not break up their homes.

We found Tilbury Dock a very dull place, but we helped to give it a push to the front, and it is now one of the busiest docks in London. At first I experienced considerable trouble in getting the work done as efficiently as in Victoria Dock, but in the course of a short time the disturbing elements found their level, and we all settled down as happily as if we had never known any other dock.

We had been at Tilbury nearly two years when I was taken suddenly ill with an attack of angina pectoris when going down by the early train one cold winter's morning. I have been in a surgeon's hands several times during my life, but I had then, for the first time, to call in a physician. I had a good record for health, but this attack made a great change, and although I was only laid up for a fort-night on this occasion, I have never since regained my former robustness.

After this illness I felt quite unable for the task of being here, there, and everywhere at once, as had formerly been my wont, nor could I stand night work, and came to the conclusion that I was not doing justice to my employers, so in March, 1905, I resigned my appointment.

The firm whom I had served for thirty-eight years gave me a very handsome testimonial, and I also received presentations from the office-staff and other business friends. To my great surprise and gratification my men at Tilbury Dock presented me with a handsome meerschaum pipe; a memento of which I am very proud.

And now I have picked up my moorings by the side of the sea on which I first embarked over half a century ago, and, in the words of the old chanty, "I'll go no more a-roving." My life has been full of varied experiences in many climes, and I hope that this account of them has—in spite of its short-comings—interested, and at times amused, all those who have followed my yarn.

THE END.

BOOKS

PUBLISHED BY

ALEXANDER GARDNER,

PAISLEY.

UT VIVAS · EVIV · VIVAS · A G

Publisher & Bookseller
by
Special Appointment

To Her late Majesty
Queen Victoria.

A LIST OF BOOKS

PUBLISHED BY

ALEX. GARDNER, PAISLEY.

Aitken.—Love in Its Tenderness. By J. R. Aitken. 6s.

Anderson.—Morison-Grant.—Life, Letters, and Last Poems of Lewis Morison-Grant. By Jessie Annie Anderson. 4s. 6d.

Anderson.—Verses at Random. By Thistle Anderson (Mrs. Herbert Fisher). 2s. 6d. nett.

—— Dives' Wife, and other Fragments. By Thistle Anderson (Mrs. Herbert Fisher). 2s. 6d. nett.

Anton.—The Flywheel: and What Keeps Us Steady. By Rev. Peter Anton. 3s. 6d. nett.

—— Staying Power: Reconsiderations and Recreations. By Rev. Peter Anton. 3s. 6d. nett.

A. O. M.—Two Brothers. By A. O. M. 2s. 6d.

Auld.—Lyrics of Labour and other Poems. By Thomas C. Auld.

Ayles.—Gillicolane. By Grueber Ayles. 4s. 6d.

Aytoun.—The Braes o' Balquhidder. By Douglas Aytoun. 6s.

Ballads of the Scottish Border. With Introduction and Notes. 1s. nett. Paper cover, 6d. nett.

Ballingal.—A Prince of Edom. By J. Ballingal, B.D. 2s. 6d.

Barclay.—A Renewal in the Church. By Rev. P. Barclay, M.A. 2s. 6d. nett.

Beatty.—The Secretar. By W. Beatty. 6s.

—— The Shadow of the Purple. By W. Beatty. 2s. 6d.

"Belinda's Husband."—Plain Papers on Subjects Light and Grave. By "Belinda's Husband." 2s. 6d. nett.

Beveridge.—Sma' Folk and Bairn Days. Translated from the Norse by the Rev. John Beveridge, M.A., B.D. Second Edition. 3s. 6d.

Bilton.—The Four Gospels. By Ernest Bilton. 2s. 6d.

Blair.—The Paisley Thread Industry and the Men who Created and Developed It. By Matthew Blair. 6s. nett.

—— The Paisley Shawl and the Men who Produced It. By Matthew Blair. 7s. 6d. nett.

—— A Short History of the Glasgow Technical College (Weaving Branch). By Matthew Blair. 2s. nett.

Bogatsky.—A Golden Treasury for the Children of God. By Rev. C. H. V. Bogatsky. Cloth, 2s. Cloth gilt, 2s. 6d.

Boston.—A Soliloquy on the Art of Man-Fishing. By Mr. Thomas Boston, A.M. 1s. 6d. nett.

Brown.—To Those About to Marry: Dont! Without a Practical Guide. By M. Harriette Brown. 1s. nett.

Brownlie.—Hymns of the Holy Eastern Church. Translated by Rev. John Brownlie. 3s. 6d. nett.

———— Hymns from the Greek Office Books: Together with Centos and Suggestions. Translated by Rev. John Brownlie. 3s. 6d. nett.

———— Hymns from the East. Translated by Rev. John Brownlie. 3s. 6d. nett.

———— Hymns of the Apostolic Church. With Introduction and Biographical Notes. By Rev. John Brownlie, D.D. 3s. 6d. nett.

Buchan.—The Ballad Minstrelsy of Scotland. By Patrick Buchan. 5s.

The Songs of Scotland. Chronologically Arranged. 5s. Uniform with above.

Burns.—The Selected Works of Robert Burns. Edited by Rhona Sutherland. Crown 4to. 430 pp. With Illustrations. Price 5s. and 7s. 6d. nett.

Bute.—Coronations — Chiefly Scottish. By the Marquess of Bute, K.T. 7s. 6d. nett.

———— Essays on Foreign Subjects. By the Marquess of Bute, K.T. 10s. 6d.

———— Seven Essays on Christian Greece. Translated by the Marquess of Bute, K.T. 7s. 6d.

Caird.—Sermons. By the late Rev. J. Renny Caird, M.A. With Memoir, by Rev. Robert Munro, B.D. 3s. 6d. nett.

Calder.—Poems of Life and Work. By Robert H. Calder. 2s. 6d. nett.

Campbell.—Notes on the Ecclesiastical Antiquities of Eastwood Parish. By the late Rev. George Campbell. 12s. 6d. and 25s. nett.

Campbell—Popular Tales of the West Highlands. By the late J. F. Campbell, Islay. Four vols. 7s. 6d. each.

Campbell.—The Elder's Prayer-Book. By Rev. Wm. Campbell, B.D. 1s.

Carslaw.—Heroes of the Scottish Covenant. By Rev. W. H. Carslaw, D.D.

      Vol. I.—James Guthrie, of Fenwick.
          II.—Donald Cargill, of the Barony, Glasgow.
        III.—James Renwick, the last of the Martyrs.
    1s. 6d. nett each. The three vols. in one, 3s. 6d. nett.

———— Six Martyrs of the First and Second Reformations. By Rev. W. H. Carslaw, D.D. 2s. nett.

———— Exiles of the Covenant. By Rev. W. H. Carslaw, D.D. 2s. nett.

Chalmers.—Chalmers' Caledonia. 25s. and 40s. per vol. Vol. VIII.—the Index—sold separately, 15s. and 25s. nett.

Cheviot.—Proverbs, Proverbial Expressions, and Popular Rhymes of Scotland. By Andrew Cheviot. 6s. nett.

"Claverhouse."—Gretna Green and Its Traditions. By "Claverhouse." 1s. nett

Colvin.—Bell Roger's Loon, and other Stories. By Margaret Colvin. 1s. 6d.

Cook.—In a Far Country. By Rev. Thomas Cook, M.A. 3s.

Craib.—America and the Americans. By Rev. A. Craib. 3s. 6d.

Craigie.—Scandinavian Folk-Lore. By W. A. Craigie, M.A., F.S.A. 7s. 6d.

Crawley-Boevey.—Beyond Cloudland. By S. M. Crawley-Boevey. 5s.

Cupples.—The Green Hand. By George Cupples. 2s. 6d.

Darling.—Songs from Silence. By Isabella F. Darling. 2s. 6d. nett.

Downie.—The Early Home of Richard Cameron. By J. Downie, M.A. 1s. nett.

Drummond.—Life of Robert Nicoll. By the late P. R. Drummond, Perth. 5s.

Edgar.—Old Church Life in Scotland. By Andrew Edgar, D.D. 7s. 6d.

———— The Bibles of England. By Andrew Edgar, D.D. 7s. 6d.

Eyre-Todd.—The Glasgow Poets. Edited by George Eyre-Todd. 7s. 6d. nett.

Fergusson.—Alexander Hume. By R. Menzies Fergusson, M.A. 5s. nett.

———— A Student of Nature. By R. Menzies Fergusson, M.A. 4s. nett.

———— A Village Poet. By R. Menzies Fergusson, M.A. 3s. 6d. nett.

———— Rambles in the Far North. By R. Menzies Fergusson, M.A. 3s. and 2s.

———— Logie: A Parish History. By R. Menzies Fergusson, M.A. 2 vols. 15s. nett. each vol.

———— The Viking's Bride, and other Poems. By R. Menzies Fergusson, M.A. 3s.

Ferguson.—The King's Friend. By Dugald Ferguson. 3s. 6d.

Fergusson.—The Poems of Robert Fergusson. Edited by Robt. Ford. 5s. nett.

Fife.—And I Knew It Not. By David Fife. 3s. 6d. nett.

Findlay.—Medici Carmina. By William Findlay, M.D. 3s. 6d. nett.

——— Ayrshire Idylls of Other Days. By "George Umber." 5s.

——— In My City Garden. By "George Umber." 6s.

——— Robert Burns and the Medical Profession. By William Findlay, M.D. ("George Umber.") 6s. nett.

Fittis.—Curious Episodes in Scottish History. By R. Scott Fittis. 6s.

—— Heroines of Scotland. By R. Scott Fittis. 6s.

—— Romantic Narratives from Scottish History and Tradition. By R. Scott Fittis. 6s.

—— Sports and Pastimes of Scotland, Historically Illustrated. By Robert Scott Fittis. 5s. nett.

Fleming.—Ancient Castles and Mansions of Stirling Nobility. By J. S. Fleming, F.S.A. 21s. nett.

Ford.—American Humourists. Selected and edited by Robert Ford. 3s. 6d.

—— Auld Scots Ballants. 6s.

—— Ballads of Bairnhood. Selected and edited by Robert Ford. 5s.

—— Ballads of Babyland. Selected and edited by Robert Ford. 5s.

—— Children's Rhymes, Games, Songs, and Stories. By R. Ford. 3s. 6d. nett.

—— Ford's Own Humorous Scotch Stories. 1st and 2nd Series, 1s. each nett. Both Series in 1 vol., 2s. 6d. nett.

—— Poems and Songs of Alexander Rodger. Edited by Robert Ford. 3s. 6d. nett.

—— Tayside Songs and other Verses. By Robert Ford. 3s. 6d. nett.

—— The Harp of Perthshire. Edited by Robert Ford. 15s. and 7s. 6d.

—— Thistledown. By Robert Ford. 3s. 6d. and 1s. nett.

—— Vagabond Songs and Ballads of Scotland. Edited by R. Ford. 5s. nett.

—— Miller's "Willie Winkie," and other Songs and Poems. Edited by Robert Ford. 3s. 6d. nett.

—— The Heroines of Burns. By Robert Ford. 3s. 6d. nett.

—— Popular American Readings. Popular English Readings. Popular Irish Readings, Popular Scotch Readings. Edited by Robert Ford. 1s. each. Also in one vol., 4s.

Forsyth.—Elocution : Simple Rules and Exercises for Correct and Expressive Reading and Reciting. By John Forsyth. 1s. 6d. nett.

Gardner's Verse for Schools. Parts I. and II. 6d. nett each part.

Gentles.—A Plea for the Restoration of Paisley Abbey. By Rev. T. Gentles, D.D. 1s.

Gough.—Scotland in 1298. Edited by Henry Gough. 21s.

—— The Itinerary of King Edward the First, as far as relates to his Expeditions against Scotland, 1286–1307. By Henry Gough. 2 vols. 30s. nett.

Granger.—The Average Man, and other Sermons. By the late Rev. William Granger, M.A., Ayr. 3s. 6d. nett.

Greethead.—Our Future. Edited by Miss Greethead. 1s. 6d.

Grey.—The Misanthrope's Heir. By Cyril Grey. 6s. nett.

—— The Manse Rose. By Cyril Grey. 3s. 6d.

Grosart.—The Verse and Miscellaneous Prose of Alexander Wilson, the Ornithologist of America. Edited by Rev. A. B. Grosart, LL.D. 12s. 6d.

Hall.—The Art of Being Happy. The Art of Being Healthy. The Art of Being Successful. By Rev. Charles A. Hall. 1s. nett each. In one vol., 3s. nett.

—— The Manly Life, and How to Live It. By the Rev. Charles A. Hall. Cloth, 1s. ; Paper Covers, 6d.

—— "The Divinity that Shapes Our Ends." By Rev. Charles A. Hall. 1s. nett

Hall.—Edith Watson. By Sydney Hall. 3s. 6d.

Hanton.—Drifted Northward. By T. Hanton. 1s.

Harvey.—Scottish Chapbook Literature. By William Harvey. 3s. 6d. nett.

Hatherly.—A Treatise on Byzantine Music. By Rev. S. G. Hatherly, Mus. Bac. (Oxon.). 6s. and 4s.

—— "God Save the Queen." Supplementary to Dr. Hatherly's Treatise. 2s.

Henderson.—Anecdotes and Recollections of A. K. H. B. By Rev. D. R. Henderson, M.A. 6d. nett.

Henderson.—Lady Nairne and Her Songs. By Rev. George Henderson, M.A., B.D., Monzie, Crieff. 2s. 6d. nett and 2s. nett.

Hewat.—Half-Hours at the Manse. By the Rev. Kirkwood Hewat, M.A., F.S.A. (Scot.), Prestwick. 3s. 6d.

—— In the Olden Times. By Rev. Kirkwood Hewat, M.A., etc. 4s. nett.

Hill-A-Hoy-O. By a "Country Cousin." 2s. 6d.

Hogg.—A Tour in the Highlands in 1803. By James Hogg. 2s. 6d.

—— Memoir of James Hogg, the Ettrick Shepherd. By his daughter. 5s.

Holmes.—The Teaching of Modern Languages in Schools and Colleges. By D. T. Holmes, B.A. 2s. nett.

—— Literary Tours in the Highlands and Islands of Scotland. By D. T. Holmes, B.A. 4s. 6d. nett.

Hume.—The Practice of Sanctification. By Alexander Hume, B.A. 1s. nett.

Hutcheson.—Maisie Warden. By J. D. Hutcheson. 5s.

Isobel Burns (Mrs. Begg). By her Grandson. 2s. 6d.

James.—Poems and Fragments. By Charles James. 3s. 6d.

Jamieson.—Jamieson's Scottish Dictionary. Edited by David Donaldson, F.E.I.S. 5 vols., £8 17s. 6d. ; Large Paper, £14.

—— New Supplementary Volume (being Vol. V. of above). Edited by David Donaldson, F.E.I.S. 27s. 6d. and 42s.

—— Jamieson's Scottish Dictionary. Abridged by John Johnstone, and Revised and Enlarged by Dr. Longmuir. With a Supplementary Edition, Edited by W. M. Metcalfe, D.D., F.S.A. 1 Vol., Demy 8vo, about 900 pages. The Supplementary Addition may be had separately.

Johnson.—A Journey to the Western Islands of Scotland in 1773. By Samuel Johnson, LL.D. New Edition. 2s. 6d. nett.

Kennedy.—David Kennedy, the Scottish Singer : Reminiscences of his Life and Work. By Marjory Kennedy. And Singing Round the World : a Narrative of his Colonial Tours. By David Kennedy, Jun. 7s. 6d.

Kennedy.—Reminiscences of Walt Whitman. By William Sloane Kennedy, Camden, N.J. 6s.

Ker.—Mother Lodge, Kilwinning, "The Ancient Lodge of Scotland." By Rev. W. Lee Ker, Kilwinning. 4s. 6d.

Kilgour.—Twenty Years on Ben Nevis. By Wm. T. Kilgour. 2/6 & 1/6 nett.

—— Lochaber in War and Peace. Illustrated. By Wm. T. Kilgour. 7s. 6d. nett.

King.—Shipwreck Wood : A Story of "Some that lift and some that lean." By Carrol King. 2s.

Laing.—The Buke of the Howlat. By Dr. Laing. 12s. 6d.

Lamont.—Poems. By J. K. Lamont. 2s. 6d.

Latto.—Hew Ainslie : a Pilgrimage to the Land of Burns. Edited by Thomas C. Latto. 6s.

Latto.—Memorials of Auld Lang Syne. By Thomas C. Latto. 4s. 6d. and 2s. 6d.

Law.—Dreams o' Hame, and other Scotch Poems. By James D. Law. 6s.

Lumsden.—Thoughts for Book Lovers. By Harry S. Lumsden. 2s.

Macbremen.—Breezes from John o' Groats. By MacBremen. 3s. 6d.

—— The Death of Lady Wallace : a Poem. By MacBremen. 1s.

Mac Cormick.—Oiteagan 'o n Iar (Breezes from the West). By J. Mac Cormick. Edited by M. Mac Farlane. 2s. 6d.

Macdonald.—The Husband to Get and to Be. Edited by G. G. Macdonald. 1s. nett.
————— The Wife to Get. 2s. 6d. nett.
McClelland.—The Church and Parish of Inchinnan. By the Rev. Robert McClelland, minister of the Parish. 3s. 6d. nett.
M'Ewen.—Life Assurance. What to Select. By Robert M'Ewen, Cambus. 3d.
Macfarlane.—The Harp of the Scottish Covenant. Poems, Songs, and Ballads collected by John Macfarlane. 6s.
Macintosh.—Irvindale Chimes. By John Macintosh. 4s. nett.
Macintosh.—A Popular Life of Robert Burns. By John Macintosh. 2s. 6d. nett
Mackintosh.—The History of Civilisation in Scotland. By John Mackintosh, LL.D. 4 vols. £4 4s. Calf Extra, £5 5s. Large Paper, £6 6s.
Mackay.—Where the Heather Grows. By George A. Mackay. 2s. 6d.
Mackean.—The King's Quhair. Done into English by Wm. Mackean. 3s. 6d.
Macleod.—Satan's Fool. By A. Gordon Macleod. 4s. 6d. nett.
Macleod.—Wallace : a Poem. By Neil Macleod. 1s., post free.
M'Gown.—Ten Bunyan Talks. By G. W. T. M'Gown. 2s. nett.
————— A Primer of Burns. By G. W. T. M'Gown. 1s. nett.
M'Kean.—The Young Naturalists. A Book for Boys and Girls. By Minnie M'Kean. 1st and 2nd Series. 1s. each.
M'Kellar.—Greece : Her Hopes and Troubles. By Campbell M'Kellar. 1s.
MacKenzie.—History of the Outer Hebrides. By William C. MacKenzie. 12s. 6d. nett. Large Paper, 21s.
MacKenzie.—The Lady of Hirta. By Wm. C. MacKenzie, F.S.A. Scot. 6s.
————— A Short History of the Scottish Highlands and Isles. By Wm. C. MacKenzie. New Edition. 5s. nett.
MacKenzie.—History of Kilbarchan Parish. By Robert D. MacKenzie, minister of the Parish. 21s. nett. Large Paper, 35s. nett.
M'Kerlie.—History of the Lands and their Owners in Galloway. By the late P. H. M'Kerlie, F.S.A. Scot., F.R.G.S., etc. 2 vols. 25s. nett.
MacLaine.—My Frien' the Provost. By Hew MacLaine. 6d. nett.
McMillan.—Mainly About Robert Bruce. By Alec McMillan, M.A. 1s. nett.
MacNicol.—Dare MacDonald. By E. R. MacNicol. 5s.
Macpherson.—History of the Church in Scotland. By Rev. John Macpherson, M.A. 7s. 6d.
Macrae.—A Feast of Fun. By Rev. David Macrae. 3s. 6d.
————— Book of Blunders. By Rev. David Macrae. 1s.
————— National Humour. By Rev. David Macrae. 3s. 6d.
————— The Railway Chase, and other Sketches. By Rev. David Macrae. 1s.
————— Popping the Question, and other Sketches. By Rev. David Macrae. 1s. The above two volumes in one, 2s.
Mather.—Poems. By James Mather. 4s.
————— Poems. Second Series. By James Mather. 5s. nett.
Maughan.—Rosneath : Past and Present. By W. C. Maughan. 5s.
————— The Garelochside. By W. C. Maughan. 7s. 6d.
————— Picturesque Musselburgh and Its Golf Links. By W. C. Maughan. Cloth, 1s. 6d. Paper covers, 1s. nett.
Menzies.—National Religion. By Rev. Allan Menzies, D.D., St. Andrews. 5s.
Menzies.—Illustrated Guide to the Vale of Yarrow. By James M. Menzies. 1s. 6d. nett.
Menzies.—Provincial Sketches and other Verses. By G. K. Menzies. 2s. 6d. nett.
Metcalfe.—SS. Ninian and Machor—the Legends of, in the Scottish Dialect of the Fourteenth Century. By W. M. Metcalfe, D.D. 10s. 6d. nett. On Whatman Paper, 15s. nett.
————— A History of the Shire of Renfrew from the Earliest Times down to the Close of the Nineteenth Century. By W. M. Metcalfe, D.D., F.S.A. 25s. nett. On Whatman Paper, 40s.

Metcalfe.—History of Paisley. By W. M. Metcalfe, D.D. With Illustrations and a Map of Paisley. 7s. 6d. nett.

——— Charters and Documents relating to the Burgh of Paisley. By W. M. Metcalfe, D.D. 21s. nett.

——— Ancient Lives of the Scottish Saints. Translated by W. M. Metcalfe, D.D. 15s. On Whatman Paper, 25s.

——— Pinkerton's Lives of the Scottish Saints. Revised and enlarged by W. M. Metcalfe, D.D. 2 vols. 15s. per vol.

——— The Natural Truth of Christianity. Edited by W. M. Metcalfe, D.D. 5s.

——— The Reasonableness of Christianity. By W. M. Metcalfe, D.D. 5s.

Metcalfe.—The Great Palace of Constantinople. Translated from the Greek of Dr. A. G. Paspates, by William Metcalfe, B.D. 10s. 6d.

Miller.—Selections from the Works of Hugh Miller. Edited by W. M. Mackenzie, M.A., F.S.A. (Scot.). 3s. 6d.

Mitchell.—A Popular History of the Highlands and Gaelic Scotland. By Dugald Mitchell, M.D., J.P. 12s. 6d. nett.

Mitchell.—Jephtha : a Drama. Translated by A. G. Mitchell. 3s. 6d. nett.

——— John the Baptist : a Drama. Translated by A. G. Mitchell. 3s. 6d. nett.

Moffat.—From Ship's-boy to Skipper. By H. Y. Moffat.

Moody.—"Buy the Truth !" and other Addresses. By Rev. Andrew Moody, D.D. 2s. 6d. nett.

Morison-Grant.—Protomantis, and other Poems. By L. Morison-Grant. 6s.

Motherwell.—Poems and Songs. By William Motherwell. 6s.

Mowat.—Search Light. By G. H. Mowat. 2s. 6d. nett.

Munro.—Burns' Highland Mary. By Archibald Munro. 3s.

Munro.—Schleiermacher. By Robt. Munro, B.D., Old Kilpatrick. 4s. 6d. nett.

Murray.—A Handbook of Psychology. By J. Clark Murray, LL.D., F.R.S.C., M'Gill College, Montreal. 7s. 6d.

——— An Introduction to Ethics. By J. Clark Murray, LL.D., etc. 6s. 6d.

——— A Sketch of the Life and Times of the late David Murray, Esq., Provost of Paisley. By his son, J. Clark Murray, LL.D., etc. 4s.

——— Solomon Maimon. Translated by J. Clark Murray, LL.D., etc. 6s.

Murray.—Kilmacolm : a Parish History. By Rev. Jas. Murray, M.A. 6s. nett.

——— Life in Scotland a Hundred Years Ago. By Rev. James Murray, M.A. Second and Enlarged Edition. 3s. 6d. nett.

Murray.—The Black Book of Paisley and other Manuscripts of the Scoti-chronicon. By David Murray, LL.D., F.S.A., Scot. 12s. 6d.

Mursell.—The Waggon and the Star. By Walter A. Mursell. 2s. 6d. nett.

——— Two on a Tour. By Walter A. Mursell.

Naismith.—The Young Draper's Guide to Success. By W. Naismith. 1s. 6d. nett.

Nicolson.—Tales of Thule. By John Nicolson. 2s.

Ochiltree.—Redburn. By Henry Ochiltree. 5s.

On Heather Hills. 2 vols. 21s.

Patterson.—The "Cyclops" of Euripides. Edited by John Patterson, B.A. (Harvard), Louisville, Kentucky, U.S.A. 4s. 6d.

Perin.—Divine Breathings. By Christopher Perin. 1s.

Phelps.—The Still Hour. By Rev. Austen Phelps. 6d.

Phillips.—Cora Linn. By J. G. Phillips. 3s. 6d., post free.

——— James Macpherson, the Highland Freebooter. By J. G. Phillips. 3s. 6d.

Philp.—The River and the City. By Rev. George Philp, Glasgow. 6d.

Pride.— A History of the Parish of Neilston. By Dr. Pride.

Rae-Brown.—The Shadow on the Manse. By Campbell Rae-Brown. 3s. 6d.

Reid.—A Cameronian Apostle. By Professor Reid, D.D. 6s.

Reid.—Poems, Songs, and Sonnets. By Robert Reid (Rob Wanlock). 5s.

Reid.—Problems of this Life—Social and Sacred. By W. Reid. 2s. 6d. nett.

Renfrewshire. Archæological and Historical Survey of the County, under the direction of several eminent antiquaries. Lochwinnoch. With numerous Plates. 2 vols. 25s. per vol. Large Paper, 37s. 6d.

Renfrewshire—Geographical and Historical. 3d.

Renwick.—Poems and Sonnets. By James Renwick. 2s. 6d.

Rigg.—Nature Lyrics. By James Rigg. 2s. 6d. nett.

Roberts.—A Short Proof that Greek was the Language of Christ. By the late Professor Roberts, D.D., St. Andrews. 2s. 6d.

Robertson.—Jockie, and other Songs and Ballads. By A. S. Robertson. 1s. 6d.

Robertson.—Practical First Aid. By Wm. Robertson, M.D., D.P.H. 1s. 6d. nett.

———— The Stone of Dunalter. By Wm. Robertson, M.D., D.P.H. 3s. 6d.

Robertson.—The Lords of Cuningham. By Wm. Robertson. 5s.

Ross.—Highland Mary. Edited by John D. Ross. 2s. 6d.

—— Random Sketches on Scottish Subjects. By John D. Ross. 2s. 6d.

—— Round Burns' Grave. The Paeans and Dirges of Many Bards. Gathered together by John D. Ross. 3s. 6d.

Ross.—In the Highlands, and other Poems. By G. R. T. Ross. 3s. 6d. nett.

Ross.—Kingcraft in Scotland. By Peter Ross, LL.D. 6s.

Roy.—Lilias Carment ; or, For Better for Worse. By Gordon Roy. 6s.

Russell.—Three Years in Shetland. By Rev. John Russell, M.A. 3s. 6d.

Scotland Eighty Years Ago. Thirty-two Fine Copperplate Etchings of the Chief Towns and their Surroundings. £5 5s. to subscribers only.

Scott.—Lectures for Club and Cloister. By A. Boyd Scott. 3s. 6d. nett.

Seath.—Rhymes and Lyrics. By Wm. Seath. 3s. 6d. nett.

Silver Aims and Golden Anchors. A Text-Book. 1s. nett.

Simpson.—Familiar Scottish Birds. By A. Nicol Simpson, F.Z.S. 2s.

———— Familiar Scottish Animals. By A. Nicol Simpson, F.Z.S. 2s.

———— Familiar Scottish Sketches. By A. Nicol Simpson, F.Z.S. 2s.

———— Bobbie Guthrie : a Scotch Laddie. By A. N. Simpson, F.Z.S. 2s. 6d. nett.

Skinner.—That Loon o' Baxter's. By Rev. J. Skinner. 2s.

Smith.—The New Testament in Braid Scots. Rendered by Rev. Wm. Wye Smith. New Edition. 6s. nett.

Smith.—Scottish Athletic Sports. By W. M'Combie Smith. 1s. 6d.

Smith.—The Dalbroom Folks. By Rev. J. Smith, M.A., B.D. 2 vols. 6s.

Snodgrass.—Wit, Wisdom, and Pathos, from the Prose of Heinrich Heine. Selected and translated by J. Snodgrass. 6s.

Souper.—The Disciple of Love. A Poem. By W. Souper. 2s. 6d.

Stenhouse.—Lays from Maoriland. By William M. Stenhouse. 3s. 6d. nett.

Stephen.—Divine and Human Influence. By Rev. R. Stephen, M.A. 5s. nett.

Stewart.—The Church of Scotland. By Richard Morris Stewart. 7s. 6d.

Story.—Health Haunts of the Riviera and South-West of France. By Very Rev. Principal Story, D.D. 3s.

—— St. Modan of Rosneath. By the Very Rev. Principal Story, D.D. 2s.

Sturrock.—Our Present Hope and Our Future Home. By Rev. J. B. Sturrock. 2s. 6d. nett.

Symington.—Hints to Our Boys. By A. J. Symington. 1s. 6d.

Symington.—The Story of the Covenanter Church. By A. Balfour Symington, M.A. 1s. nett.

Tannahill.—Poems and Songs of Robert Tannahill. Edited by the late David Semple, F.S.A. New Edition. 3s. 6d. nett.

Taylor.—The Autobiography of Peter Taylor. 3s. 6d.

Taylor.—Twelve Favourite Hymns : their Messages and their Writers. By Rev. Wm. Taylor, M.A. 2s. nett.

The Knight of Snowdon ; or, The Saxon and the Gael. 2s. 6d.

The Leading Aisles. 2s. 6d.

Thomson.—The Dunfermline Hammermen. A History of the Incorporation of Hammermen in Dunfermline. By Daniel Thomson. 5s. nett.

Tweeddale.—Dunty the Droll. By John Tweeddale. 1s.

Urie.—Reminiscences of 80 Years. By John Urie.

Veitch.—The Dean's Daughter. By Sophie F. F. Veitch. 3s. 6d.

Warrick.—The History of Old Cumnock. By Rev. John Warrick, M.A., Free Church, Old Cumnock. 7s. 6d. nett.

Watt.—Selected Metrical Psalms and Paraphrases. Selected and edited by R. MacLean Watt, M.A., B.D. 1s. nett.

Whyte.—Naigheachdan Firinneach (True Stories). Vols. I. and II. Translated into Gaelic by Henry Whyte ("Fionn"). 3s. 6d. per Vol., nett.

Mac-Choinnich.—Eachdraidh a' Phrionnsa; no, Bliadhna Thearlaich (The Jacobite Rising of 1745). Le Iain Mac-Choinnich. New Edition. 5s. nett.

Williamson.—Cartsburn and Cartsdyke. By G. Williamson. 25s. and 42s.

——— Old Greenock. Second Series. Uniform with above.

Woodrow.—Gardening in the Tropics : being a Sixth Edition of "Gardening in India," adapted for all Tropical or Semi-Tropical Regions. By G. Marshall Woodrow, late Professor of Botany.

Wright.—Laird Nicoll's Kitchen, and other Sketches of Scottish Life and Manners. By Joseph Wright. 2s. 6d. nett.

Young.—Scotch Cameos. By John Young. New Edition, 1s. and 1s. 6d.

MANUALS FOR THE HOUSEHOLD.

Cookery for Working Men's Wives. By Martha H. Gordon. 1d.; post free, 2d. Large Type Edition, 3d.; post free, 4d.

Indigestion. By Florence Stacpoole. 2d.; post free, 2½d.

Our Babies, and How to Take Care of Them. By Florence Stacpoole. 3d.; post free, 4d.

The Home Doctor. By Florence Stacpoole. 3d.; post free, 4½d.

THE "JENNY WREN" SERIES. 6d. each. Post free, 8d.

A Treatise on the Cooking of Big Joints.
Dainty Dishes for Dinners, Luncheons, and Suppers.
Dishes of Fishes : How to Prepare Them.
Sauces, Seasonings, and Salads.
The Art of Preparing Puddings, Tarts, Jellies, etc.
The Art of Preparing Soups, Stews, Hashes, and Ragouts.
The Complete Art of Dinner-Giving.